13.95

The Actor at Work

PRENTICE-HALL SERIES IN THEATRE AND DRAMA
Oscar G. Brockett, Consulting Editor

The Actor at Work, Revised and Enlarged
ROBERT L. BENEDETTI

Century of Innovation:
A History of European and American Theatre and Drama Since 1870
OSCAR G. BROCKETT AND ROBERT R. FINDLAY

Creative Play Direction
ROBERT COHEN AND JOHN HARROP

Children's Theatre: A Philosophy and a Method
MOSES GOLDBERG

Creative Dramatics for the Classroom Teacher
RUTH HEINIG AND LYDA STILLWELL

Play Directing: Analysis, Communication, and Style
FRANCIS HODGE

Introduction to Theatre: A Mirror to Nature
ORLEY I. HOLTAN

Theatre in High School: Planning, Teaching, Directing
CHARLOTTE KAY MOTTER

Playwriting: The Structure of Action
SAM SMILEY

Three Hundred Years of American Drama and Theatre:
From Ye Bare & Ye Cubb *to* Hair
GARFF B. WILSON

REVISED AND ENLARGED EDITION

The Actor at Work

Robert L. Benedetti
California Institute of the Arts

Prentice-Hall, Inc., Englewood Cliffs, New Jersey

Library of Congress Cataloging in Publication Data

BENEDETTI, ROBERT L
    The actor at work.

    (Prentice-Hall series in theatre and drama)
    Includes bibliographical references.
    1. Acting. I. Title.
PN2061.B39 1976   792'.028   75-29376
ISBN 0-13-003665-X

This book is dedicated with love to my parents.

Prentice-Hall International, Inc., *London*
Prentice-Hall of Australia Pty. Limited, *Sydney*
Prentice-Hall of Canada, Ltd., *Toronto*
Prentice-Hall of India Private Limited, *New Delhi*
Prentice-Hall of Japan, Inc., *Tokyo*
Prentice-Hall of Southeast Asia Pte. Ltd., *Singapore*

Contents

Exercises

For One or Two People

Group Exercises

Preface

It was in 1965 that Oscar Brockett convinced me to write a book on acting using the techniques I was developing in my classes. It took much longer than I had imagined it would; three years of writing, testing, and rewriting. The trouble was that the ideas and the form of their expression refused to stand still; every day, some new thought or phrase would strike me, and I took to jotting them down on scraps of paper. Later, I would unload my pockets, and slowly piles of crumpled notes turned into the final manuscript. I often despaired of really finishing the thing, and even as the last galley proofs were mailed I thought of Alan Schneider's maxim about productions: they're never finished, only abandoned.

But even after I had "abandoned" the book to its fate, I still found those cryptic notes in my pockets at night; my daily stint with pen and paper, a discipline begun out of necessity, had become a habit—or rather, more than a habit, a *need*. The agony of fashioning living ideas out of piles of dead words had become a way of working things out, of giving form and purpose to the often chaotic and always unfinished business of teaching young people to act. The pile of crumpled notes, or reworked pages, grew.

Many found their way into a second book called *Seeming, Being, and Becoming.*[1] While *The Actor at Work* had been about *how* to act, this new book was about *why* there are actors. I had begun to wonder about that as I watched more and more young people, despite declining college enrollments in many other fields, signing up for acting classes. Why this rising interest, in the high schools, the colleges, the professional programs, the studios? Why all these young people wanting to join what is obviously an endangered species?

[1]*Seeming, Being, and Becoming* (New York: Drama Book Specialists/Publishers, 1975).

Something, I thought, is revealing itself, some ancient value of acting for which our culture has a growing need. That value, I decided, is the actor's ability to define his existence, to determine with clarity his identity. His performance can remind us of our spiritual capacity to cope with our identities; whatever a play may tell us about who we *are,* the actor's ability to transform himself into a new reality can teach us something about who we may *become.* When in our history have we more needed confidence in our individual mastery over our existence?

Even after this idea about the *why* of acting had been worked out in detail, however, there was still a big pile of notes left. Most of these were more *how* notes, things that I wished I had put into *The Actor at Work* in 1965, but that I simply hadn't known then. Some were notes about specific improvements and additions in the text: the new section on "centering," for example. Then too, over two hundred people who had used the book had written comments full of good suggestions: changes in the lesson on emotion, for example, came from these.

But still a mountain of notes remained, notes that were simply beyond the material treated in the book as it was, and these confirmed my lingering sense of incompleteness; I had treated expressive skills, I had treated analytical skills, but I hadn't been able to say much about how an actor puts the two together.

True, I did (and do) disclaim that a book can teach the creative act itself, and it is only in the creative act that form and substance are completely synthesized; but I now understand much more about the methodological principles that help the actor to pursue his creative discoveries. If we cannot ensure creativity, we can at least communicate those amenities of work that may encourage inspiration, and this is the subject of the new third part of *The Actor at Work,* which appears in this second edition.

The new section, like the two original sections, is based upon exercises developed in my acting classes over a period of time, and a number of my colleagues and students have made significant contributions to the ideas and exercises contained in part 3. To all of them, my deep thanks.

The mountain of crumpled notes is gone for now.

NOTE TO MY FEMALE READERS

I regret that our language has no neuter pronoun. I am aware of the constant use of the male "his" and "actor" in this book, and I hope that you will understand that I am using these words in the sense of "his *or her*" and "actor *or actress.*" To have actually replaced all the pronouns with these phrases would have made for very clumsy style, and the noncommittal pronoun "one's," as in "one's acting," seems to me terribly stuffy. As much as possible I have tried to say merely "your acting," for that is what I mean.

There is a great deal that is sexist in our theatre; a recent survey of the media revealed that only 17 percent of all the roles on television or in films are for women. Unfortunately, the percentage of women's roles in drama is even smaller, as anyone who has tried to find plays with more than four women's roles can attest.

Women in our culture face some special problems in the training process as well as in performance. I have tried to structure my exercises so as to make them equally useful to men and women, but we all have a long way to go toward a nonsexist theatre. Let us begin!

HOW TO USE THIS BOOK

No book, including this one, can teach you to act. It is doubtful that anyone has ever been taught to act, or to dance, or to paint, or to compose; only the skills of art can be taught, not the creative act itself.

A good acting teacher provides a sound foundation of necessary skills; he also instills the self-discipline by which these skills may be mastered; he communicates the methodology for the application of these skills. He does all this with a personal concern for the student, wishing to liberate whatever talent the student possesses, and with an ethical concern for the theatre as well, wishing to help the student realize the humanistic purposes underlying the theatrical endeavor. But when he is being honest with himself, his greatest fear is that he may stifle some talents while nurturing others. In any art, the teacher-student relationship is a fragile, mysterious blending of inspiration and constraint, of unfettered roamings of the imagination and unyielding insistence on the precise detail of form. It doesn't take much to upset the balance of such a relationship.

Mutual respect and careful trust are indispensable to the teaching relationship, as is an overriding recognition by teacher and student alike that it is the excellence of the created work that is at all times the greatest concern. Your teacher's aim is to help you to realize yourself within the demands of the theatrical art, not just for your sake but also for the sake of the contribution that you may someday make to the theatre. And that is also why I have written this book for you; to provide experiences and insights that may help you to begin fulfilling that promise so that you and the theatre may both prosper.

The book is in three parts. The first deals with expressive technique and takes a strongly organismic approach, drawing material from many fields such as Gestalt psychology, kinesics, linguistics, social psychology, and various Oriental philosophies. In this part, I try to relate the basis of theatrical discipline to the inherently dramatic aspects of everyday expressive behavior.

The second part of the book treats in considerable detail the techniques of textual analysis. An actor without insight into the specific qualities of his text is missing an important source of creative inspiration, since every play presents its own problems and demands its own solutions; moreover, every play contains the seeds that generate those solutions if the actor is craftsman enough to apply the appropriate interpretive and expressive skills to realize them. This craftsmanship is the necessary antecedent of artistry.

The new third part of *The Actor at Work* explores the principles involved in putting your expressiveness and your analytical insights to work in the process of creation. It is during this process, as you join your partners in developing the shared focus that permits your personal energies to flow freely into the created scene, that the truly creative aspects of acting are most evident.

These three parts are called "The Actor's Tools," "The Actor's Blueprint," and finally "The Actor at Work" because my aim is to help you understand what your job is, what skills you need to do it, and what principles underlie the methodologies of work that you may adopt in relation to a given role. Remember, however, that none of this is a "formula" to be blindly followed, nor can any of it guarantee that you will develop stageworthy acting ability. The synthesis of understanding and expressiveness in a living performance is a mysterious and deeply personal phenomenon.

THE EXERCISES

The most important element of this book is the series of exercises that accompany each lesson. These are meant to be training devices, *not* performance techniques; their aim is to sensitize you in various ways, to focus your awareness on fundamental principles, and to provide experiences that will serve as a program of self-discovery and self-development in graduated stages. They are arranged roughly according to the "natural" acquisition of these skills, beginning simply and moving toward greater complexity and subtlety. The experiences they provide are essential to a true understanding (in the muscles as well as in the mind) of this book's point of view.

It is especially important that you do the exercises innocently, without expectation of a specific result. These exercises have no "right" outcome, so try not to analyze or premeditate the experience they offer. Just *do it.*

Doing it, unfortunately, is not so easy; you will often catch yourself merely "going through the motions" of an exercise, or acting out your *idea* of it instead of committing yourself to a vivid new experience. There are several reasons for this: first is fear; fear of an unknown experience and of what you may discover about yourself, as well as your conditioned fear of academic failure. Hence you experience a tremendous pressure to deliver a "safe" and "acceptable" result.

Another source of trouble is your ingrained habit of showing others your effort instead of actually surrendering to the work at hand. This began when Mom or Dad or some teacher asked you a long time ago to do something, and you were eager to please them, even though you weren't terribly interested (or even happy) about the thing you were doing; your activity therefore became not so much real effort as a *display of effort* that said "look at me doing this." In acting class we call this "look at me" attitude *indicating;* you *indicate* by showing us that you are doing something instead of really doing it. This is to be avoided not only because it looks and feels false on stage, but also because it prevents you from having a deep and meaningful experience of your task.

Another common source of trouble is sheer laziness. These exercises are not easy, even when they are simple. Stage activity is always heightened beyond everyday life in some way, and activity that seems comfortable to you by the standards of everyday life is usually not "enough" for the stage; eventually, when you have become stage "wise" and experienced, the range and clarity of behavior required for the theatre will start to seem natural to you, but it will always require an expenditure of real energy.

On the other hand, avoid the extreme of those who try *too* hard and "muscle" their way through the exercises. Part of the actor's skill is that he assimilates his special abilities into a free-flowing, organic *naturalness.* Beware not only of saying "look at me doing this" but also of saying "look how hard this is!"

Likewise, avoid overcomplicating the exercises in your mind; follow the spirit of the instructions and *enjoy* the experiences that follow. There will be no apocalyptic revelations; the heavens will not open and deliver ultimate theatrical truth in a clap of thunder. In fact, the results of the exercises are seldom immediate and can be properly measured only by their cumulative, long-range effect. Young actors are often so eager to *act* that they rush through the process of *learning to act;* don't be too much in a hurry!

Examine your early reactions to the exercises. At first you may regard them as "silly," or at best ineffective. Such resistance toward committing yourself to a program of physical, vocal, and spiritual development probably springs from those same inhibitions you are attempting to overcome.

You more than likely have such defenses against any kind of public involvement, and it is the actor's first attitudinal task to realize that he is often called upon to behave in a *private* manner within a *public* situation.

WORKING CONDITIONS

You should wear loose clothing or, even better, leotard and tights when you do the exercises. Besides permitting you freedom of movement, a rehearsal "uniform" (like those shown in the photographs) will enhance your sense of discipline; the uniform proclaims that you are ready and committed to work. It will also help your teacher and your classmates to observe your work and remind you that you must involve *all* of your body in it.

If conditions permit, I advise working barefoot or in ballet slippers to get a more direct feel of the floor. Long hair should be worn back, out of the face, to discourage those annoying, unconscious fiddlings at the hair that are so distracting in a performer. As a matter of safety, avoid wristwatches and jewelry; glasses should be secured with an athletic band.

Many of the exercises, especially those in the first lessons and in the lesson on voice, are meaningless unless performed with regularity over a period of time. I would recommend incorporating these specialized exercises into one of the good, all-purpose exercise programs available and to pursue them on a *daily* basis. The body learns, and is limbered and strengthened, only at a set rate; there are no shortcuts. An interruption in your exercise discipline will impair the momentum of your development.

Almost all the exercises in this book can be done in ordinary surroundings and without special equipment; many can even be done at home. When you can, however, work under the watchful eye of your teacher or with an exercise partner who fully understands the work; you can help each other a great deal by supplying an objective point of view of each other's work and progress.

Although these exercises are largely drawn from types of therapeutic psychology, I must stress that this book makes no therapeutic claims. Acting is a rigorous discipline, and my approach is designed (and has been extensively class-tested) for efficacy alone.

There are, nevertheless, many benefits of this kind of work awaiting the serious young actor, none of which relate to fame and success. Descartes said that reading good books was like conversing with the greatest minds of history, minds that had distilled their experience and wisdom in their art; we who perform good plays go a step further: we actively participate in the experience of peoples, places, and ages which have been shaped and condensed by the artistic consciousness of great playwrights. Theatre is the most human of all the arts, and we, and our audience with us, can expand our humanity through our art in ways denied us by everyday life. In turn, our extended sensitivity can reveal to us the unseen and unsuspected vibrancy of the human condition that is the raw material of all great drama.

Which brings us, finally, to the reading of some great plays. Throughout, I have tried to use examples to illustrate points taken from a few plays of various representative types. One of the great difficulties in teaching acting is that acting students are familiar with so few plays, so if you will take time at the outset to read the following plays, from which almost all my examples are drawn, you will benefit much more from the examples themselves: Shakespeare's *King Lear* and *Romeo and Juliet,* Brecht's *Mother Courage,* Miller's *Death of a Salesman,* Albee's *Zoo Story,* and Beckett's *Endgame.*

A good journey to you!

To the Teacher

This book was written to save your valuable class time for personal contact with your students—to help you minimize talk and maximize work time. It offers exercises and discussions of *principles;* it does not offer *formulas* or *rules.* Help your students to treat the book as a source of ideas and inspiration for their explorations and self-discoveries.

The ideas and exercises presented in the book are arranged "organically," but you should feel free to assign lessons and exercises in the sequence which seems best for you and for the flow of the class's work. For example, it might be appropriate to begin an advanced class with part 2 or part 3, or to teach part 1 concurrently with either part 2 or part 3. If your school's curriculum offers separate analysis or interpretation work, part 2 is an excellent basic interpretation text.

This enlarged edition was intended to offer *two years* of course work. In a school which offers only one year of acting work, I suspect that part 1 and elements of part 3 would be the wisest choice of material, with the possibility of making concurrent assignments in part 2 for home study.

In a two-year curriculum, I would suggest this format:

One semester or two quarters on part 1.
One semester or one quarter on part 2.
One semester or two quarters on part 3.
One semester or one quarter of scene work.

In any case, *do not rush!* It is more important that what is done be done well than that the entire sequence be completed. Let the work take its natural course.

Many of the basic exercises, like the first ten, are more beneficial if they are repeated regularly over a long period of time. Think of the work as being *cyclical* rather than *sequential;* like the breath itself, we must *return to center* after each excursion into a new experience.

Finally, be sure your students read and understand the opening section on How to Use This Book, as well as the introductions to each of the parts; we all know the tendency to skip prefaces and other introductory material. (And please be sure that each exercise is read as well, even if it is not used in class.)

IDEAL WORKING CONDITIONS

Few schools offer the acting teacher as much class time as we all would like. I have found six or seven hours per week (assuming additional time for voice and movement work) to be optimum for a conservatory situation; most schools get along with much less. If you have a choice, I suggest that fewer but longer working sessions are preferable to the same amount of time split into standard "fifty-minute hours." I have found ninety minutes to be a real minimum for an acting class, with two or three hours even better. In most situations we would be very happy with two class sessions per week, each three hours long. This schedule gives the class sufficient time to develop momentum while also giving the student time to prepare work between classes.

Few schools offer spaces which are appropriate to a serious acting class; certainly the traditional classroom (especially one with fixed chairs) is useless. Often we are better off in a gymnasium, in a dance studio, or on a stage—*if* the class need not continually move about to make way for sets or other events. Look about your school for a space which can be your "home" and which has (or can be provided with) any of the following qualities:

1. A sprung floor (wooden) or tumbling mats.
2. A modicum of stage-type lighting when needed, even if this means simply mounting two or three spotlights or PAR lamps on the walls.
3. Mirrors, either wall-mounted or on rolling mounts. Extremely cheap closet mirrors can be wall-mounted. Use your ingenuity— let the class help to create and maintain its working space and don't depend on the janitors!
4. Basic rehearsal furniture and a cabinet, box, or closet full of basic hand props and costume pieces.
5. A changing room nearby and lockers for clothing and valuables.
6. A phonograph or tape recorder. There are many creative ways of using music in your exercise work. A portable videotape

system is a useful luxury, but avoid close-ups (which encourage "facial" acting) and concentrate on full-body shots; the best result of videotape experience is that the student begins to relate his subjective kinetic experience to his actual appearance. (Most common remark at the first video session: "Gee, I thought I was moving more than that!")

SUGGESTED CLASS PROCEDURES

The best way to develop self-discipline in your students is to run a regularly disciplined class with certain standard procedures. I have found the following to be both reasonable and productive, as well as an excellent preparation for professional discipline in later life:

1. Absolute promptness in beginning all classes. I have gone so far as to lock the door at the appointed hour; latecomers are not admitted and must submit excuses before the next class. It is not long before everyone is in place, ready to work, at the proper time.
2. Strict policies on absenteeism, requesting advance notice of absences whenever possible.
3. A basic class uniform: I require leotards and tights, sweatshirts, or other clothing which does not restrict movement and provides a reasonable view of the student's body (especially of the mid-torso). If the floor permits, bare feet or ballet slippers are the rule; long hair on men and women is tied back or secured with a headband to keep it from obscuring the face or falling into the eyes.
4. All eating, drinking, and smoking are prohibited within the studio except at specified times.
5. Perhaps most important, a regular warm-up ritual begins each class. The length of the ritual depends on the time available; the first ten exercises in *The Actor at Work* can be performed in about twelve minutes. Once carefully learned, the ritual can be performed by the students with no verbal instructions at all; as an alternative, members of the class can take turns leading exercises.

Avoid the time-wasting temptation to continuously do new exercises; not only is time wasted in giving new instructions, but the students lose the maturing discipline of repeating basic exercises until a profound level of experience is reached. Whatever your favorite warm-up, or whatever series of preparatory exercises you evolve for your class, the real purpose of the warm-up is just what the name implies—it is a preparation for work, not an end in itself. Follow this "scenario" for any warm-up:

1. Centering and touching stillness.
2. Encouraging good alignment.
3. Clearing the mind and giving full awareness to the Here and Now and to the work of the day.
4. Gradual limbering, starting the energy flowing.
5. Lifting inhibitions (encouraging organic flow).
6. Letting sound flow easily; no good warm-up should be silent!
7. Moving steadily into states of increased activity, but always beginning from *deep muscle* involvement (which tends to be massive and slow) and moving toward *surface muscle* activity without losing the support of the deep muscles. This can best be done by keeping the breath an unobtrusive (and largely unconscious) but essential aspect of all levels of the exercise sequence; when the breath is inhibited, deep muscle involvement ceases.
8. Allowing the exercise sequence to move the student into relationship with his space and his partners.
9. Giving the sequence a conclusion of its own, but avoiding tiring the student. Try to let the warm-up lead directly into the work of the day.
10. Finally and at all cost, avoiding rote activity. The student should be alert, focused, and pursuing a playable intention during all exercise work.

SELECTION OF MATERIAL FOR CLASSROOM SCENES

So few students have an adequate grounding in dramatic literature that this is usually a real problem. I suggest that you create a list of representative plays which—over a period of time—your students will read. Draw your examples from these plays and allow students to select exercise material from them as well; in this way you will avoid the common occurrence of students doing speeches and scenes from plays they have not read carefully. (I feel very negative about the various "scene books" on the market; they invite students to work on scenes out of the context of the whole play.)

In the exercises in parts 2 and 3, it is useful if the student will stick with the same speech and (in part 3) with the scene from which the speech comes. While a solo speech or even a sonnet may be convenient for beginning analysis work, a speech from a scene is much better; after all, we are training actors, not platform performers.

Exercise material should be short: speeches not more than three minutes, scenes or scene segments not more than six or eight. Longer scenes usually do not repay the class time invested in them (until advanced work, of course, when they are indispensable); a shorter piece can usually be criticized more effectively. The speech, scene, or scene segment must, of course, have a clear shape and single central focus. Take the time to work over your students' selections with them at the beginning; this time will be handsomely repaid later.

The level of the material chosen has never seemed to me to be as crucial as many teachers think; I have successfully used Shakespeare in beginning classes, for example. The popular notion that students should begin with realistic scenes featuring characters "close" to their real selves seems to me an open invitation to the student to base his earliest work on unexamined personal habits and mannerisms. On the other hand, avoid the extreme of one major professional program, which required that all second-year actors perform a Restoration play or a play of equivalent verbal complexity! Moderation in all things . . .

Certainly you should not permit students to select material from inferior plays, but don't disparage selections from reputable commercial products either, and if the student's talent warrants, consider good musical plays as well. In any case, the material should have sufficient literary merit to repay the investment required by the exercises. Short playlets like those contained in Pinter's *Trouble in the Works* are very useful and have the added advantage that the classwork of the term might produce a short performance or other informal showing—but *do not* set this up as a goal (or even mention the possibility) until it is clear that the class is on a firm and level footing.

CLASS CRITIQUES AND EVALUATIONS

Ongoing class critiques are essential, but they must be kept within reasonable limits. Don't fall into the trap of talking one three-minute scene to death while twelve other students try to stay awake. Set a time limit for your critique and for class discussion. I do encourage class discussion of exercises, so long as these rules are followed:

1. Be a stern moderator; don't let anyone monopolize the discussion.
2. Cut off instantly defensiveness or offensiveness in anyone; we seek the truth, not personal victories.
3. Give every point of view (within the above limits) a fair hearing. Most importantly, put all attractive ideas *to the test immediately.*

In other words, critiques should be *reworking* sessions, not just talk fests.

4. Insist, within the bounds of respectful behavior, on honest and direct criticisms. Your students will quickly tune out if they see faults being whitewashed; students want expert, direct, and honest criticism. We must respect them enough to assume that they can take it—for if they can't, they are better off out of the theatre anyway.

5. Help the class to create a supportive environment by keeping critiques and discussions objectively balanced between positive and negative commentary. Too often a "critique" is judgmental only in the negative sense and not truly analytical of success as well as of failure.

The last point above is especially important in our culture where students seem to be trained to respond only to negative comments. How difficult it is to say "yes" and have our students believe us—the hidden response is often "Fine, thanks a lot, but now tell me what was wrong!" Help train your students to recognize good work and to let it *speak for itself.*

Finally, we come to the painful subject of evaluation, which for most of us means grading, even in a pass/fail system. In my experience, the ensemble nature of acting means that a class tends to learn more from itself than it does from the instructor; notice, in the history of older training programs, how "vintage years" seem to occur, in which a given class had that magical chemistry by which each member of the class was supported and enhanced by membership in that particular peer group. For this reason, you *must* jealously guard the quality of the peer group by cutting out the drifters and the dilettantes and—more painfully—the hard-working but untalented students. If you are in the common but unenviable situation of having no control over admission to your class, you can at least fail (or politely ask to leave without failing) those students who don't deliver the goods. You will quickly earn a reputation as a serious, exacting, but fair teacher, which will serve you almost as well as the ability to audition your students, and your best students will have the pride of knowing that your continued commitment to them is a meaningful reflection on their development.

We must also strike a humane balance between evaluation of a student according to abstract professional criteria and evaluation within the context of the student's potential. As a practicing actor and director, however, I lean toward the stern professional criteria. Acting is, to put it mildly, a lousy way of life and we do no one a favor by allowing him to delude himself into a doomed career. Our country presently employs fewer than one-fifth of all its existing "actors," and even outstanding talent is no guarantee of a happy theatrical life. The sad fact is that if actors were deer, we would have to shoot more than half the herd.

Even a very talented student may not benefit from your particular method of teaching. If this is the case, be direct and honest and convince him or her to seek more useful tutelage, even if that means changing schools. Know too when it is time for a talented student to "leave the nest."

Above all, avoid the extreme empathy of accepting every student failure as your own. "Where did I go wrong with him," we ask ourselves time after time. Spare yourself; you cannot teach everything every student needs and you are only in very limited ways a parent to your students. Fulfill your sense of duty and creativity, and *insist that the student fulfill his.*

TEN USEFUL PRINCIPLES

1. Never encourage the student to please *you.* The student's task is to explore the problem you have defined; the search must be his, not yours.

2. Insist on sufficient preparation; stop any exercise which is obviously ill-prepared. Teach your students the true extent of an actor's homework, the work which must be done outside rehearsal time.

3. Talk as little as possible; let the students *do* as much as possible. Side-coaching is a difficult but useful art once you and your students become used to it.

4. When you do talk, try to give your notes in *active* terms with an indication of an external focus—that is, talk about the *doings* of the exercise.

5. Never outline the "desired results" of an exercise, as this will ensure "playing for results" rather than true exploration. Try to banish "desired results" from *your* mind; when an exercise is done, accept what has really happened and treat it. If nothing has happened, find out why or set a condition which will make something happen. In short, be in the Here and Now just as much as you want your students to be. You are a guide and efficator, not a manipulator.

6. Never *justify* an exercise. When a student demands justification, he or she either is hiding from the exercise or has simply failed to have the experience which the exercise offers. Don't waste time explaining what "should" have happened and why; try something else until justification becomes unnecessary.

7. Keep the focus of the class on the work, not on the student. Acting students are narcissistic and introspective enough without

being encouraged in these largely unproductive perceptual postures.

8. To help keep the focus on the work, try to center each class session around a theme of exploration: "Today we will explore space," "Today we will explore the way in which we use space in the expression of relationship," and so on.

9. Inculcate the attitude that classwork *is* acting, not merely a *preparation for* acting. Help the student to know that theatre happens whenever and wherever we make it happen, not just on a stage at 8:15 P.M.

10. Most important, ALWAYS BE LEARNING YOURSELF! Teaching is the best education available; the teacher who has ceased to learn, to make discoveries in almost every class, is useless to himself and to his students—and to the theatre. When you feel it going stale, try something new: get out and *do,* get up and act alongside your students, find something which touches your joy in the work. You have nothing of real value to teach without it.

Acknowledgments

To Dr. Robert S. Breen of Northwestern University for his insight into the underlying relationship of social acting and stage acting, which is the foundation of this book; to Dr. John C. Edwards of the University of New Hampshire for the technique of polarization exercises; to Dr. Oscar Brockett of Indiana University for the idea to write this book, and for his generous help over the three years it took to do the job and during the two years of work on this second edition; to my colleagues at the training programs in which I have been privileged to teach: at the University of Wisconsin–Milwaukee, Carnegie-Mellon University, Yale School of Drama, York University, the National Theatre School of Canada, the University of California at Riverside, and the California Institute of the Arts. Thanks also to the following, whose ideas and exercises have found their way into this book: Fran Bennett, Nathaniel Branden, Richard Brown, Jacques Burdick, David Calderisi, Joseph Chaiken, Carmen deLavallade, Paul Draper, Jim Edmondson, Carol Egan-Lech, David Feldshuh, David Flaten, Earle Gister, Al Huang, the Institute for Research in Acting, Mordecai Lawner, Charlotte Lee, Judith Leibowitz, Michael Maley, Bob Parks, Margery Phillips, Roger Pierce, Richard Schechner, Paul Sills, Viola Spolins, Peter Stelzer, Jewel Walker, Ronald Watkins, and Daniel Yang. Thanks too for the ideas from the many books quoted—books which I hope you will read for yourself.

Finally, thanks to my wife, who kept me at this and put up with a lot in the process, and most of all deep thanks and reverence to my students, who have really taught me about acting.

The Actor at Work

PART ONE

The Actor's Tools

An actor creates, with his body and voice, sights and sounds that contribute to the artistically patterned experience we call a play. In his preparation and performance, he redefines himself and enters new realms of experience that extend and enhance his sense of aliveness. His ability to "become anew," and the meaningfulness of the experience offered by his play, move the spectator to a similar enhancement of his own spiritual vitality.

The theatre is a physical place, and all its meanings, philosophical or psychological insights, emotions—all that may be communicated by a play —first reach the spectator as the physical sensations that the actor creates. These physical sensations are the result of careful preparation; behind them lie careful study of the playscript and complex interpretive decisions by the actor and his director which are intended to express the deepest vitality of the play in a form accessible to the sensibility of the contemporary audience.

But before the playwright's conception or the director's interpretation can live, the actor must translate them into meaningfully patterned sensations communicable to his audience. Until this has been done, theatre can exist only on an intellectual or literary level; the skill of the actor in creating expressive sensations is what makes theatre a potentially full human experience, the "liveliest" among all the arts.

The actor's job is threefold: first, he must develop his *expressiveness,* reaching deeply into his being and creating from his everday feelings a highly responsive and versatile system of reactions; he must also master the technical skills of the stage until he is absolutely in control of the

1

theatrical environment, completely free to bring the vitality of his responses into a creative synthesis with the form provided by his script and to communicate this synthesis to his audience with the utmost effectiveness.

Second, he must develop the skills of *analysis* which will teach him to penetrate the surface of his script and to uncover its hidden riches.

We must add to this list a third "unteachable" but essential skill of the good actor, his "instinct" for *role-playing.* It is this imaginative ability to put himself truly in the place of a fictitious character in a meaningful way that provides the vitality of all good acting. This activity of role-playing is not unique to the stage actor; it is one of the common and necessary activities of everyday social life. As you begin developing yourself as a stage actor, you will find that a great deal of your skill as a "social actor" will be useful. You are probably already more skillful at projecting a semifictitious characterization to an audience than you might think.

Around the turn of the century, psychologist William James suggested that our personality is a complex structure consisting of an "I" and several "me's." Each of us has a good many roles, or "me's," which we play in various situations. Your roles as son or daughter, as student, as employee, as friend, all call upon you to modify your behavior at different times, to present yourself differently. Your sense of identity, your "I," is your sense of the continuity that lies behind these various performances and ties them together into one personality. If you have ever been forced to perform two different social roles at once (visits by parents to their children at college often occasion such uncomfortable situations), you know how radically different some of our "me's" can be from each other. Our sanity depends, in part, on keeping our various "me's" in their proper place and holding on to a strong sense of "I."

A contemporary social psychologist, Erving Goffman, has analyzed social behavior as if it were a dramatic performance. He finds that most of us have a highly developed ability to play successfully the role demanded from us at each moment:

It does take deep skill, long training, and psychological capacity to become a good stage actor. But this fact should not blind us to another one: that almost anyone can quickly learn a script well enough to give a charitable audience some sense of realness in what is being contrived before them. And it seems this is so because ordinary social intercourse is itself put together as a scene is put together, by the exchange of dramatically inflated actions, counteractions, and terminating replies. Scripts even in the hands of unpracticed players can come to life because life itself is a dramatically enacted thing. All the world is not, of course, a stage, but the crucial ways in which it isn't are not easy to specify. . . . In short, we all act better than we know how.[1]

Your skill as a social actor gives you a firm foundation upon which to build. But your theatre training must be intensive and specialized; as Goffman says, anyone can quickly be taught to give some sense of life to a part, but that is a very different thing from becoming a really good stage actor. As an "actor" in everyday life, you have practiced for years just to portray yourself. The stage actor must give artistically intensified performances of a whole range of extraordinary characters, often quite different from himself, and "living" in very different worlds. The good actor is rarely "himself" on stage; he has put himself *into* his character, rather than forcing the character to conform to his own habitual manner of expression and thought.

We have already named the three basic skills necessary to you as an actor: *physical and vocal mastery, analytical insight into your text, and the ability to synthesize these concepts and techniques in role-playing.* Each of these skills is dependent upon the others; without any one, the other two are useless. The complete actor strives to achieve all and disciplines himself in each area.

Here in the training program we can begin by providing you with some of the tools you need to become an actor. We can help you work on your voice, on your bodily expressiveness; we can help you develop an intelligent and sensitive relationship with the plays you perform; we can teach you techniques of concentration and role-playing. All this will take time; your formal training will barely prepare you to start *becoming* an actor. It is very important that these "first steps" of yours be good ones. Bad habits, shortcuts, gimmicks, and false values are the results of impatience and are difficult to correct later.

Patience and a sense of striving together—being able to accept the momentary failure for the sake of the long-range success—are the attitudes that the young actor must nurture. The pressures of our educational system and of the professional theatre are against these attitudes, as is the normal desire of all of us to be "successful" right *now.* Resist your desire to be an overnight star and instead explore a variety of approaches and experiences. Most of your explorations will lead up blind alleys, but it is

better to suffer momentary disappointments now than to commit yourself
to an approach or an attitude that will hopelessly limit you later.

> "Poetry," said Wallace Stevens, "is a process of the personality of the
> poet." Creative work is a training of each individual's perception according
> to the level on which he is alive and awake; that is why it is so difficult to
> evaluate. And it should be difficult. In art, perception is embodied: in dust,
> in pigment, in sounds, in movements of the body, in metals and stone, in
> threads and stuff. Each product, each goal, is an intermediate moment in a
> much longer journey of the person.[2]

Discipline also involves regularity. Your work, especially on technical
skills, must be a *daily* affair. Stanislavski, looking back late in his life, had
this to say:

> Let someone explain to me why the violinist who plays in an orchestra on
> the tenth violin must daily perform hour-long exercises or lose his power to
> play? Why does the dancer work daily over every muscle in his body? Why
> do the painter, the sculptor, the writer practice their art each day and count
> that day lost when they do not work? And why may the dramatic artist do
> nothing, spend his day in coffee houses and hope for the gift of [inspiration]
> in the evening? Enough. Is this an art when its priests speak like amateurs?
> There is no art that does not demand virtuosity.[3]

You must have the patience to work *each* day, to let your techniques and
understanding develop slowly. Learning to act is the development of pa-
tient, persistent self-discipline.

The growth of your vocal and physical expressiveness and your ability
to comprehend the life of a character are skills that, in fact, you will never
fully master—and this is, paradoxically, one of the greatest joys of acting.
You will never be "finished"; you will always be learning and changing.
Change, especially for the theatre artist, is necessary for continuing vitality.

The aim in the first part of this book is to start you out on the very long
road toward the development and maintenance of your skills. Learning to
make careful decisions and the development of a serious and disciplined

[2]Copyright © 1964 by Mary Caroline Richards. Reprinted from *Centering,* by Mary
Caroline Richards, by permission of Wesleyan University Press (p. 25).

[3]From *My Life in Art* by Constantin Stanislavski, translated by J. J. Robbins, Copyright
1924 by Little, Brown & Co. and 1952 by Elizabeth Reynolds Hapgood. Used with the
permission of the publishers, Theatre Arts Books, New York, and Geoffrey Bles Ltd., London.

working attitude at this stage of your career will be two of the most important investments you will ever make. Remember: the word *craft* comes from the German word *Kraft,* which means *power.*

Contacting Yourself: Relaxing, Concentrating, Limbering, Sensing Wholeness

"Mister Duffy lived at a little distance from his body." This description of one of James Joyce's characters applies to most of us in our everyday lives. As actors, however, we can no more maintain this distance from our bodies than could a violinist refuse contact with his violin. It is not an easy task to come to grips with one's physical existence; as one psychologist has so exactly put it, you must "invade your own privacy." This will be the purpose of the next few lessons.

While beginning to get acquainted with yourself, it will be useful to avoid distinctions like *mind* and *body*. We do not start out in life divided between a physical and an intellectual self; but as we "mature," most of us begin to think about ourselves as if we had two parts, the "mental" and the "physical." The actor, who must use his voice, body, thoughts, and feelings to achieve a unified stage creation, must strive to realize that the mind and body are one and inseparable; for him, the concept of a role and the physical realization of that role are one and the same. The ideal toward which you must work is this unity of conception and physical rendering, this indivisible wholeness that is essential to any living stage creation. The only way for you to find this integration in your work is by contacting your own existence so profoundly that the distinctions between concept and realization, mental and physical, impulse and action cease to exist for you.

Ultimately you hope to reach the point where even the distinction among the "senses," "emotion," and "body" ceases to exist. How many times directors have said to actors, "You're not seeing with your whole body!" and "You're not feeling with your whole body!" The voice especially has suffered this artificial separation from the whole body that produces it, and more often than not we could also say, "You're not *speaking* with your whole body." Once you have realized that the voice, senses, emotions, thoughts, and body are integral with one another, you will see the thread that connects the words printed on the page of your script with all aspects—verbal and nonverbal—of your ultimate performance.

6

You are working toward a realization of your actual being that is rare in our culture. We need not suggest any spiritual, moral, or philosophical reasons why such an experience is desirable for an actor; it is simply mechanical necessity that an actor explore and extend the fullest possible range of his experience, since it is this experience that will provide him with the ultimate materials of his craft. Of course, such a program of development will inevitably have a profound impact upon you:

> To reacquire the full feeling of actuality is an experience of tremendous impact, moving to the core. In the clinical situation, patients have cried out, "Suddenly I feel like jumping into the air!" And, "I'm walking, really walking!" And, "I feel so peculiar—the world is there, *really* there!" And, "I have eyes, *real* eyes!" But there is a long road . . . to such a full experience.[4]

THE BODY AND THE THEATRE

The theatre is uniquely organismic in nature. In the theatre, the "instrument" that creates the experiences—the actor's total self—is identical with the "instrument" that receives the experience—the spectator's self. It is this organismic identity between actor and spectator that makes the theatrical experience feelingful as well as comprehensible. This biological identity is expressed primarily in the nonverbal aspects of theatrical (as well as everyday) communication.

A psychologist recently found that the average adult in our culture spends only about twenty-five minutes a day in articulated speech. The rest of the time he is communicating with others (including pauses between words) he is using nonverbal means: gestures, expressions of the face, adaptations in posture and body tone, as well as the many nonverbal noises we produce, which tend (alas) to be much more common and rich in ordinary life than they are on the stage.

The picture of Willy Loman walking with bent back, sighing, shuffling through the opening scene of *Death of a Salesman,* communicates a vivid emotion as well as surprisingly specific information about Willy's situation. So, in its way, does the picture of Sheridan's Sir Anthony Absolute rushing wildly, powdered wig flying, in front of painted perspective flats. And so does the formal, precise striding of the Kabuki warrior as he employs the conventions of his theatre to reveal emotion and meaning. The highly artificialized movement required by some styles of drama is not

---

[4]Frederick S. Perls, Ralph F. Hefferline, and Paul Goodman, *Gestalt Therapy* (New York: The Julien Press, 1951), p. 41. Dell Paperback, 1964.

an obstacle to the communication of the life contained in that drama; all drama, all styles, communicate a sense of life. The genius of the actor is that he can communicate this life in the specific *form* in which it was conceived and still transmit, through the fullness of his execution of the role, the underlying common humanity essential to all great drama.

Therefore, the development of your physical tools is always geared to increasing your potential for the expression of life as well as to increasing the fidelity with which you can communicate the playwright's conception of life. For this reason, do not limit yourself to the qualities of movement you experience in everyday life, but study your body and voice to develop the control necessary for the creation of whatever forms are required of you.

RELAXATION

You first must come to terms with the actuality of your body, and the first step in contacting your body is that of relaxation. By relaxation, I do *not* mean a passive state: I mean, rather, a state in which all bodily tensions have been perfectly balanced and reduced, and in which inhibitions have been lifted. The human organism is not passive by nature: "inhibition" means literally an "in-holding." As the psychologists say, "If the inhibition is lifted, what was held in does not then passively emerge; rather, the person actively, eagerly brings it forth."[5]

When we speak of relaxation on stage, we mean that all unnecessary tensions have been removed and that the remaining energy has been purposefully focused. Only an extremely lazy actor would try to be truly "relaxed" at a time when he has such an important and complex job to do; the kind of relaxation we desire could be defined as *that state in which the actor is most ready to react to the slightest stimulus.* In other words, a state in which all inhibitions to movement or reaction have been lifted. The energy that remains, the useful energy, must be in harmonious balance so that you are free to move or react in any way required. A good way of describing the relaxed actor would be to say that he is "waiting to move."

The first step in achieving relaxation is to identify, localize, and rid yourself of all unnecessary tensions, and your first exercise will be to inspect the tensions within your body.

Note: If you have not yet read How to Use This Book *in the opening pages, please do so before beginning the exercises.*

[5]Ibid., p. 22.

Exercise 1 Playing cat

Select a comfortable position in a surrounding that is not too distracting. Do not "try to relax"; trying to relax is like trying to fall asleep—it can't be done. At best, you are trying to become aware of the tensions that prevent you from relaxing. Stretch yourself out face up, hands at your sides. Put yourself at rest by yawning and stretching.

> To see yawning and stretching at their luxurious best, watch a cat just awakening from a siesta. It arches its back, extends to the utmost legs, feet, and toes, drops its jaw, and all the while balloons itself up with air. Once it has swelled until it occupies its very maximum of space, it permits itself slowly to collapse—and then is ready for new business.[6]

Perform the role of the cat. Stretch, arch your back, extend all your limbs to their utmost, drop the jaw, wiggle the arms and hands, and breathe deeply (not once but many times), each time taking in more and more air. When a real yawn comes, encourage it; let the full natural sound of the yawn pour out. Then, settle back with your knees raised just enough to make the small of your back lie completely against the floor. Place your toes, heels, hip joints, and shoulders on two parallel lines (see figure 1). We will call this our *floor alignment.*

Now, lying in this hopefully euphoric state, pinpoint your attention on any area of your body that has failed to play the game. Perhaps it is your right hand, or the toes of your left foot, or the small of your back, or the nape of your neck, or your buttocks. Wherever tensions occur, focus the full force of your concentration upon that area until those tensions have been quelled. Continue breathing as fully as possible. Although you are not *trying* to relax, do not prevent spontaneous relaxation when it occurs. As you relax more and more, feel yourself melting into the floor.

THE HERE AND NOW

Your primary point of awareness must be the present moment, not the past or the future. Relaxation in the sense of being "ready to act" demands that

[6]Ibid., p. 134.

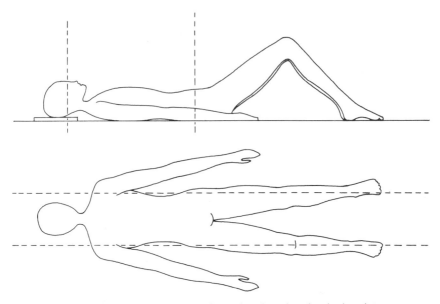

FIGURE 1   Floor alignment. A small pad may be placed under the head; in any case, the head is level, with eyes looking directly upward. The waistline is also level.

you immerse yourself in the present instant, because it is only *now* that you exist. This is more difficult to achieve than would be imagined; we tend to protect ourselves from the unknown of the immediate moment by dwelling imaginatively in the past or the future. Daydreaming and wool-gathering are almost continuous processes. We rarely risk complete contact with the present: we prefer a sense of comfortable continuity, achieved by blurring the lines that separate the present from the past and future. The past, in memory, and the future, in expectation, can both be controlled by our consciousness; but the present can be met only on its own terms. Although you can never specifically isolate it, you can put yourself in touch with the unending *flow* of the present.

> The wish to seize the present and pin it down—to mount it, as it were, like a butterfly in a case—is doomed to failure. Actuality forever changes. In healthy persons, the feeling of actuality is steady and continuous but, like the view from a train window, the scenery is always different.[7]

[7]Ibid., p. 33.

Exercise 2   Here and now

Put yourself at rest as above: while breathing comfortably, say to yourself sentences describing your immediate awareness. For example, "Right now I am lying on the floor, I am doing exercise 2, I am making up sentences, what will I do first, my right hand is a little cold," and so on. Do this as long as you can.

How far did you go? Why did you stop where you did? Was there anything you ignored or avoided? Go farther each time you do the exercise and examine the responses. Where did your awareness take you? How hard was it for you to stay completely in the present? Did you wander backward into memory, or into the future? Were your responses "physical" or "mental"? What did you avoid?

Most of these exercises have no specific "goal" and can remain useful indefinitely as warm-up exercises. The immediate purpose of this exercise has been more or less fulfilled when the temptation to wander into the past or the future has been so completely overcome that you can remain comfortably and effortlessly in the present, but even then there is more to be done. As you repeat this exercise on successive days, allow the sentences describing the endless present to fade gradually away, leaving only a *restful alertness;* your mind will be like a pool of still water, ready to reflect anything, and the lightest touch of a falling leaf will send ripples into the farthest corner of your consciousness.

FOCUSING AWARENESS

Just as the relaxed actor's body is ready to move, his mind is ready to react; it is clear and fresh, dwelling comfortably and quietly in the here and now, observing watchfully the endless flow of the present. Like the cat before the mousehole, he is perfectly still, without tension, but ever alert. We have already called this relaxed but energized condition one of *restful alertness.*

In this state of restful alertness you will be able quickly to focus your full attention, to *concentrate.* "To concentrate" means literally "to come to a common center," so that in a concentrated state your awareness may flow freely toward a given point or into a given pattern.

We commonly misunderstand concentration, thinking of it as a narrow *limiting* of the awareness and a condition involving *strain.* Neither is the case; think instead of your awareness as a quiet energy that flows into a

FIGURE 2

meaningful pattern of "foreground" and "background." The "foreground" is the thing you are perceiving, and the "background" is everything else. This is not a rigidly fixed relationship, but rather one involving choice and training of the awareness. For example, figure 2 is a well-known illustration of figure/ground patterning: what do you see in it? The drawing may be interpreted in two ways; you may even alternate the "foreground" and "background" at will. You do not cease to perceive the background while concentrating on the foreground; rather, you perceive one *because* of the other, seeing both simultaneously in a meaningful pattern. Your awareness may flow into the pattern called "vase" or into the pattern called "faces."

As you train yourself to control your awareness while still remaining flexible in your ability to accept new patterns, you will begin to perceive each emergent pattern with greater vividness. It is this clarity and acuteness of pattern perception that we commonly call good "concentration." The actor needs this ability because he is called upon to be aware of many things simultaneously on the stage and to assimilate all of his awareness into one vivid and useful pattern. When he is able to focus his full awareness freely into such a useful pattern, it becomes his "theatrical reality."

As difficult as this may sound, it is actually accomplished without great effort; your awareness, like any of your other energies, will flow naturally if you lift the inhibitions that impede its flow, if you can open yourself to immediate experience. For this reason, the ability to concentrate is related to the ability to relax; relaxation frees the consciousness to flow freely and flexibly into new and vivid patterns of experience. For the actor, relaxation and concentration are two aspects of one state of mind and body. As we have said, relaxation permits an immediacy and flexibility of response. Rigid perceptual habits are obstacles to flexibility in this sense; you must free yourself of such habitually rigid patterns of perception. You must be able to shift from "vase" to "faces" at will, and even to see both at once, or a new third pattern they form together.

Creativity, in fact, may be thought of as the ability to discover new patterns in old experiences, so that the artist must be able to suspend his habitual habits of perception and look at life with "fresh eyes," thus allowing new patterns to emerge. For the actor, this means adopting a new awareness of human behavior and experience that sees fresh meanings in them. Just as the cubist painter trained himself to "see" the geometric patterns underlying the shapes of everyday life, so the actor trains himself to "feel" the underlying, universal patterns of human experience and to find fresh and vivid expressions of these patterns in his work. You can begin to develop this freshness of perception by finding a heightened experience of your own existence.

In each of the following exercises you will be asked to give your full conscious awareness to some specific part of your body, or to some aspect of your voice, or to some quality of experience. Whatever the point of focus, begin to feel the natural flow of your awareness into it. Experience it as a "foreground" that emerges from the "background" of your total consciousness. Avoid strain, avoid premeditation; open yourself to the experience. Be alive!

The next exercise will provide a shifting point of focus through your body while also moving you further into a state of relaxation.

Exercise 3   Phasic relaxation

Begin in floor alignment. The breath is the focus of your awareness in this exercise: imagine that each inhalation is a warm, fresh energy-filled fluid flowing into your body, and that each exhalation carries away with it tension and inhibition, like a refreshing wave. Breathe deeply and easily in a slow, natural, regular rhythm; don't "act" your breathing or artificially exaggerate it. After you have done this exercise a few times, you will cease to be aware of the breath at all.

During the exercise, each successive breath will be sent into a different part of the body, awakening that area. As the breath flows into the area, let its energy cause the muscles there to contract as much as they can; then, as the breath flows out, the muscles release and the breath carries all the tensions away with it, leaving the area refreshed and at ease. The exhalation is a *letting go.*

The breath will travel from the top of the body downward, and the regular rhythm of your breathing should make the muscular contractions and relaxations flow smoothly down the body like a slow wave. Allow only one area at a time to be involved; your total awareness follows the breath into each of the following:

The forehead and scalp, furling the brow and then releasing;

The eyes at rest, closed and turned slightly downward;

The jaw, clenching, then letting it fall easily downward until the teeth are about one-half inch apart;

The tongue, extending, then lying easily in the mouth;

The front of the neck, so that the chin is drawn down to touch the chest and a stretch is felt across the back of the neck—then rolling easily back down;

The back of the neck, so that the top of the head rolls under to touch the floor and a stretch is felt across the front of the neck—then rolling slowly down and lengthening the neck;

The upper chest, swelling outward in *all* directions so that the shoulders are widened—then easily subsiding, feeling the shoulder blades spread and melt into the floor, wider than before;

The arms and hands, becoming stiff and straight as steel rods, the hands clenched into fists—then easily melting into the floor, uncurling;

The pit of the stomach, clenching, becoming a small, hard ball—then, with a sigh, releasing;

The buttocks, clenching—then releasing and widening so that the pelvis (*not* the knees) is wider than before;

The knees, stiffening as the legs straighten, the feet being pushed downward by this action—then releasing and feeling the legs melt into the floor;

The toes reach up to touch the eyes (but the heels remain on the floor) —then they release and fall into a natural position;

The heels and the shoulder blades simultaneously push downward into the floor so that the whole body lifts in a long arch—then with a sigh you slowly fall, the body lengthening as it relaxes, melting deep into the floor;

The knees are again raised, by the action of the breath, until the entire spine is flat on the floor;

Ten deep, slow, regular breaths follow, and with each breath you move more deeply into relaxation, remaining alert and refreshed. The flow of breath is a continuous cycle of energy that is stored comfortably in the lower body; with each breath this store of energy is increased. Whenever a yawn comes to you, enjoy it fully; vocalize the exhalation and let the sound of the yawn pour freely out.

As you repeat this exercise on successive days, you can begin to give yourself the instructions silently, reminding yourself of the specific activities in each phase. Keep a steady rhythm that follows the tempo of deep, relaxed breathing. Gradually the action of the exercises will become natural, and you will no longer need to think of the instructions, giving your full conscious awareness to the wave of contractions and relaxations that follow the breath through the body, awakening, refreshing, and relaxing it, making you ready for work.

LIMBERING

Having begun to remove unwanted tensions from the body, and having begun to develop a clear, watchfully alert mind, you must now proceed to lift any inhibitions to movement you may have so that your relaxed state will indeed be one of complete responsiveness. All of the exercises in the next four lessons will attack this problem in one way or another, but for now we will begin to loosen the body and make it more limber, more free in its capacity for movement.

We begin our limbering with an expanding of the joints. Like any mechanism, our skeletal structure produces friction and requires a certain degree of looseness and lubrication, which permits the parts to slide easily against one another. Our muscles are housed in sheaths of smooth tissue that permit them to slide easily; our joints have viscous fluids in them that lubricate. If distorted posture or muscular habit compresses the joints or holds them rigid, or causes the sheaths of interstitial tissue to shrink into permanent misalignment, your capacity and readiness to move is reduced; you become literally less responsive.

The following exercises will begin to lengthen and widen the torso, expanding the joints and opening bodily cavities to maximum size.

Exercise 4   Lengthening and widening (first phase)

A. *With a partner:* One partner assumes floor alignment while the other proceeds gently but firmly and steadily to lengthen and widen his torso according to the following instructions. The partner on the floor remains entirely passive, surrendering totally to the actions of the active partner, neither helping nor hindering.

1. The head is cupped gently in the hands from above, and is rolled and rocked while being gently pulled directly upward along the axis of the spine; *do not* pull the head in such a way that the chin lifts (see figure 3).

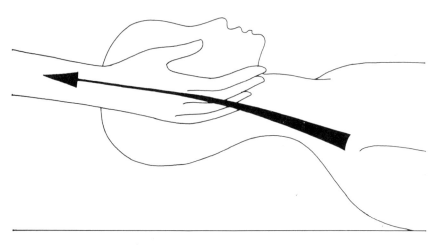

FIGURE 3

2. Placing one hand palm up under the center of partner's back and the other palm down just below the base of his neck, massage and pull gradually outward toward the side. You will see the shoulder visibly widen and flatten. Repeat with other side (see figure 4).
3. Massaging the whole of the arm, beginning well up into the armpit, draw the arm steadily downward, continuing through the hand and into the fingers. Repeat with other arm.

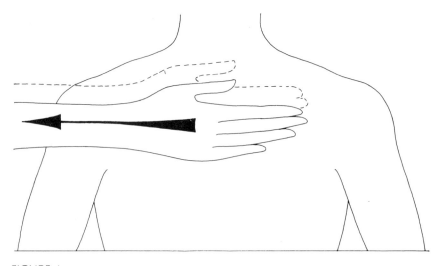

FIGURE 4

4. Repeat this same action with each leg.
5. Trade roles and repeat the exercise.

(When you and your partner have done this exercise a few times, you may recall the experience for yourself by taking floor alignment and remembering the actions of your partner's hands, cueing yourself to "lengthen" and "widen" on your own. The remainder of the exercise does not require a partner.)

B. In floor alignment, slowly rock your pelvis upward; feel the thrust as a downward, curving motion as indicated by the arrow in figure 5. The motion is a flowing undulation; one after another, each vertabra is lifted until the back is raised as far as the midback (dotted line); then it is rolled back down vertabra by vertabra in a steady motion; the back is longer when it comes down than it was when it went up. Breathe *in* on the way *down* and *out* on the way *up*, counting aloud seven counts up and silently seven counts down. Release completely between each series; begin with four repetitions.

C. Immediately after completing section B begin again but extend the upward motion until you are lifted well up onto your shoulders;

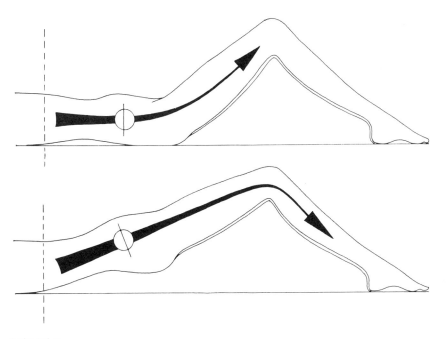

FIGURE 5

Right

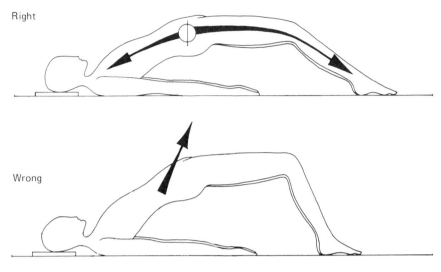

Wrong

FIGURE 6

the thrust is still downward, and your raised position should feel like a long arch from heels to shoulder as in the phasic relaxation exercise. *Do not* thrust the stomach upward, causing the small of the back to bend sharply (see figure 6). After reaching the top of the arc, lower the back, vertebra by vertebra, with a smooth motion as in section B. Leave the arms relaxed, the head free to roll from side to side. The breath and counting pattern is the same as in B.

D. In the same rhythm, roll yourself smoothly up into a forward-reaching position (vertebra by vertebra) so that the head reaches forward over the knees, leading with the arms. Feel lifted upward out of the top of the head in a lengthening motion. Keep the shoulders wide. Repeat four times (see figure 7).

E. Lie flat with the arms stretched upward on the floor above the head. Without lifting any other limb, reach the right leg across to the left as far as you can in the direction of the arrows in figure 8. Do the same with the left leg, and with each arm.

F. Stretch in all directions at once, again playing cat, then fall easily back into the floor alignment position. Let the noise of your stretches be full and natural. Again, encourage any yawn that occurs spontaneously, letting the sound pour freely out. The yawn is a good friend to us in our work.

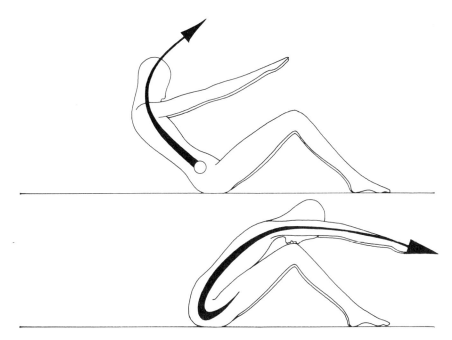

FIGURE 7

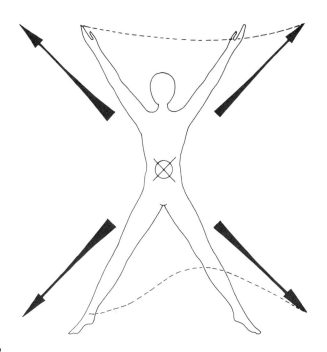

FIGURE 8

19

SENSING WHOLENESS

When you have completed the series of four relaxation exercises as a single uninterrupted experience, you can let the liberated consciousness explore its new freedom within the body.

Our bodies seem complex when we think of all the organs and systems operating in a delicate balance and cooperation, but there is a way in which our whole organism, body as well as consciousness, can be experienced as a unified whole with each part, each sensation, fully integrated. The actor strives for such a sense of wholeness because the stage demands total responsiveness simultaneously from all the aspects of his organism; only an integrated, "together" organism can supply such responses.

Exercise 5 Getting it together

In the restful state following the preceding exercises, lying in floor alignment, with the eyes closed:

A. Let your conscious awareness roam at random throughout the body;
B. Mentally measure the distances within the body from point to point; are all your dimensions as big as they can be without forcing?
C. Become aware of all kinds of paired relationships within the body; explore the connections between various sensations and parts of the body. What does the stomach do when you breathe, what does your tongue do when you clench your buttocks, etc?
D. Finally, breathing very easily and feeling the warm energy of the breath flowing into and out of the body, *make a neutral sound* without effort or change in the breath stream; simply "let" a sound be there for a moment. What bodily activities support the sound? Do you see what a tiny change is required to produce sound? Do you truly experience sound as an aspect of the breath, and the breath as an aspect of the wholeness of your mind and body?

The body is not a "thing," remaining static; it is a continuous process of change. Yet for all its dynamism and seeming complexity, it is at any moment also a single, totally unique, and harmonious entity. So, too, all of the activities of which you are capable—motion, sound, consciousness itself—express this same wholeness; they are all aspects of the total organism, and all spring from the same common source.

This sense of a common source, or *center,* from which all our expressive activity springs, can provide you with an important understanding of your wholeness. When your center becomes felt and fully energized, you will begin to move, to sound, even to think in a more integrated way, with greater continuity and effectiveness. This sense of the center is, for the actor, rooted in a literal, specific recognition of a physical center from which all your impulses to move or to sound flow outwardly into the external world.

This physio-vocal center is deep within the body, in an area roughly three finger-widths below your navel. It is here that the breath (and therefore the voice) originates, as well as all large motions of the body. This area is the literal center of gravity of your body. If you withhold this area of the body from a full and easy participation in everything you do, you will inevitably look and sound "stiff" and "superficial"; the movements and sounds you will produce will not be deeply motivated or complete because they will not be originating from the true center of your being.

The essential experience in realizing your wholeness, then, is to contact and energize this deep center, and to begin to feel every motion and sound as having its roots in it. The next lesson will help you to begin freeing and enjoying your center as you begin to move and to produce sound.

Lesson 2

Contacting Yourself: Centering, Aligning, Moving, and Sounding

Incarnation: bodying forth. Is this not our whole concern? The bodying forth of our *sense of life?* . . . We body forth our ideals in personal acts, either alone or with others in society. We body forth felt experience in a poem's image and sound. We body forth our inner residence in the architecture of our homes and common buildings. We body forth our struggles and our revelations in the space of theatre. That is what form is: the bodying forth. . . .[8]

This thought is from a book called *Centering* by Mary Caroline Richards. She is a poet, translator of Antonin Artaud's theatrical writing, and a potter; as a potter, she knows how the centering of the clay upon the wheel is essential to creation in that art, for only from perfectly centered clay can the motions of the wheel and of the potter's hands bring the flow of the pot's shape freely and naturally toward its ultimate form. As a poet, she also knows how the experiences of one's life must touch a personal center before they can in turn flow outward, be bodied forth, in the form of a poem. We teachers of acting, and we actors, also know how the actor, in the deepest way, must center himself; as he touches his center he, like the clay, is liberated to flow outward into new forms that are profoundly organic expressions of his life experience.

Your center is a *source* of energy; as that energy flows outward into a new form through your stage actions, you begin to *experience yourself anew.* As the new form of thought and behavior required of you by your play becomes more demanding, it extends you further from your "ordinary" self, and as you come to experience this new form of yourself more fully, it summons new energies from you. Thus your center as a source of energy, the external forms that those energies may take, and the process of action

[8]Copyright © 1964 by Mary Caroline Richards. Reprinted from *Centering,* by Mary Caroline Richards, by permission of Wesleyan University Press (pp. 38–39.)

by which energy flows from your center into observable outer form are in fact all aspects of one indivisible *process of becoming* that expresses your fullest personal potential within your art.

It is this unity of *energy source/energy flow* that will sum up the term *centering.* There are many ways in which this idea will be important to you, and in this lesson you will explore its physiovocal aspects; later you will see that it has spiritual and psychological aspects as well. A feeling of centeredness is a *total* experience of the *total* self.

When you begin to study characterization you will find that your ability to engage and modify your sense of center in order to bring it into conformity with the character's quality of center will be a primary tool of characterization. Your aim in learning to center yourself, in fact, is to make all your human energies accessible and controllable in the process of creation.

When your stage creation has grown from your own center, and when the form of your characterization is filled with the energy which flows from this center, then (and only then) will it glow with the unmistakable vitality of true life. Without the engagement of your deepest energies in your stage creation, your work can only appear empty, a mere superficial form; however technically skilled or interpretively accurate your performance may be, it will fail to speak to your audience with the unmistakable ring of *authenticity.*

Whatever kind of play, whatever "style" of theatre you are engaged in, your work must be *authentic.* This word literally means *self-authorship,* or *to be the author of yourself,* and this is a beautiful summation of the actor's creative purpose. Your deepest task is to be *trans-formed,* to allow your total personal energies to flow into a new form, to *re-define* or *re-author* yourself so as to serve a precise and meaningful artistic function within the demands of your play. Your analytical and expressive skills provide you with an understanding of the character and the means to realize it, but the form can be brought to life only by your ability to contact the source of your deepest energies and to permit them to flow easily into the character. It is this ability that also gives you the marvelous opportunity to experience yourself anew, to live many lives, each of which is an enhancement of your own; and this is the ultimate reward of the actor.

SOUNDING

The happy, effective workman is often the noisy one; humming, singing, laughing, grunting, his effort usually flows into his work via sound as well as motion. The student of karate learns this—that the outward flow of energy from our deepest center naturally carries the breath, and hence the voice, with it. We often inhibit this natural flow out of fear, or anxiety,

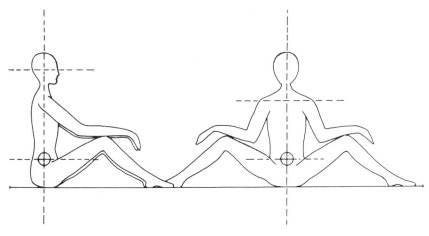

FIGURE 9   Sitting alignment.

or because our upbringing has taught us to restrain our natural capacity for sounding. The actor, however, must recapture the naturally integrated and simultaneous quality of moving, breathing, and sounding.

The following exercise will give you an experience of the breath flowing from (and back to) your center, carrying sound and motion with it.

Exercise 6   Giving sound

Sit up, directly on the bony points you can feel just below the surface of each buttock; spread your legs as wide as is comfortable, with the knees slightly raised. Feel lifted out of the top of your head so that your back and neck are long and wide. The head is level, eyes ahead, and the waist is level also. We will call this our *sitting* alignment. You should do this exercise as a continuous flow, not as a series of positions; the tempo and flow of the exercise are determined by slow, deep breathing, and each cycle uses one complete breath.

A. Breathing out, reach forward and down, keeping the back and neck long, and shoulders wide. Imagine that you are bowing to someone sitting at the back of a theatre.
B. As you begin to breathe in, draw the breath into the lower part of the body by drawing the small of your back to the rear and scooping "energy" into the funnel formed by your legs with your hands.

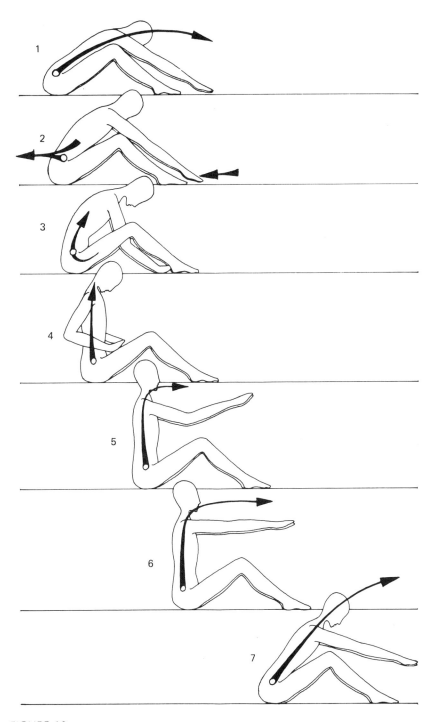

FIGURE 10

C. As the breath begins to fill you, you feel its warmth and power flowing up from your deep center. Follow its upward movement with your hands.

D. As the breath rises in the body it lifts you, straightening and lengthening the upper torso and neck, lifting the head, widening the shoulders and the throat as it flows upward like a wave moving you in a slow undulation. You unfurl like a fern opening.

E. The breath then flows into the outer world, with the feeling and sound of a yawn; you are giving this sound to that person sitting at the back of the theatre, and you accompany it with an unfolding gesture of the arms toward him. Your eyes are alive; you "see" him.

F. As the power of the breath begins to diminish, you easily close the mouth so that the "ah" sound of the yawn becomes an "m," and you experience a tingle in the mouth and nose areas. As the breath and sound begin to die away, the body again bows forward and down, the back still long and wide, arms reaching forward to scoop in a new quantity of breath energy.

G. As the breath and sound are completely used up, the body has sunk low in its bow, and the cycle begins again. At no time do you strain or pinch the voice, for the breath always lifts the head, widens and relaxes the throat, and pours easily out with the feeling of a yawn.

As the breath enters and leaves your body in this exercise, feel the continuity of inward and outward breaths as two aspects of one cycle; change over easily from one to the other so that the entire exercise becomes one unbroken, flowing experience with no "sharp corners," only smoothly curving patterns of time, energy, motion, and sound. The smooth flow of the sound produces a trisyllable word, "ah-oh-m" or *om*. The exercise then concludes:

H. When you have completed enough cycles of this exercise to feel the full integration of breath, motion, and sound in an unbroken pattern, hold in the erect position and begin to produce as continuous a tone as you can, pausing easily for breath. (If you are in a group, the entire group should produce one continuous, harmonious sound, and each member of the group should feel himself part of the group sound and the group sound part of him.) In a group or alone, begin to feel the space around you vibrating with your sound. As you continue to produce sound, feel the vibrations of that sound spreading into every part of your body: out of the neck into the head and chest, into the back, the stomach, the buttocks, into the arms and hands, into the legs and feet, into the scalp. As each area of the body opens to the vibration, let the easy energy of the sound lift you and open you so that you rise first to your knees, then to a standing position. Feel the sound radiating from *every* part of your body!

Examine your experience during sounding: were there parts of your body that did not join in the vibration? Did you have a new sense of the capacity of your entire organism to join in the action of sounding? Did you keep a sense of the sound flowing from your center? Did you feel more in touch with yourself and with the space around you, as if your sound were literally reaching outside yourself in a tangible way? Are you now more alert, refreshed, and relaxed?

STANDING ALIGNMENT

Just as we experienced relaxation as *a readiness to react,* so our aim in aligning and centering the body is to put ourselves in the most responsive physio-vocal condition. We are *not* interested in "correct" posture or voice, for there is no "correct" voice or posture for the actor until they are determined by the demands of his characterization; here we are merely working to achieve a *neutral but energized* condition from which we are ready to move in any way necessary to fulfill the demands of our dramatic task.

As you stand, focus your awareness on your skeleton. In the course of man's evolution, the skeleton has begun (and is still) adapting itself to an erect posture, so that we can stand against the force of gravity with a minimum of muscular strain. Imagine the bones as building blocks that, if each is set properly above the one below, can almost stand erect by themselves.

This sense of bringing each part of your body into the proper position to permit its weight to flow directly downward through the body into the ground will not only give you stability, it will also place you in the most responsive alignment from which movement or sound in any direction is free and easy.

The following sequence of exercises will give you a direct experience of this alignment and centeredness. We begin by examining the structure of the body as it relates to movement.

Exercise 7   Finding the joints

A. With your partner, standing and facing each other: help each other to find the two joints in the spinal column; one is high in the head, inside the hollow that runs up the back of the neck and underneath the bony ridge that can be felt at the top of this hollow. The joint itself is inside the head roughly level with the eyes. The other joint is at the base of the spine, roughly on a level with the hip joints. Find the hip joints by lifting each leg and feeling for them; they are higher than you may suppose, roughly level with your center.

It is common to think that the spine has many "joints" in it, but in fact only these two, at top and bottom, are true joints. The rest of the spine is capable of considerable flexibility, of course, but too often we try to make small areas of the spine do the work of joints; for instance, we commonly behave as if our back were jointed at points A and B in figure 11, while it is actually jointed at points X and Y.

The result of this widespread misuse of the spine in our culture is equally widespread back and neck trouble. For the actor, however, the bad effects of this misuse are even more severe; you can see immediately how bending the back at point B causes your abdomen to be constricted, severely limiting the action of the diaphragm and thus limiting your breath support and freedom. Likewise, bending the neck at point A causes you to crush the voice box, disturbing the natural production of vocal tone. In the next section of the exercise, try to loosen and expand the true joints in your spine and to feel yourself moving easily, fluidly, from them. Notice how your sound can remain full and free when you move in this way.

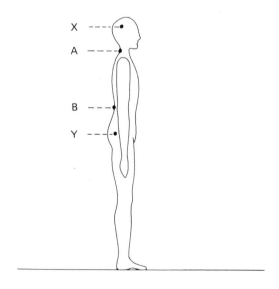

FIGURE 11

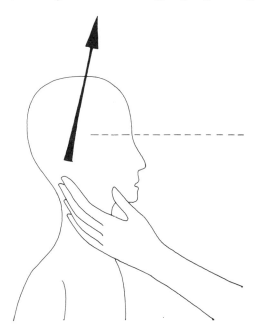

FIGURE 12   Be sure that the head remains level as it is lifted.

B. Again facing each other, one partner reaches out and cups the other's head in his hands, as in figure 12. Gently, he lifts slightly upward along the central axis of the body. The partner being lifted lets himself "hang" loosely, like a medical student's skeleton on a spring. As partner slowly moves the head in many directions and through space, the hanging partner lets his loose body respond easily and gives sound, experiencing his sound through a variety of motions. Change roles and repeat.

(After you have experienced these exercises with partner, you may repeat them alone by remembering the feeling of partner's lift; the remainder of the exercise does not requre a partner.)

C. Moving on your own with the memory of partner's lift, explore the balance of your body when it moves as a single system hinged at these joints and at the knees: walk by simply moving the knee forward (not up); sit and rise by maintaining continuous balance between these joints. Let sound accompany your outgoing breath. ALL MOVEMENT AND SOUND ORIGINATE IN YOUR CENTER AND FLOW EFFORTLESSLY UP THE SPINE AND OUT THE TOP AND FRONT OF YOUR HEAD AS IF PARTNER WERE STILL LIFTING YOU.

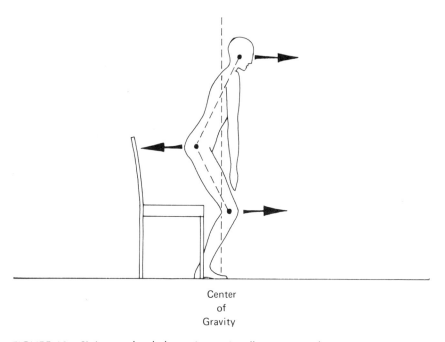

Center
of
Gravity

FIGURE 13   Sitting so that balance is continually maintained.

In these exercises, all movements originate from your deep center and flow into the outer world. Specifically, energy flows upward through your spine and out the *top* of the head; this is the point at which the spine would protrude from the scalp if it were extended upward; for most of us it is also the center of the whirlpool-like swirl in our hair. You and your partner can help each other to determine this point. When you are lifted upward from this point, your head remains perfectly level, with the chin neither lifting toward the ceiling nor dropping toward the chest.

In the next exercise, we translate this upward lift along the central axis of the body into an "unfolding" motion that can help to teach us good standing alignment.

Exercise 8   Hanging yourself up

Bend at the hip joint, and let the entire top half of the body fall forward and downward, so that you are folded like a rag doll hanging from a string tied to the base of its spine. Don't strain; simply hang as limply as you can with the knees locked (but not tense). If necessary, partner may hold you at first. Imagine now that the string has been moved up one vertebra, and you are now hanging from a point a few inches further up your back. Steadily, the "string" moves up your back, vertebra by vertebra; the head and arms hang loosely as you straighten up until the head at last floats upward as the "string" reaches the last of the small vertebrae in the neck and comes out the top of the head. The overall movement is of an undulation or wave motion as you "uncurl" into *standing alignment* (see figure 14). You will feel taller and lighter, you will have a sense of openness, and the distance from your ears to your shoulders will be greater. Avoid "pushing" up from below; try to feel yourself "pulled" up from above.

These exercises may have revealed tensions and distortions in your body of which you were not previously aware. Everyone has some habitual, unconscious way of holding the tensions of everyday life in his muscles; over a long period of time the tendons and connective tissue within the body may become distorted under the influence of these habits, result-

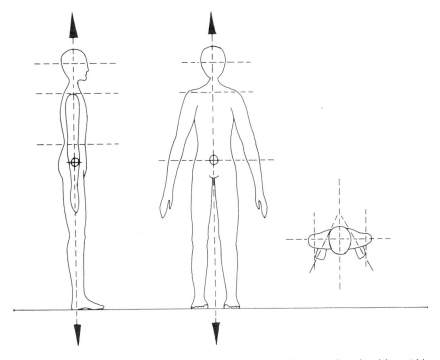

FIGURE 14   Standing alignment. The feet are comfortably spread to shoulder width. If the knees are bent, they will move out directly over the toes.

ing in a semipermanent misalignment and inhibiting of one part of the body or another.

Inhibitions, you see, are not only "mental" attitudes; they come to reside in the body in a variety of physiological ways. Most commonly, "taboo" areas of the body may fall into disuse because we withhold them from everyday activity rather than risk violating socially "acceptable" behavior. The genital areas most obviously suffer in this way, and they are a special problem for the actor, since the lower abdomen is the source of most gestural and vocal impulses; but there are other areas of the body that may also be inhibited for any number of reasons: the inner thighs, the toes, the underarms, the neck, or the back, for example.

Disused areas are often somewhat shrunken or pinched. In the other extreme, areas of which we are acutely aware but about which we may have some fear or embarrassment may be overdeveloped or held rigidly by tight muscles. Perhaps in your adolescence you were motivated to thrust out your chest, or your pelvis, or your jaw (or, alternatively, to withdraw one or another of these areas). Years later, even though this social motivation has ceased to operate, you may find these earlier muscular patterns still operating, literally "built in" to the body; the shoulders still pinched forward or back, the pelvis tilted, the head forward or back of center. Such muscular patterns may even have become expressive habits for you, ways in which you continue to confront and react to life.

While such habitual physical patterns are part of your personality, it will be necessary to your development as an actor that you bring these patterns within your conscious artistic control and that you be able to restore your self, your body and mind, to an undistorted or "neutral" condition. If you do not, you will carry these uncontrolled habits of body (and therefore of mind as well) into every character you play, appropriate or not.

Working with a partner or before a large mirror, check yourself: is one shoulder higher than another, or wider? Does your pelvis rock to one side as you stand? Most commonly you will find that your waistline, viewed in profile, tilts down toward the front, making your abdomen protrude and your back sway. Perhaps your chest is somewhat sunken, drawing your shoulders forward; or, in the other extreme, the shoulder blades pinched together and the shoulders drawn back. Everyone has a symptom, or symptoms, of this kind; find yours. Be particularly careful as you exercise to keep your head, chest, and waistline level.

Do not be overly concerned with your findings, however; everyone has some distortion from "perfect" alignment, and such distortion is not in itself a major obstacle to your development as an actor. However, you can use these symptoms to trace habitual bundles of tension, or to identify disused areas of your body; try to relate each of your alignment symptoms to the habitual posture or inhibition that produced it. You will probably also find in our later vocal work that these bodily misalignments cause many vocal problems.

As you continue your exercise program day after day, give special attention to these problems; in your daily life as well, "catch" yourself when you notice yourself falling into the old habits. A "trigger" word that you say to yourself, like "lengthen," or "center," is sometimes valuable as a self-reminder. Do not, however, *force* yourself into alignment; merely try to break the old habits and let the body's natural sense of balance reassert itself. This is a very gradual process of *un*doing, not *doing,* and over a period of months you may begin to notice improvement.

These suggestions, of course, pertain only to common misalignments. If you have a severe problem, you may want to consult an expert therapist. The Alexander Technique is one of several good therapies that help to align and liberate the body; other recommended techniques include Structural Integration (Rolfing), Patterning, and Bioenergetics. You should consult only licensed, reputable practitioners by contacting national accreditation centers for each type of therapy, or by consulting an osteopath or orthopedist. Avoid home remedies!

MOVING AND SOUNDING FROM CENTER

Your relaxed and aligned body is ready to move, your energy is ready to flow spontaneously from your deepest center. This energy, flowing into the outside world, may take a variety of external forms: its visible aspects are movements, its audible aspects are sounds and words, its psychological aspects are emotions. All of these are only different modes of the same energy; any impulse may flow into any of these forms or into all of them simultaneously, and all of these forms—movement, sound, and feeling—are as integral to one another as you are to yourself. To whatever degree your movement, sound, and feelings are not integral with one another, you are less whole and less accessible to yourself in your work, and your work will inevitably exhibit this same fragmentation.

But it is easy and simple to continue sensing wholeness or centeredness, and you begin with the simplest of exercises:

Exercise 9   Finding center

Align yourself as in the previous exercise.

A. Move either foot out to the side about two feet; rock from foot to foot, feeling your center of gravity moving from side to side. Gradually come to rest on center like a pendulum coming to rest.

B. Move either foot forward about two feet; find your center with front-to-back motions in the same way.

C. Move your center around rotationally, exploring the limits of various stances. Feel the weight of your body flowing into the ground out of your center through the legs; feel "rooted," as if your weight were a root reaching into the ground beneath you.

D. Bring the feet together and explore the center.

E. Imagine a cord entering the top of the head and attached to your center; "lift" yourself upward in small jumps by "tugging" on this cord.

F. Jump to a specific place by *lifting* the center, then *putting it down* on the destination. You land perfectly centered, stable and without jiggling, but *lightly*. At no time in your jump do you lose your center.

G. Walk to a specific place by lifting the center up through the top of the head, holding it up while you walk, and setting it down at the destination.

GROUNDING

As you begin to sense your physical center, feel the way in which energy flows from it into even the smallest movements. Notice that, like any energy, your energy radiates outward in all directions at once, *downward* as well as upward. Feel how your energy flows into the ground. Imagine yourself standing on a mirror. Below you is your other self with its own center; imagine a bond between your center and that in your mirror image. This imaginary bond of energy is like a *root,* giving you stability, strength, and nourishment.

As your energy flows into your root, it also flows upward, so that your rootedness permits you to stand taller, to be stronger. As you move, your rootedness moves with you; you "detach" your rooted center, and at your destination you "plant" or ground yourself again. Continue your exercise:

H. Select a destination; lift your rooted center, move to the destination, and plant yourself there.

I. Move continuously, alternating between a "plowing" and a "floating" sense of weight; as you "plow," your main energy thrust is downward into the root; as you "float," your main energy flow is upward out of your center. As you plow more, begin to "burrow"; as you float more, begin to "fly."

J. Gradually work between these two extremes, alternating quickly from one to the other, and finally find a balance between them.

During this exercise in centering, you began to move through space by "lifting" your rooted center, moving, then "planting" your rooted center at your destination. Review this experience; did it give you a heightened sense of clarity and purposefulness in your movements? Does better contact with the ground make you feel more whole and secure, and yet more open and responsive?

An actor moving from one point to another on stage goes through much the same process as the musician playing a note on his instrument. The actor chooses his destination, just as the musician selects the pitch he intends to produce. Then, deep within him, the first energy of the movement is initiated, just as the musician's muscles produce the breath that causes the reed of his instrument to vibrate. So, too, the energy for your movement is initiated deep at the center of the body, where the largest muscle systems intersect. This initial vibration travels, expands, and is amplified by your body. Finally, the movement, like the sound of the instrument, erupts into the outside world in all its fullness. When the destination has been reached, the energy that initiated the entire process is expended and the movement ceases, just as the musician's note dies away when his breath is stopped. The exact quality of the movement, just like the timbre, amplitude, and color of the musical sound, is determined by the nature of the instrument (your body) and the way in which the instrument is played.

This is all a way of saying that movements on stage must be clearly defined and *phrased,* that their shape must be self-contained—a beginning, a middle, and an end—and that they must be economical. Even if your character's mode of movement should be vague, purposeless, and confused, your *portrayal* of that kind of movement must be translated into clear and purposeful stage terms. You are not learning how to move "beautifully" or "correctly"; you are learning how to control your movements fully to serve your stage purpose in a forceful and economical way. If your character is ugly, awkward, or confused, you must present beautifully defined ugliness, forcefully purposeful awkwardness, or an absolute clarity of confusion.

Having had a literal experience of your center as it relates to balance and grounding, you will now explore the center as the source of the energy that produces breathing, motion, and sound.

Exercise 10   Moving and sounding from center

A. Align, center, and ground yourself as in the previous exercises.

1. Breathe easily, slowly, feeling the breath as an expansion and a release of the center. As you breathe in, the center becomes larger and you feel yourself expanding in all directions; as you breathe out the center is effortlessly released, and it draws to itself the energy of the breath you have just taken. Feel each breath as a gathering, a harvesting of energy by your center.
2. Become quietly aware of the breath rising and falling in the body from the center.
3. As the breath travels outward, *make sound* lightly; do not disturb the breath, simply allow it to vibrate. This is your voice: *your vibrating breath carrying energy from your center into the outside world.*
4. Reach effortlessly with your vibrating breath into the world around you.

B. Put yourself, at random, into a new position; sit, or bend over, or lean to one side. Repeat the above exercise in this new position and experience the breath flowing through this newly shaped pathway; what changes are there in the voice? Explore a variety of positions, but avoid strain; simply let the breath vibrate as it flows out of the center in each new bodily composition.

C. Begin moving from your center, allowing the breath to vibrate so that the energy of each motion is *the same energy that produces your vibrating breath.* Your sound becomes simply an *audible* aspect of the *visible* energy of your motion; it flows easily as the motion flows, as the breath flows, and it takes on all the changing qualities of the motion and breath.

D. Come gradually to stillness and let each breath vibrate: feel the vibration of the sound spreading into every part of your body so that the sound fills you; feel it begin to radiate from every surface of the body into the space around you. Your sound fills and warms that space, and as you breathe in again that same space comes in, bringing that warmth and sound with it. Experience the *sounding out* and the *gathering in* as two apsects of one, continuous cycle.

E. Stand vibrating and, alone or with the aid of a partner, check every surface of your body with a light fingertip touch; are there "dead spots" that are not participating in the sound, no matter how faintly?

Those areas of your body that are not available for sounding will relate in some way to the distortions and inhibitions that you identified during your alignment work; examine each and find the relationship. A disused abdomen will cause a shallow, unsupported tone because the breath is not flowing freely from center; a rigid or pinched chest and shoulders will withhold those areas from sound, robbing the voice of the deep resonances that give it richness; a tense neck and jaw may pinch the tone and force it into a narrow channel, causing a strident or sharp quality.

Whatever your findings, you see that vocal and physical qualities are integral with one another, because the breath, the body, and the voice are all integral. As you begin to gain freedom and ease in one you will enhance the others, enhancing too a quality of *mind* important to your work, for your consciousness is itself a partner in this same wholeness.

All this is not accomplished quickly and requires regular discipline. You will find that the ten exercises you have performed so far can be done in a smooth, unbroken sequence; I recommend using this sequence of exercises as a "warm-up" prior to each working session, and even as a regular morning exercise. Let each exercise flow into the others so that the sequence becomes one unbroken experience; the ten exercises, in other words, are really one long exercise that you will be able to complete in roughly ten minutes. Don't rush, don't strain; enjoy yourself! This can be one of the ways that, each day, you do something nice for yourself, something that lets you know that you like yourself—that what you are *becoming* is worth the effort.

Lesson 3

Contacting Your Environment

In the first two lessons you worked at contacting yourself, becoming more aware of the world inside your skin. It would be unfortunate, however, if your idea of awareness and organic wholeness were restricted to self alone.

Your organism functions within an environment, and you can have no meaningful sense of yourself without a heightened awareness of the world *outside* your skin. Furthermore, the behavior you will eventually portray on the stage is *expressive;* it reveals itself externally in the ways your character copes with places, things, and other characters. We may say, in fact, that one of your main jobs as an actor is to make the consciousness of your character visible and audible, turning his private world into a public experience.

This is why we strive to bring your *innerness* and your *outerness* into unity, to help you to bring your deepest impulses directly to the "surface," and also to make yourself immediately accessible to stimulation so that you are in a perfectly *reactive* condition. This direct reciprocity between your innerness and outerness is based upon your ability to contact your world, to feel yourself an integral part of it. Philosopher Alan Watts put it this way:

> We suffer from a hallucination, from a false and distorted sense of our own existence as living organisms. Most of us have the sensation that "I myself" is a separate center of feeling and action, living inside and bounded by the physical body—a center which "confronts" an "external" world of people and things, making contact through the senses with a universe both alien and strange. Everyday figures of speech reflect this illusion. "I came into this world." "You must face reality." "The conquest of nature." This feeling of being lonely and very temporary vistors in the universe is in flat contradiction to everything known about man (and all other living organisms) in the sciences. We do not "come into" this world; we come

out of it, as leaves from a tree. As the ocean "waves," the universe "peoples." Every individual is an expression of the whole realm of nature, a unique action of the total universe.[9]

Your sense of wholeness, then, depends also on your sense of oneness with your environment. When you are fully related to your environment, able to receive from it and give to it with immediate spontaneity, you will begin automatically to provide the kind of revelations of "inner" process that your job requires.

The most basic and omnipresent aspect of your environment is the literal, physical *space* you occupy, which occupies you as well. The way in which you relate to this space is an important part of your expressive behavior, and developing an open and responsive relationship to life "outside" can start with an effort to contact your immediate space.

Exercise 11   Swimming in space

Relaxing and placing yourself in alignment, begin to move continuously (that is, without any specific destination) around your space.

A. When you are moving freely and effortlessly through space, concentrate your whole attention on the fluidity of your movement, becoming aware of the physical actuality of the space itself as you move through it. Boccioni's sculpture of a man walking (see figure 15) shows a figure frozen in time, and behind it trail the aerodynamic patterns of the space through which it was moving. Become aware of the eddies and currents in space that you yourself are making. Uncover as much of your skin as possible, and feel the resistance of the air as you move through it. Swing yourself wildly about, swimming in the ocean of air.

B. Now concentrate your attention on the fact that the space is not only outside your skin, but comes inside your skin as well. Each breath takes in space. You are not only swimming through space, but *space is swimming through you.* The air through which you are moving is a fluid, and in every joint and cavity of your body there is also fluid. Swim until you feel at one with your space, moving through it, it moving through you, overcoming its resistance, as well

[9]Alan Watts, *The Book: On the Taboo Against Knowing Who You Are* (New York: Random House, 1972), p. 6.

FIGURE 15 Umberto Boccioni, "Unique Forms of Continuity in Space" (1912). Collection, the Museum of Modern Art, New York. Acquired through the Lillie P. Bliss Bequest.

as being carried along by it. As you move, you carry along with you, in orbit as it were, a certain amount of space, which influences your momentum. An acute awareness of this will help you to move smoothly, so as not to violate the momentum of your "envelope" of space (unless, of course, such violent movement is demanded by your role). As you walk and approach objects or other people in the room, sense the way in which you must change direction, pulling your space with you, pushing against space in a new direction in order to avoid collision.

C. Now become aware of the total space of the room and all the objects including yourself that it contains. Concentrate fully on the way in which your movements influence the total shape of the room. See how every movement of your own and every movement of every other person in that space influences the total space.

STAGE IS A STAGE IS A STAGE

Everything that happens on stage . . . happens on a stage. The famine in ancient Thebes, the capture of Joan of Arc, a fight in a waterfront bar, God confronting mankind, mankind confronting nothingness; it all happens on *a stage.* The actor can make a stage seem like any place, any time; but— it is, first of all, a stage. Until you have come to grips with the physical reality of the total stage, you have no foundation upon which to build further; the stage is your space, your environment, your *world* as an actor. You must work in the here and now; the stage is the "here."

The space of the stage is not only an environment for your work, it is also one of the *materials* with which you create. The stage and all the objects and sensations it offers to you can support you in your work if you accept and contact its reality. Certainly there may be useless, perhaps even distracting aspects of your stage environment, but when you learn to use your *real* stage environment to help you create an *imaginary* world, you try to find a way for each thing to help you. Many things that might seem distractions or obstacles to you at first can turn out to be valuable helpers if you find an imaginative way to use them. You need not ignore any aspect of your environment (everything you ignore moves you one step further out of your here and now), nor must you have hallucinations and "really" see things that aren't there. Instead, you control your reactions to the things that are there and make them fit your artistic purpose.

A child can look at a floating twig and see a great ocean liner, and he doesn't have to deny the existence of the twig in order to do so; he simply transforms his interpretation of what he is seeing. Yet when student actors are asked to visualize a scene, they invariably close their eyes, or stare off blankly into space, as if the things they really see around them hinder their ability to pretend. They have lost the child's ability to contact and accept reality, and then *use* it to create an even more vivid illusion.

This ability is well worth regaining. The actor must continually relate to things on stage as if they were something else, but he must not lose touch with the reality of his situation in the process. Let us say that those hot spotlights are supposed to be a moonlit sky; only a madman would fail to recognize the lights shining in his eyes, or the rows of people where a meadow ought to be. The actor accepts these sensations in all their reality and then reacts to them *as if* they were sky and meadow. In this way, your responses can always be real, though the form in which they are expressed is artistically controlled.

We discussed concentration as involving the ability to let a "foreground" emerge from a "background," and you can see this same principle at work here; like the child, you must contact and accept your immediate reality, allowing it to generate new associations in you so that a new "foreground" emerges from it at will. The "illusion" you create is therefore not at all unreal; it is rooted in a tangible but reinterpreted reality.

Working in this way requires that you work continuously in the here and now, avoiding the common trap of projecting a premeditated image on your stage world rather than accepting and working from what is really there. In the next exercise you will begin to use your environment without premeditation.

Exercise 12   Action, object, emotion

A. Put yourself at rest and in alignment. Take a deep breath, hold it, then thrust your body and your breath outward at the same time, moving suddenly and *without plan*. Continue your random movements, allowing them to change, until you discover some pantomimed object "touching" some part of your body. Don't let your mind decide what it is to be; let your muscles, in their random movement, suggest it to you. Keep asking your body, "Since you are moving like that, what might you be holding, standing upon, rubbing against?" and so on. When you have discovered an object, begin to *use* it until an emotion grows in you. Again, *don't plan* the emotion, but let it be suggested to you by your activity. *How hard is it to avoid planning ahead? Can you see how much more "real" and imaginative the discoveries are that are truly made by the muscles?*

B. Continue the exercise, but relate to real objects and the room itself; what new realities can you find around you? Play, like the child in the attic who turns the old trunk into a sailing ship, and the beams and rafters into masts and spars.

STAGE TERMINOLOGY AND TYPES

What is a stage? It is any area in which actors create for their audience the patterned experience called drama. The spatial relationship of stage and audience is what spells the difference between one sort of stage and another. While your immediate concern may be the stage proper, that stage is only an artificially separated area within the larger theatre. It is this *total* theatrical space that is your true working area, and the stage derives its meaning only from its relation to this total space.

During some periods of theatrical history the stage floor was sloped, or "raked," for a heightened illusion of perspective and for improved visibility of actors standing at the rear of the stage. For this reason we still speak of "*down*stage" as being toward the audience, and "*up*stage" as being away from the audience, since the stage floor was actually sloped in this way. Some modern productions have revived the raked stage.

Lateral directions are determined by the right and left of an actor as he stands facing the audience. Thus "stage right" is the same as the audience's left. *Downstage right* means toward the audience and to the actor's right (see figure 16). This basic system of giving directions is used on most types of stages.

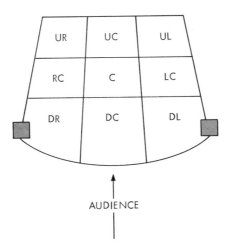

FIGURE 16   Traditional directions on a proscenium stage.

Exercise 13 Saying hello to the stage

After learning the terminology for stage locations (figure 16), move about on your stage announcing to the audience area your location, destination, and whatever you find on your travels. For example, "I am now standing upstage right, and I am noticing a bump in the floor here, and now I am crossing slowly down left, crossing center, where I see a floor marking from some past show, and now I am crawling in the down right area, seeing a different kind of flooring here, with old stage screw holes in it. . . ." Take your time and see how mich of the stage area you can explore, concentrating fully on contacting the area and announcing your findings. Someone listening to a tape recording of your voice should be able to recreate exactly your movements and discoveries.

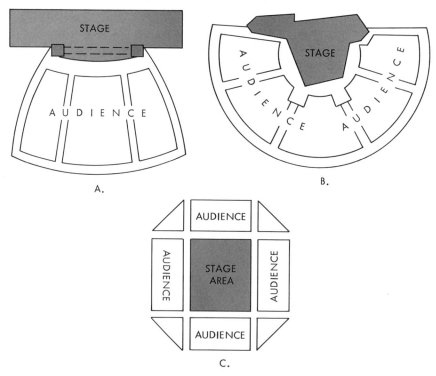

FIGURE 17 Types of stages: (A) traditional proscenium; (B) modern thrust; (C) full-round or "arena"; (D) environmental, viewed from above. (In the setting [opposite page] for the author's production of Kafka's *The Trial* at the Yale Drama School, the audience and the action were intermixed on various levels and in various spaces; scenic design by Eugene Warner.)

Stages come in many sizes, shapes, and types. Anyone who has played "on the road," moving from one theatre to another, has had a vivid experience of the importance of an actor's responsiveness to his theatrical space. Never before has such a wide variety of stage types, each of which demands a somewhat different spatial attitude, confronted the actor. The basic types are four—*proscenium, thrust, arena,* and *environmental*—though there are many "in-between" variations (see figure 17).

Proscenium. The traditional proscenium stage features an arch through which the audience sees the action. This "picture frame" developed as a way of establishing a frame of reference for settings painted in perspective (hence the word *pro-scenium* meaning *in front of the scene*).

The actor on the proscenium stage must realize that his audience is limited to one side of his playing area, and he must accommodate himself

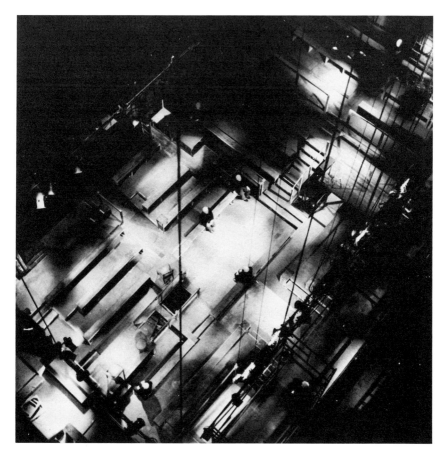

D.

to this fact. Standing behind the sofa during a crucial scene may not be a good idea, and neither is creeping continually upstage so that everybody else has to turn their backs on the audience in order to speak to you (hence the dreaded charge of "upstaging"). But the possibilities of good proscenium movement are greater than you might think, and it is certainly *not* necessary to "cheat out" at all times as if you were more interested in speaking to the audience than to the person on stage with you (some actors are, of course). And don't underestimate how much acting you can do with your back. Strindberg said it was beyond his "wildest expectation" that he should ever see an actor's back during an important scene. So while you must accommodate your movement and positioning to the audience's location, you must also do so *without destroying the internal logic of the stage space you inhabit.*

Thrust. Recently the thrust stage (so called because it "thrusts" into the midst of the audience) has come into great popularity. It features the same stage/audience relationship as the Classical and Elizabethan theatres. It puts the actor into a close proximity with his audience but limits the use of scenery. For this reason, it is very much an "actor's" theatre, and plays that, like the classics, utilize description and imagistic poetic devices instead of scenery and furniture seem more at home here than do realistic ones.

The actor's movement on a thrust can be described in the same way as on a proscenium stage, though here he is liberated from the audience's presence on only one side and is freer to form three-dimensional patterns. He has the added responsibility, however, of relating his movement to three sides and keeping himself open to audience view, or at least distributing his presence equally to all sections of the house. This quickly ceases to be a problem when the actor realizes that the thrust provides a freedom to be used in an active, total way. The increased sense of audience participation inherent in the thrust stage inspires a warm and active sense of actor/audience contact, which makes such accommodation easy and natural.

Arena. The arena and other types of full-round stages stand at the opposite extreme from proscenium stages. Here the actor enters through the audience area, either down the aisles or from an opening cut into the sloped audience area. The actor's problem of keeping open to all sections of the audience is more acute here than on a thrust stage, not only because of the additional audience encirclement, but also because there is no "home base" to which the actor can relate. In thrust stages, the existence of a clear upstage area gives the actor some sense of direction; there is still an upstage and downstage. But in full arena, there is no upstage and downstage, or right and left, and the actor must remember that he always has his back to someone. Scenes requiring the actors to sit for prolonged periods, for example, are especially difficult here. But the full-round does offer a sense of intimacy unlike any other type of stage, and such theatres are usually quite small. For this reason, audiences tend to expect a more detailed and subtle type of performance here.

Environmental. While most stages are of the three basic types described above, we see increasingly the creation of special environments for specific productions that may even abandon entirely the separation of stage and audience. Here, of course, the proximity of the audience demands total commitment and attention to detail.

Whatever stage you are on, your adaptation to the positioning of the audience, to the vocal demands of the shape and size of the house, and to the configuration of the stage are essential.

EXPLORING YOUR SPACE ON STAGE

The theatre is a physical space, and your treatment of that space is an important aspect of your performance. Your movement through the space of the stage and your spatial relationship to the setting and other actors should express a meaning and logic of their own. This sculptural or *plastic* aspect of theatre is usually the main responsibility of the director and designer, but the actor's spatial sensitivity is equally important for several reasons.

First, good stage movement depends upon extremely subtle adjustments, which the actors are often in the best position to make. Second, the spatially sensitive actor can understand and sometimes even assist his director much more than the sort of actor who seems unaware of where he is on stage. Finally, strong spatial awareness provides an actor with a basic channel of communication with his fellow actors. Your sense of your stage space is part of your overall awareness of the here and now, and your ability to share space with your fellow actors is part of your ability to contact them and help the *ensemble* to operate in the here and now as well.

Realizing "where you are" on stage provides a point of physical contact between you and your environment that anchors and focuses your concentration and gives a firm basis in physical fact for the *experience* that you construct upon that reality. In this way, the experience that you create is made more "real," more tangible, by its derivation from your physical actuality on stage.

Group Exercise 1   Searching: I

A. Place yourselves at random throughout the stage space. Touch the physical environment with as much of your skin as you can:

slither, crawl, roll. Move in a large circle from your position around as much of the theatre (audience area included) as you can cover, and back again. Do not deviate from your path no matter what objects you encounter (including other people), and fully explore all sensory qualities of each object and surface that you cross, all the time keeping as much physical contact with the theatre as possible.

B. With as much of your skin uncovered as possible, aggressively attempt to influence one another's space as you move continuously through the stage area. See what effect you can have on others by sweeping by them, pushing space at them, and so on, and what effect they can have on you.

C. All close your eyes and, keeping them closed, move very slowly throughout the stage space trying not to touch any physical object or person. Search with your skin, hearing, and smell for open space; crawl, stretch on tiptoe—whatever is necessary to find the most uninhabited space—but you must keep moving. See how, through practice, you can move with fewer and fewer collisions. Move more and more freely. *Any object or person touched must be identified by name before moving on.*

SHAPING MOVEMENT FOR THE STAGE

Having contacted your stage environment, begin now to explore the ways in which your bodily, vocal, and spiritual energies may be used within this space. Your relaxation and movement exercises were meant to eliminate *unnecessary* tensions, which inhibit your responsiveness and freedom of movement; but tension itself, *properly used,* is an essential ingredient of theatrical performance. Tension, in this positive sense, is energy that has not yet been released in muscular activity, or energy that is balanced by an opposing force. Such unreleased energy is in a state of dramatic tension or *suspense* (a term that describes energy "held or prevented from proceeding"); the suspense is over when the energy is released in a completed action.

This principle applies equally to very small actions (like a single breath) and very large and complex actions (like the plot of a play). The moment when the energy that has been "prevented from proceeding" is just *on the verge* of being released is the moment of the greatest suspense. The stronger the held-back energy, the greater the suspense. The moment of suspense asks a question: how will the held-back energy release itself? What will happen?

Such a moment of suspense, when the outcome of an action hangs in the balance, is a *crisis* (a "turning point"). Most theatrical actions are shaped in this way: the action builds up energy and momentum until it reaches a crisis, it is held there in suspense, and then released. Aristotle even described the plots of plays in this way; the period of rising energy he called the "raveling," as it built up to the crisis, and the period of falling energy that followed the crisis he called "unraveling" (our theatrical term *dénouement* is French for "unraveling").

The large pattern of action that forms the plot of a play is composed of a number of smaller units of actions, each of which has its own pattern of rising energy, crisis, and release. Each of these units of action is composed of yet smaller ones, and so on. Any large action is a collection of smaller actions linked in a purposeful way; usually the release of energy following one crisis forms the beginning of a rise toward the next crisis, and so on until the overall pattern has been fulfilled. If you can master the simplest of action-patterns and purposefully link them to other simple patterns, you can create limitlessly large and complex overall patterns (this will be discussed further in part 3).

Body movement is not the only way you express dramatic action on stage, but it is one of the most important and is our immediate concern here. From your heightened muscular participation in your pattern of actions can come a profound experience of your stage task.

The most basic body movement-pattern is that of a single breath. It clearly has a period of rising tension (inhaling), a crisis (a momentary holding of the breath), and a release (exhaling). Try taking a breath so as to heighten its dramatic potential: involve the entire body in the rise, crisis, and release pattern; start as "empty" as you can and rise to a high crisis; prolong the crisis, feeling the full strength of the held-back energy; and then release completely. A single breath can be an exciting theatrical event!

You heighten the "drama" of the breath by intensifying the pattern of its action in two ways: first you involve as many muscles as possible (and remember that a muscle can be at work without actually moving a great deal, so that *all* our muscles can help support even the smallest action). This gives your body a chance to *resonate* the action fully, just as a musical instrument sounds richest when all of its parts join in vibrating the tone. Next you *extend the dynamic range* of the action by making the contractions smaller and the extensions larger, stretching the low and high points of the action farther apart.

Try taking another dramatic breath; when you have reached the prolonged crisis, see what determines the "right" moment to let the breath out (besides simply not being able to hold it any longer). If you are responding to the shape of your whole action-pattern, the way in which you *exhale* will be determined by the way in which you have *inhaled*. In other words, each segment of an action-pattern should be proportioned to the others, in whatever way is appropriate to the whole. This porportioning of the rise, crisis, and release of an action, and the way in which it is linked to other actions, is a principal factor of stage *rhythm.*

Rhythm is the patterned flow, the rise and fall, of energy through time. It is the great unifying factor that gives cohesiveness to your work. Whatever the quality of the actions you perform, rhythm not only proportions them, it also integrates you with your actions. Rhythm is deeply rooted in your breath, in your existence, and will work for you if you simply let it.

Exercise 14   Punctuating movement

Perform the following sequence of actions, attempting to realize fully the dramatic potential of each. Remember the two basic ways of intensifying action-patterns: *resonate* them by involving all your muscles in them, and *expand their dynamic range* by making the contractions small and tight, the expansions large and open. In each case identify the crisis; treat all that goes before as a preparation for the crisis and all that follows as a result. Prolong the crisis itself without breaking the overall rhythm of the action.

1. A single breath.
2. Five breaths building up to a scream.
3. A single step. (In this and each following example continue to involve the breath, inhaling during the rising action, holding the breath during the crisis, and exhaling during the release. You might like to try the actions with and without this parallel breathing to see how much the breath contributes to a sense of rhythm and to clarity of movement.)
4. Five steps building to a leap.
5. Lowering your body into a chair (realize here how the pattern can be effectively reversed; a "falling" or contracting movement can express a rising segment of action, and vice versa).
6. Five steps leading to sitting in a chair.
7. Finally, choose for yourself an action from life that is complete without being complex (for example, swatting a fly, getting a book off a shelf, changing a light bulb, or getting into a hot bath).

PATTERNING YOUR SPACE ON STAGE

Your stage space is a potent tool when put to work properly. Your movement through your space, considered by itself, is abstract; though it may have the same kind of abstract beauty as kinetic sculpture or modern dance, its effectiveness as theatrical movement depends on its relation to a meaningful context. Here are two exercises to help you examine both the abstract beauty of stage positioning and its poential meaningfulness *as an expression of relationships between people.*

Group Exercise 2 Patterns: I

As a group, put yourselves at rest and in alignment. Then all begin to move aimlessly, concentrating on the spatial pattern the group is forming within the room. As a basic pattern begins to emerge, join it until all members of the group are involved. As soon as everyone has joined in, stop all movement, concentrating on this emergent pattern. Then, on individual impulse, change your position so as to alter the basic pattern or your relationship to it. Continue doing this until the group has stopped in a new pattern, whereupon you all resume movement in the new pattern. Then go in motion and, on individual impulse, break from the new pattern until it has disintegrated. The exercise may then be repeated. The group may possibly happen upon a group identity suggested by a discovered pattern, and such a discovery should be played out.

This exercise expresses the power of spatial relationships for their own sake; your group was making a sculpture of the space of the stage. Now move on to experience the use of space to carry energies flowing between characters in specific relationships.

Exercise 15 Patterns: II

With another member of the class, select a simple relationship (for example, mother/son, husband/wife, employer/employee, policeman/demonstrator, and so on) and begin, without further planning, to move in relationship to each other around the stage. Use no words. Do not begin with a specific situation or plot. Simply move until a pattern begins to emerge that seems to you both expressive of your relationship. Pursue this pattern until it becomes fixed; let your individual qualities of movement be influenced as well.

What has your movement taught you about your characters and their situation that you didn't know before? What did you communicate to your

FIGURE 18   A patterns exercise.

audience? How did your stage space and the location of your audience affect your movement? Did you use your space as a vehicle for your relationship?

Exercise 16   Patterns: III

Using the relationship developed in Patterns: II, one partner should select a simple message with a strong emotional potential (for example, "I'm not mad anymore," or "You've just won a million dollars"), and without telling the other what it is, try to use your shared space and your movements to communicate the message. Use no words or signs of any sort; try to use only spatial means. When the partner begins to understand the message, he uses space to try to communicate his reply (for example, "I'm still mad," or "I don't believe you"). He can test his understanding of the message by testing the appropriateness of his reply. Again, attempt to use only *spatial* means. What patterns of movement emerged?

The planned use of space in a stage performance is called "blocking." Good stage blocking should reflect basic character relationships as well as the underlying action of the scene expressed as spatial cause and effect. Though the director is primarily responsible for blocking, the actor's responsiveness to stage movement makes his blocking truly expressive and not merely "dead" motion. Even without a director's help, you should be able to utilize your stage environment to create spatially logical patterns that express the action of your scene, your relationship to other characters, and as a vehicle to help you make contact with your fellow actors as teammates.

Lesson 4

Contacting Each Other

Other people are the most important part of our environment. The way they act upon us, the way we act upon them, and the way in which we react with each other make up the dynamic social process that largely shapes us and determines our mode of expression. This social process is of special importance to the actor, since the form of drama is an artistically heightened and ordered permutation of this social interaction. Just as we are influenced greatly by those around us in everyday life, so a dramatic character is formed largely by the way in which he relates to the other characters in his play and to the play as a whole.

As we watch a character on the stage, we get a great deal of information about him not only from what *he* does, but also from how all the other characters relate to him. In fact, the common idea that the actor's job is to create *his character* is somewhat erroneous; it would be truer to say that *all the actors must create all the characters* in the play, for personality on the stage, as in life, is rooted in dynamic interaction with other personalities and the environment.

If you have ever been on stage with someone who failed to relate appropriately to you, you will know how difficult it is to overcome the false impression that another actor may create regarding your character; on the positive side, you may also have experienced the effortless joy of working with someone who always gave you what you needed to help you create your character. In fact, there are very few difficulties you will ever encounter in creating a role that can be solved entirely by your own effort; more often than not, the solution to a problem lies "out there," in your working relationships with your fellow actors. In short, on the stage *we create each other more than we create ourselves.*

It is also true that a play, as a sequence of events, moves forward only as a result of truthful relationships between the characters as they interact moment by moment. "Acting is reacting" is an old theatrical dictum, and a true one. Most of what you will ever do on stage will be in reaction to something someone else does, or some intention of your own; your reaction will in turn serve as an action evoking its own reaction, and so the play moves. This means that the transfer of energy from one actor to another through the *action-reaction/action-reaction* chain is the main motive force moving the play forward; until each actor is truly acting and reacting with each of the others as fellow workers, the transactions between the characters cannot be vivid and forceful, and the play as a whole cannot move forcefully.

A stage production, then, is successful only when it is the harmonious blending of the efforts of many artists. Acting is strictly a *team* activity, and an important part of your discipline must be learning to work *with* your fellow actors. During your training, your individual skills will properly receive your attention and effort, for a team depends on the individual skills of every member, and you will serve your fellow actors best by becoming as good an actor as *you* can be; but you can develop the highest level of individual technique and still never participate in the truest artistry of the theatre if you remain incapable of working effectively within the creative ensemble. As playwright August Strindberg commented a century ago,

> No form of art is as dependent as the actor's. He cannot isolate his particular contribution, show it to someone and say, "This is mine." If he does not get the support of his fellow actors, his performance will lack resonance and depth. He will be held in check and lured into wrong inflections and wrong rhythms. He won't make a good impression no matter how hard he tries. Actors must rely on each other. Occasionally one sees an exceptionally egotistic individual who "upstages" a rival, obliterates him, in order that he and he alone can be seen.
>
> That is why rapport among actors is imperative for the success of a play. I don't care whether you rank yourselves higher or lower than each other, or from side to side, or from inside out—as long as you do it together.[10]

When things have gone well—when the play, the actors, and the director have worked as an ensemble, and the audience has likewise given of itself—then there occurs one of those rare moments when true theatre lives; all these human energies flow to form one energy that is greater than the sum of its parts. Everyone participating in the experience begins to receive more than he has given, and we feel ourselves truly moved beyond ourselves; this is the deepest wonder of the theatre, and it depends entirely on the actors' *teamwork.* Even in a scene in which your characters are

[10]August Strindberg, "Notes to the Members of the Intimate Theatre (TDR Document)," trans. Everett Sprinchorn, *The Tulane Drama Review* 6, no. 2 (Nov. 1961), p. 157. This material is also copyrighted by *The Drama Review,* 1967.

opposed or even disassociated with one another, you and your fellow actors must maintain a team relationship "underneath" the scene reality. This team relationship depends particularly on two points: first, that communication between actors must exist on all sensory levels, since the complete theatrical experience involves all the senses; and second, that this communication must be free of all inhibition. For the first point, all theatrical communication is at some point sensual. There is no ESP in the theatre; what is communicated, be it emotion or meaning, must be tangible, must be heard, seen, or felt before it can be experienced and interpreted by the audience. For the second point, you must act *totally*, making available not only all your senses but all parts of your body as well; it is the actor's job to behave *in a private manner in a public situation*, and you must overcome the social taboos that may restrict the completeness of your performance. This in no way means that you must abandon your moral standards; it simply means that you must accept the highly physical nature of acting and behave accordingly.

EXPERIENCING RELATEDNESS

We have already discussed the way in which your sense of a separate "I" bounded by the physical body is a limited understanding of your actual participation in the whole realm of nature; you are integral with your environment, and it with you. Our ideas of an "inner" and an "outer" world are only different modes of perception, different attitudes toward experience; in actual fact our "innerness" is part of the outer world, or rather the world is *one world*, which we merely experience as "inner" and "outer." As M. C. Richards points out,

> The innerness of the so-called outer world is nowhere so evident as in the life of our body. The air we breathe one moment will be breathed by someone else the next and has been breathed by someone else before. We exist as respiring, pulsating organisms within a sea of life-serving beings. As we become able to hold this more and more steadily in our consciousness, we experience relatedness at an elemental level. We see that it is not a matter of trying to be related, but rather of living consciously into the actuality of being related. As we yield ourselves to the living presence of this relatedness, we find that life begins to possess an ease and a freedom and a naturalness that fill our hearts with joy. . . .[11]

Just as the breath has been the basis for most of the exercises so far, you will now begin to explore relatedness through your breathing.

[11]Copyright © 1964 by Mary Caroline Richards. Reprinted from *Centering*, by Mary Caroline Richards, by permission of Wesleyan University Press (p. 39).

Exercise 17   Trading breath

A. Relaxed and in sitting alignment, breathe easily and slowly, experiencing the breath as described in the quote directly above.

B. Sit facing your partner; one of you breathes in, then out; as he breathes out, the other gently begins to breathe in. The breath flows between you like warm water flowing from one vessel into another and back again.

C. As you feel energy passing with the breath you are sharing, let the breath vibrate as you give it.

D. When you are comfortably sharing the energy of your voices, let your vibrating breath begin to form itself into words—any words, but truly spoken to partner as you give him the energy of your breath. Listen as you receive partner's breath/words; let a thought pass between you, let it be shared by you both as you share the energy of the breath.

You may have the experience, after some practice with this exercise, of receiving and giving energy to and from your partner on a fundamental level; once this contact has been established, this energy can become sound, then the sound can become words, and the words—of course—carry thought. Thought can be given and received as the very air you breathe!

When a dramatic scene is flowing as it should, there will be this same unbroken cycle of shared energy between the actors; sometimes it will be expressed as the words of the dialogue, sometimes as motion, sometimes as silent looking, but always the energy will flow, being given and being received. When the connection is broken, the scene dies and the characters die.

When next you work on a scene with a partner, try this same exercise, and allow the words that are formed to be those of the dialogue. Of course, the dialogue in actual performance will not move with the regular rhythm of breathing, but this exercise can give you a *feeling* of relatedness within the specific form and rhythms of the scene.

WEIGHT AND RELATIONSHIP

The physical center you experienced in lesson 2 is important to your sense of relationship on stage, for we tend to relate to one another from our centers. To see the truth of this, try an experiment: stand so that your pelvis is pointed directly at your partner, then turn your head (without turning your body) so that your face points at someone off to one side.

Now—who are you "facing?" That is, with whom do you seem to have the strongest relationship, your partner or the person to one side?

Take the experiment further: turn your face back toward your partner and speak to him; the person at your side interrupts by asking a question, and you turn your head to him and answer; then you turn back to the original partner and continue. Did you feel that your basic relationship with partner was only *suspended* while you spoke to the person at your side, so that the side conversation was only a "parenthesis" within the unbroken relationship with partner?

Again, speak to partner, but this time when the person at your side interrupts, turn your pelvis toward him as you speak. Do you feel that you have now established a *new* relationship, that the original relationship with partner has been broken?

What we do with the actual weight of our bodies, in real life and on the stage, is the most fundamental expression of our relationships with other persons, and the weight of the body is literally at our center.

We also tend to express *how* we feel about someone by the way we dispose our weight toward or away from him. Imagine yourself in the first stages of an argument that threatens to become a fight; you are confronting your opponent with your hands raised, and you appear to be ready for combat. In this situation, rock your pelvis forward, toward the opponent; do you feel more truly ready to attack? Now rock your pelvis away from the opponent, so that your center of gravity shifts backward; do you feel on the defensive, perhaps only pretending to fight?

There is no type of relationship where weight is not given or taken, and there is no way for you to "fake" a relationship if you fail to involve your true weight in it in some way. Have you ever seen student actors trying to do a love scene, perhaps even an embrace, while both were holding their weight back? Neither the actors nor the audience can have a truthful sense of the relationship if either partner is falsifying the participation of his bodily center.

Exercise 18   Falling

A. Partner stands in relaxed alignment and you stand about three feet behind with one foot thrust back for stability (see figure 19). Without tension, partner falls backward into your arms, and you gently raise him back up to his feet. He falls only a short way at first, then gradually further and further until you are catching him only a few feet above the floor. If partner becomes frightened and

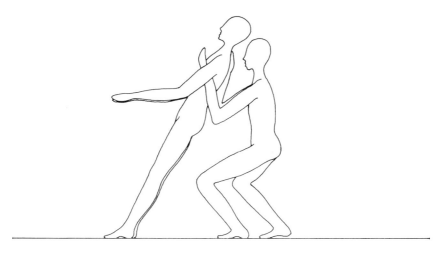

FIGURE 19   Falling.

"breaks" his body on the way down, or remains tense as he falls, speak to him and encourage him. Then reverse roles. CAUTION: DO NOT ATTEMPT THIS EXERCISE UNLESS YOU ARE CONFIDENT OF BEING ABLE TO CATCH PARTNER, FOR SERIOUS INJURY COULD RESULT.

B. Explore a variety of relationships with your partner in which the giving or taking away of the weight changes the "meaning" of the relationship. Exaggerate the shifting of weight at first, then bring it into the range of everyday behavior. By watching other partnerships at work, determine what degree of exaggeration is demanded by the stage.

Your sense of relationship on the stage is not restricted to a single partner, of course, and here is a group exercise that symbolizes in physical terms the way in which all the members of an ensemble must be supported by all the others.

Group Exercise 3   Levitating

A. In groups of seven or nine: one person lies flat on his back, eyes closed, arms at his side; the rest kneel in two lines of three or four at either side (see figure 20a). You all begin to breathe in unison,

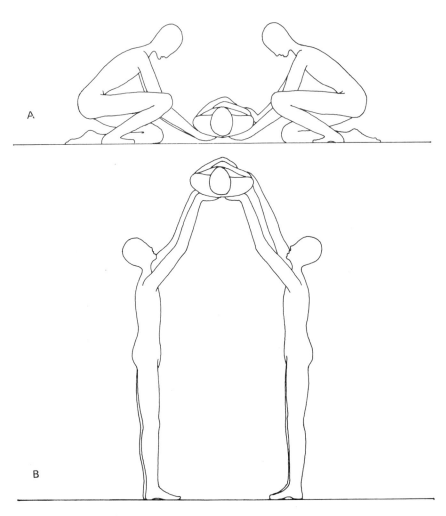

FIGURE 20   Levitation.

then as you breathe in you *gently* and *slowly* lift the person, who remains perfectly level. The sensation for the person being lifted is one of *floating* upward. The upward motion continues until the person has floated as high as the group can reach (see figure 20b). At this point the group breathes out (having held the breath during the lifting) and breathes in again. As the group breathes out the second time, the person is allowed to float *slowly* back down to earth, as if he were lying on a balloon from which the air has gradually escaped. The group should experience its shared breath as the source of the energy that causes the levitation.

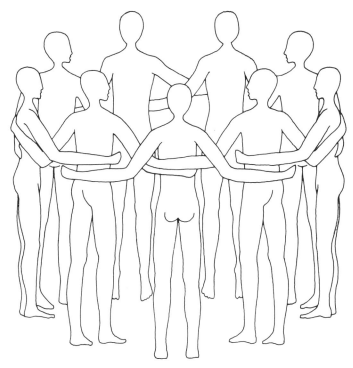

FIGURE 21   Position for group jumping exercise.

B. In one large group: stand in a circle, facing inward. Each puts his arms around the persons on either side, holding them at the small of the waist. The group begins to breathe in unison, and each feels the movement of the breathing of the people he is holding. As all breathe out, the group bends its knees *slightly* so that it sinks a bit; then, as the group breathes in, each member lifts those he is holding. DO NOT LIFT YOURSELF; LIFT ONLY THOSE YOU ARE HOLDING, AND ALLOW YOURSELF TO BE LIFTED BY THEM. As the rising and falling motion becomes stronger the group begins to vocalize the word "higher" as it breathes out. Each member gradually tries to lift those he is holding off the ground as he breathes in. Allow the natural rhythm of the group to lead you into a gradual acceleration until you all leave the ground!

Do you see how these exercises symbolize the way in which a cast must work together? *When all the energies of the group are focused rhythmically on the common goal, the resultant energy is greater than the sum of its parts; when all lift, all will be lifted.* And remember too: the audience is part of the team.

LEADING AND FOLLOWING

We not only support each other in our work, we also actively lead and follow each other through a performance. The chain of action and reaction that moves the play flows as transacted energy through all the actors, but at any given moment one or another of them will be "carrying the ball." It is crucial to the momentum of the play that energy be received and passed on from actor to actor in the most useful way possible, so that you receive and give to each other the kind of stimulation you each need to perform your tasks at any given moment; since acting is reacting, you must help each other by supplying actions that help to elicit the required reactions from your partners.

This transfer of energy from actor to actor can be described as a continuous process of leading and following, in which all the actors are both leaders and followers simultaneously. This may sound illogical, but the next sequence of exercises will give you the experience of this simultaneous interdependence of actors and will explain the importance of your sensory responsiveness to your partner in achieving such active relatedness.

Exercise 19   Leading and following

A. BLIND LEADING. You and your partner lightly interlace fingertips up to the first joint; partner closes his eyes, and you silently lead him around the room. As you gain confidence and control, begin to move faster and extend the range of your travels. Soon you can run! If your situation permits, you can even take a trip to some distant destination. Reverse roles and repeat for the trip back.

B. SOUND LEADING. Begin as above, but when you are well underway, break physical contact and begin to lead partner by repeating a single simple sound or word. Again, extend your range and speed. Run!

Check yourselves in these exercises: as follower, are you really walking and running—that is, have you truly committed your weight to your movement—or are you only "pretending" to move while still holding your weight cautiously back? As leader, are you truly helping the blind partner to follow?

Watch other partnerships at work: do you see how intense, how *connected* to each other they seem? Our listening and seeing of one another on stage should always have this kind of literal intensity; you are leading and following each other during a scene just as much as you are in this exercise!

Group Exercise 4   Searching: II

All stand together in a clump at the center of your space and close your eyes. Then all spin about a few times until you are disoriented; next, move slowly in whatever direction you are facing until you reach a wall or other obstacle. Avoid touching anyone else; feel your way with all of your nonvisual senses. When all have gone as far as they can (and still have not opened their eyes), begin to search for your partner using a new, single sound. You must identify every person you touch before moving on, until at last you and partner find each other. When you are together, stand and wait in silence for all to finish.

In this exercise you were not led, but had to find your own way toward partner's sound. Did you feel lonely while searching, and relieved when you found partner? Don't be the kind of actor who makes his stage partners feel lonely!

As you have experienced in these exercises, connectedness depends in part on the acuteness of your perception of each other; you must truly *see, hear,* and *feel* your partner at all times. As simple as this may seem, such significant seeing and hearing are fairly rare on the stage. As a way of avoiding the "here and now" and maintaining selfish control of their individual performances, some actors only *pretend* to see and hear the other actors on stage; actually, they are only superficially aware of their teammates. They are reacting instead to their prepared projection of what they would *like* their partner to be doing, not to what is actually before them. While such premeditated, false reactions might *appear* correct to an audience, the ensemble effort and therefore the play as a whole must inevitably suffer. Sometimes the selfish actor "gets away" with it, but only at the sacrifice of the fullest potential of his art.

Exercise 20   Mirror sequence

A. You and partner decide who is "A" and who is "B." Standing and facing one another, "A" begins to move while "B" mirrors him in every detail. Trying to keep the partnership moving in unison,

"A" makes slow "underwater" movements that "B" can mirror. The movements flow organically in a continuous, changing stream; avoid repeated patterns. Notice how the movement is the vehicle for the communication; the bigger, more total, and more continuous the movement is, the easier it is to stay together. Notice also that the communication must be a two-way street; "B" can be a better mirror when "A" is also responding to him.

At a signal from the group leader, the roles are instantly reversed *with no break in the action.* "B" is now the leader, "A" is the follower. Continue moving *from center;* feel yourselves beginning to share a common center through your shared movement, and with it comes a common breath. Vocalize the breath and continue to share this common sound, which arises organically from your movement.

The roles are reversed a few more times by a signal from the group leader; each time the leadership role changes, the movement and sound continue without interruption.

At last, there is *no leader;* neither "A" nor "B" leads, but both follow, and the partnership continues to move and make noise together. At another signal, both close their eyes for a few moments, while continuing to move. How well did you stay together?

Are there areas of your bodies that are not involved in the game? Did you begin to share emotions as well as noises and movements? Above all, were you really seeing and hearing each other?

B. Begin again, but this time "A" makes noise (without moving) that *makes* "B" move; "A" uses his sound as a tangible, physical force to control the movement of his partner. Again, at a signal from the group leader, the roles are instantly reversed *with no break in the action.* Gradually, the follower begins to "talk back" to the leader (with sounds but not words). Finally, both join in a moving pattern of continuous action and reaction—no longer a mirror, but a continuous sound and motion that flows simultaneously from both, who are now leader and follower at once.

Change partners often; try forming groups of three, four, and more persons, following the same process of allowing each to lead, then moving without a leader.

Group Exercise 5   Making contact

A. *Blind study.* All close eyes and move freely around the room, striving to vary movements continuously (walking, crawling, rolling, turning, swinging, jumping, and so on). All must avoid contact with

FIGURE 22   A group contact exercise.

others as they move; if contact takes place, the people who have touched must remain absolutely glued together at the point of contact, moving as a unit in a way determined by the strongest member. There is no limit to the size of the groups thus formed, and the eventual winner of this game would be the last single person not yet glued to someone else.

B. *Stealing movements.* All start by doing individual free-movement improvisations, trying to find new ways of moving. When someone sees another's movement that he likes, he "steals" it by moving in and mimicking it until the person from whom the movement is stolen abandons it. You must give up your movement shortly after it is stolen and find a new movement by stealing someone else's motif. All must be in constant change and constant awareness of others' movements.

C. *Tug of war.* Each member of the group "makes" a piece of pantomimed rope. Standing in a long line, each piece of rope joins those on each side to form one long rope. Breaking in the center, the group then becomes two teams and has a tug of war. At no time can the rope stretch or break. How real can the rope become as a group creation?

This last exercise is a splendid image of stage reality; the rope ceases to be real if *any* member of the group fails to maintain his section, and there is nothing the rest of the team can do to overcome such a gap. If you have ever seen a good scene ruined by someone who wasn't "pulling his weight," you will know that the entire movement of the play was interrupted at that moment. This is why the old theatrical adage that "there are no small parts—only small actors" is so true: the momentum of the play's energy may be broken by any actor, no matter how "small" his role in terms of number of lines or time on stage.

THE INTERRELATIONSHIP OF SOCIAL AND AESTHETIC REALITIES

So far we have been stressing the need to contact your physical reality in space and time; how will this help you in creating the "illusion" of your role? How does your personal reality relate to your stage creation? In answering this question, we must beware of the vagueness of terms like *illusion* and *reality.* It is difficult to say where theatrical illusion begins and reality leaves off. Theatre, at its best, transcends the narrow definition of these terms; it is a place where illusion and reality mix inseparably. For the actor, in fact, there is no such thing as illusion; everything that happens on a stage has its own reality, regardless of what it may also evoke from those who witness it.

The trouble with the idea of "illusion" in theatre, as in other arts, is that the "illusion" of art is often more "real" than "reality." Tennessee Williams puts it beautifully when his character Tom in *The Glass Menagerie* says to the audience:

> I am the opposite of a stage magician. He gives you illusion that has the appearance of truth. I give you truth in the pleasant disguise of illusion.[12]

[12]Tennessee Williams, *The Glass Menagerie* (New York: Random House, Inc.), scene i.

Let us abandon the distinction between reality and illusion and speak instead of various *levels* of reality that coexist within the theatre, each of which contacts the audience in its own way but also interacts with the other realities.

Instead of "illusion," we will use the term "aesthetic reality." This phrase implies that the product of the performance, the thing that used to be called the "illusion," is itself *real*. If you think back to successful performances you have seen, you will remember characters created by the actors that had a reality *of their own*, not necessarily "better" or "worse" than the reality of the actors themselves as real people, which you also remember, but that existed simultaneously in a different way.

We will call the "reality" of the actors themselves the "social reality," referring to the identity between actors and audience members as human beings existing *within the same social sphere*. The theatre itself has a physical existence, a social reality, as a place within which aesthetic reality is created and communicated. The *aesthetic reality* refers primarily to the created *character* and the world of his play, while the *social reality* refers primarily to the *actor*, his theatre, and his witnesses.

Think back to a performance you have seen recently. Try to list all the sensations you, as an audience member, had in the first ten minutes.

1. Which sensations were related to the social reality?
2. Which related to the aesthetic reality?
3. Which related to both?
4. How did each of your sensations contribute to your experience of the play? Were some helpful and others harmful? Can you really distinguish between levels of reality at those moments when the play is working well?

Having substitued this idea of *levels* of theatrical reality for the usual distinction between "illusion" and "reality," we see that the various levels are simultaneous aspects of a unified experience with each level serving a necessary purpose. The social reality binds you and your audience together: on a basic level, you accept the presence of your audience as real people and are sensitive to their responses to your performance; likewise, they accept you as a real human being and are sensitive to you as a performer. You may sometimes be tempted to ignore this social reality, or even to consider it antithetical to the aesthetic reality, but there is no incompatibility between social and aesthetic realities. The plays of Bertolt Brecht, for example, are designed to remind the audience continually that they are really in a theatre, watching actors performing; other playwrights very different from Brecht—Arthur Miller, Thornton Wilder, Samuel Beckett, Eugene Ionesco, Robert Bolt, Jean-Claude van Itallie, and many others—also manipulate, each in his own way, the social reality of the actor and the theatre itself as an overt and purposeful element of the total theatrical experience. This use of the social reality within the structure of a performance is usually a way of inviting the audience to take a more active, creative role—in effect, to become a cocreator with the actor.

In fact, an attitude that is the hallmark of much recent theatre (and of contemporary arts in general) is that there is no *essential* difference between the artist and the spectator. The aim is to make the social reality and the aesthetic reality combine so thoroughly that the result is a new kind of experience, one that transcends both the social relationship of audience and actor and the aesthetic relationship of audience and character by combining them into a unique *theatrical* experience.

It is important, therefore, to accept the audience's presence. If you ignore your social relationship to the audience, if you pretend that there really isn't anyone out there watching you, you cut yourself off from vital avenues of communication that can be utilized for the benefit of your creation, a creation in which the audience must participate. The play must not remain trapped either "behind the fourth wall" or in the "mind's eye" of the audience, but it must be free to exist within the total theatrical environment, free to receive the contributions of both spectator and actor.

Of course, this is only a general principle; each play requires a different emphasis *within this general idea.* The stage life of some plays, especially naturalistic ones, is relatively self-contained and partially independent of the audience's response; other plays, like Brecht's, require the audience's full participation. Most plays adopt a *variable* position. There are a good many different kinds of theatre, each kind requiring its own particular mode of communication between stage and audience. An important part of the actor's (and director's) job is to discover and establish the particular kind of stage/audience relationship that each play demands. You should, therefore, keep in mind that your relationship with your audience is in part an expression of the play's style and the director's production concept, and you should not allow a narrow, fixed attitude toward the theatrical environment to limit this relationship.

A word of caution is in order: except in those plays in which the audience's presence becomes an overt element of the play's structure through such devices as direct address (dialogue with audience members), actors mingling with the audience, and so on, the audience's reaction is not the immediate *purpose* of your performance. Even in such plays, the audience is treated artistically as a "character" in the play. Therefore, *your immediate task on stage is always to fulfill your character's dramatic objective, not to create a response in our audience.* Your audience's response is certainly important, and you shape your performance with an eye toward audience response; but when you are actually performing, your immediate concentration is on *what* you are doing, not on the audience's response to it. Your task is your *foreground;* your audience is the *background* against which you work.

It will be best to think of the audience's presence as *part of your stage environment.* To be in touch with your total environment, you must also accept the audience just as you accept your fellow actors. You, your fellow actors, and your audience are all teammates working *together* to create the drama. You do not "play for the sake of" your audience, any more than you "play for the sake of" your fellow actors. You are *all* working together toward the same goal.

This paradoxical idea of working with complete commitment to your stage reality while simultaneously accepting the audience's presence as a part of your working environment was summed up by Stanislavski in the term *public solitude.* It implies a *dual* and *simultaneous consciousness:* full concentration as if you were totally within the world of the play *as well as* effortless acceptance of the presence of your witnesses and your obligation to them. The key to this attitude is to be in the here and now (which includes relating to the audience) while also giving full "foreground" focus to your dramatic task.

Lesson 5

Bodily Gesture

The word *express* means "to push out." When you have a feeling or idea, it is natural to *externalize* it, to "push it out." Your expressive activity is part and parcel of your feeling and thought; the process of externalization goes on even when you are alone, for although your expressive behavior communicates your feelings to others, it is also an organic and automatic part of your feelings themselves.

When you have an impulse, feeling, or reaction, it arouses an energy at your deep center that then naturally flows outward, reaching the outer world in many forms: words, sounds, motions, postures, inflections, and so on. Broadly speaking, any external sign of a feeling or thought may be called a *gesture.* We will, for purposes of examining them systematically, break the wide range of gesture down into two main types: *bodily* and *vocal,* referring to gestures that can be *seen* and those that can be *heard.* This lesson treats bodily gestures; the next lesson will examine vocal gestures and will divide them further into two subtypes, *verbal* (the speaking of words) and *nonverbal* (the many sounds we make, as well as matters of inflection and emphasis that affect the emotional meaning of the words we speak).

Since your playwright usually will have provided your verbal gestures in the words of his script, your creation will consist mainly of the nonverbal aspect of your performance—the physical gestures, posture, inflections, facial expressions and so on. As you will see in part 2, the verbal language of the text is rich in implications about nonverbal gesture, which are helpful in the creation of a specific role, but even before you have learned the techniques of textual analysis, you can begin to explore the expressive possibilities of gesture as a means of communication.

GESTURE AND COMMUNICATION

Our culture has a large shared vocabulary of many types of gesture that we use to augment and often to replace our verbal communication. Some gestures have fairly consistent meanings when they appear in similar situations and thereby serve as a symbolic system; hence the term, *body language*. In their symbolic function, gestures provide a *physical analogy* for actions or feelings being expressed or described. While our *verbal* language provides a system for the communication of fairly precise meanings, our *gestural* language provides information about feelings and actions with greater expressiveness than words alone.

> Gestures achieve their highest degree of analogical value in emotional expression, but they also continue to serve as simple indicators in traffic, in games, and in love. Gestures have a communicative range from the universal down to the idiosyncratic; they may substitute for words or accompany words.[13]

A great deal of study has been devoted to the whole system of verbal language; until the last decade, however, the study of nonverbal gesture received little attention. Many physiologists and psychologists are now very interested in body language, and this area of study has been given the name *kinesics* by Professor Raymond Birdwhistle. He defines this new field as "the study of body motion as related to the nonverbal aspects of interpersonal communication." Several of his basic premises are of tremendous importance to the actor:

A. No motion is a thing in itself. It is always a part of a pattern. There is no "meaningless motor activity."
B. Until otherwise demonstrated, body motion patterns should be regarded as socially learned.
C. No unit of motion carries meaning per se. Meaning arises in context. It is the physiological similarity of our bodies and the generally similar influences of our environment that cause many gestures to develop roughly standardized meanings within our culture.

Here is a brief example of nonverbal expression at work as observed by Professor Birdwhistle. He recorded this encounter (he calls such encounters "scenes") and describes the nonverbal action just as a playwright would give "stage directions."

> (*The situation is that a guest of honor at a party arrives forty-five minutes late. Three couples besides the host and hostess have been waiting. The doorbell rings.*)

---

[13]Wallace A. Bacon and Robert S. Breen, *Literature as Experience* (New York: McGraw-Hill Book Company, 1959), p. 29.

HOSTESS: Oh! We were afraid you weren't coming; but good. (*As the hostess opened the door to admit her guest, she smiled a closed-toothed smile. As she began speaking she drew her hands, drawn into loose fists, up between her breasts. Opening her eyes very wide, she then closed them slowly and held them closed for several words. As she began to speak, she dropped her head to one side and then moved it toward the guest in a slow sweep. She then pursed her lips momentarily before continuing to speak, nodded, shut her eyes again, and spread her arms, indicating that he should enter.*)

GUEST: I'm very sorry; got held up you know, calls and all that. (*He looked at her fixedly, shook his head, and spread his arms with his hands held open. He then began to shuffle his feet and raise one hand, turning it slightly outward. He nodded, raised his other hand, and turned it palm-side up as he continued his vocalization. Then he dropped both hands and held them palms forward, to the side and away from his thighs. He continued his shuffling.*)

HOSTESS: Put your wraps here. People are dying to meet you. I've told them all about you. (*She smiled at him, lips pulled back from clenched teeth, then, as she indicated where he should put his coat, she dropped her face momentarily into an expressionless pose. She smiled toothily again, clucked and slowly shut, opened, and shut her eyes again as she pointed to the guests with her lips. She then swept her head from one side to the other. As she said the word "all" she moved her head in a sweep up and down from one side to the other, shut her eyes slowly again, pursed her lips, and grasped the guest's lapel.*)

GUEST: You have? Well, I don't know. . . . Yes. . . . No. . . . I'd love to meet them. (*The guest hunched his shoulders, which pulled his lapel out of the hostess' grasp. He held his coat with both hands, frowned, and then blinked rapidly as he slipped the coat off. He continued to hold tightly to his coat.*)[14]

As you reconstruct this scene in your mind's eye, it is obvious that the nonverbal behavior is very eloquent; moreover, it tends to express feelings that run *counter* to the surface meaning of the words being spoken. This is an extremely important aspect of nonverbal expression: it often "counterpoints" or even contradicts our verbal expression and "safely" expresses feelings that the situation forces us to suppress; in acting terms, it often conveys the *subtext,* the feelings running beneath the surface of the dialogue.

We can deduce a great deal of information from the gestures recorded in the scene above. The "logic of the body" has, within our culture, provided us with certain conventionalized meanings that are apparent

[14]Raymond Birdwhistle, *Introduction to Kinesics* (Louisville, Ky.: University of Louisville Pamphlet, 1957), pp. 29–30.

within this scene. The clenching of the teeth beneath the smile, the making of fists, the shuffling of feet, all tend to have generalized meanings when they appear in similar situations.

Professor Birdwhistle is not the first man to engage in the observation and "decoding" of nonverbal behavior. Here is the famous detective Sherlock Holmes in action, from "A Case of Identity," by Sir Arthur Conan Doyle:

> He had risen from his chair and was standing between the parted blinds, gazing down into the dull neutral-tinted London street. . . . On the pavement opposite there stood a large woman with a heavy fur boa around her neck, and a large curling red feather in a broad-brimmed hat which was tilted in a coquettish Duchess of Devonshire fashion over her ear. From under this great panoply she peeped up in a nervous, hesitating fashion at our window, while her body oscillated backward and forward, and her fingers fidgeted with her glove buttons. Suddenly, with a plunge as of the swimmer who leaves the bank, she hurled across the road and we heard the sharp clang of the bell. "I have seen those symptoms before," said Holmes, throwing his cigarette into the fire. "Oscillation upon the pavement always means an *affaire de coeur.* She would like advice, but is not sure that the matter is not too delicate for communication. And yet even here we may discriminate. When a woman has been seriously wronged by a man she no longer oscillates, and the usual symptom is a broken bell wire. Here we may take it that there is a love matter, but that the maiden is not so much angered as perplexed, or grieved. But here she comes in person to resolve our doubts."[15]

In his book *The Silent Language,* Edward Hall comments on this passage by saying that Holmes "made explicit a highly complex process which many of us go through without knowing that we are involved. Those of us who keep our eyes open can read volumes into what we see going on around us."[16]

Group exercise 6 The science of deduction

Try playing the part of Sherlock Holmes using the hostess/guest scene recorded by Professor Birdwhistle. In a short, written description recreate as completely as you can the reasons for the behavior of both characters; forecast as well as you can the

[15]From THE SILENT LANGUAGE, by Edward T. Hall, p. 43. Copyright © 1959 by Edward T. Hall. Reprinted by permission of Doubleday & Company, Inc.
[16]Ibid., p. 42.

immediate future of their relationship. Then, as a group, compare your accounts to see what similar deductions you have made. What areas were the most commonly agreed upon, and what evidence was the most persuasive? Be specific; why did you draw the conclusions you reached from each bit of evidence?

While the science of body language is fairly new, man's interest in it is very old. One of the first studies of the "silent language" (which may have been influential on the style of acting of its time) was John Bulwer's *Chirologia and Chironomia,* written in 1644. The book calls itself a study of "the Speaking Motions, and Discoursing Gestures, the patheticalle motions of the minde." The book discussed and illustrated (see figure 23) an enormous number of feelings as expressed by nonverbal gestures. Similar attempts to categorize physical gestures for the performer were made throughout the seventeenth, eighteenth, and nineteenth centuries. Even a few modern systems of acting use, in a very modified form, a formalized approach to the physical expression of emotion by locating "emotion centers" in the body, an idea borrowed from Oriental acting and medicine.

THE ORIGINS OF BODILY GESTURE

While the actor is very often interested in the unique behavior of individual people, he is also profoundly concerned with the typical aspects of behavior that are common within his culture. As we have seen, much of our bodily language is common within similar situations, and this is because such gestures have a common bodily origin.

We can see the evolution of common nonverbal gestures from actions that were at one time *necessary* and *practical* in nature. Man's present state of development has changed his needs and has changed also the purpose of much of his physical behavior. A situation that at an earlier time had to be met with physical action is now "solved" for us by technology or our complex social structure, but the original practical behavior, in a vestigial state, still persists. It is now purely *expressive,* and no longer *functional.*

The way in which vestiges of physical behavior can live on as symbolic activity, even after the action has ceased to be practical, is explained by Charles Darwin in *The Expression of Emotion in Man and Animal* and is expanded on here by Robert S. Breen:

> Consider the expressive value of behavior that was once in our human history adaptive, but is no longer so except in a vestigial sense—for example, the baring of teeth in the preparation for attack or defense. In primitive experience, the use of the teeth for tearing and rending an enemy

FIGURE 23   An old method of indicating emotion.

was common enough, and a very effective means of adapting to an environmental necessity. Today, the use of teeth in this primitive fashion is rare, but the baring of the teeth is still very much with us. In an attitude of pugnacity, men will frequently clench their teeth and draw back their lips to expose their teeth. This action is a reinstatement of the primitive pattern of biting, though there is no *real* intention of using the teeth in such a fashion. The "tough guy" talks through his teeth because he is habituated to an attitude of aggressiveness. When he bares his teeth, it is a warning to all who see him that he is prepared to attack or to defend himself. His speech is characterized by a nasality because his oral cavity is closed, and his breath escapes primarily through his nose. Lip action in speech is curtailed because the jaw is held so close to the upper jaw that there is little room between the lips for even their normal activity. Restriction of the lip action results in the tough guy's talking out of the corner of his mouth.

When we see a person bare his clenched teeth, curl his lip, narrow his eyes, deepen his breathing, etc., we conclude that he is angry. These are the *signs* of attack in our ancestors which have become for us *social symbols expressive of an emotional state* known as *anger.* [17]

Exercise 21   Animal gestures

A. Examine your own physical functions: breathing, eating, vomiting, defecating, fighting, lovemaking, etc. Choose one, then adopt the characteristics of a prehistoric man performing the same function. When you have begun to experience the activity fully on a purely physical, "animalistic" level, begin gradually to "civilize" the behavior. Do not premeditate; let the activity itself lead you as it gradually becomes less and less practical and more and more "symbolic."

B. Reverse the procedure; select some detail of contemporary expressive behavior and gradually "animalize" it.

C. Try working again on the hostess/guest scene and, with a partner, develop this scene as it might have happened between two animals.

You will probably notice that the "animalized" version of even the most genteel behavior involves a strong participation of the lower center and appears more vivid and powerful than its civilized offspring. It is useful for the actor to reawaken his own sense of the origins of his expressive behavior for just this reason; even as you perform the "polite" contemporary behavior, your memory of the animal origins of that behavior can

[17]Bacon and Breen, *Literature as Experience,* p. 32.

serve as a source of power and deep involvement in it. This does not mean that your performance appears animal-like, but only that you have established within yourself a link with the deepest racial origins of your own behavior, which enriches your stage creation.

FUNCTIONS OF BODILY GESTURE

We can divide the language of gestures into four broad categories of gestural function:

1. Illustrative, or imitative
2. Indicative
3. Emphatic
4. Autistic

Illustrative gestures are "pantomimic" in communicating specific information ("the box was about this high and this wide").

The indicative gesture points ("it's right over there").

The emphatic gesture provides subjective rather than objective information, relating how we *felt* about something (as we say "now listen here," we pound our fist on the table or jab our finger into our opponent's face).

The autistic gesture (meaning literally "to the self") is not intended for social communication but is rather a way in which we communicate privately to ourselves. Suppose that as I listen to you speak I have hostile feelings, which for some reason I must conceal from you. With my arms crossed over my chest, I am viciously clutching the flesh under one of my armpits. In this secret manner, I am having some symbolic satisfaction in strangling you, the flesh of my armpit substituting for the flesh of your neck. While such gestures are usually hidden, they are often unconsciously perceived and recognized by the people around us.

Obviously, these four categories of gesture are not actually separate in practice and are for the convenience of our study only. Almost every gesture we make serves a combination of two or three of these functions simultaneously.

Exercise 22   Physical gesture scene

Select a simple but highly physical action. Perform it four times, each time utilizing a different kind of gesture. For example, if your action is to lift a heavy box and move it across the room, you would:

1. Illustrate lifting it, as if you were telling us about how you did it without actually doing it. You may use words together with physical gestures here.
2. Indicate lifting it. ("I'll pick it up from over there and carry it over here.")
3. Use emphatic gestures that are symbolic (rather than illustrative) as you show and tell us *how it felt* to lift the heavy box. See especially how your voice is affected.
4. Finally, perform the action symbolically and *secretly* using autistic gestures (for example, hitching up your belt as a substitute for lifting the box).

Which categories resulted in meaningful involvement in the action? Do you see why indirect and symbolic gesture is often more effective and interesting than obvious pantomime or indication?

Exercise 23   Implied gestures in the script

A. Notice how often the verbal language of a play's script makes demands of a nonverbal nature upon us. The following speech from *King Lear* demands gestures of all four types. Try performing it four times, each time emphasizing a different category of gesture:

LEAR: When I do stare, see how the subject quakes. I pardon that man's life. What was thy cause? Adultery? Thou shalt not die. Die for adultery? The wren goes to't, and the small gilded fly does lecher in my sight. Let copulation thrive, for Gloucester's bastard son was kinder to his father than my daughters got 'tween the lawful sheets. To't luxury, pell-mell! for I lack soldiers. Behold yond simpering dame, whose face between her forks presages snow, that minces virtue, and does shake the head to hear of pleasure's name: the fitchew nor the soiled horse goes to't with a more riotous appetite. Down from the waist they are centaurs, though women all above. But to the girdle do the gods inherit, beneath is all the fiends'. There's hell, there's darkness, there is the sulphurous pit: burning, scalding, stench, consumption. Fie, fie, fie! pah, pah! Give me an ounce of civet, good apothecary, to sweeten my imagination. There's money for thee.

B. Now perform an "animalization" of the speech; see how far you can go in physicalizing this speech, to the point of making it a dance.

This is only the most obvious way in which the verbal language of a text can inspire the nonverbal language of stage performance.

BODILY CENTER AND CHARACTER

The energy that flows outward from your center reaches the outer world after passing through your characteristic bodily alignment and emerges in a variety of expressive postures and gestures. We have already categorized four functions that gestures may serve; we can now characterize the various shapes that the body and its gestures may take. We will first consider how a character's energy-center can be a profound expression of his attitude toward life.

When we experimented with centeredness in lesson 2, I said that your ability to bring your own center into conformity with your character's center would be a fundamental characterizational choice. To understand this point fully, you must distinguish between your center *as an actor* and the "apparent" center you adopt *for your character.* Remember that true centeredness is a quality of wholeness and stability in the personality, but that stage characters are rarely stable, well-adjusted people; since "normal" people are not terribly interesting on stage, dramatic characters are usually abnormal in some way and therefore "uncentered" or functioning from an "unnatural" center of energy, both physically, vocally, and even psychologically. Your job, then, is to use your own deeply centered energies to support your portrayal of an abnormally centered character, allowing your energy to flow "internally" from your true center into an *apparent* center from which your character relates to the world.

I can suggest five primary character centers that, by bodily logic and by cultural tradition, are each associated with a different sort of person: head (the cerebral and/or sexually repressed person), chest (the sentimental, or even the "militaristic" person), stomach (the indulgent person), genitals (the libidinous, or perhaps the naive person), and anus (the sexually withdrawn, "constipated" person). See figure 24a. We have all known people who tend to relate to the world from one of these centers and who carry with them their own unique variations on the basic theme of their center; observe some of your aquaintances from this point of view. Think also of some specific dramatic characters and imagine how this idea of centers would apply to each. What center might Amanda in *The Glass Menagerie* have? Falstaff? The Fool in *Lear*?

Try adopting various centers for yourself and see what experiences result.

ENERGY STRUCTURE AND CHARACTER

The character's apparent center (head, chest, etc.) is the source of his impulses or energy; we must further consider the dynamic nature of this energy and the pathways through which it flows on its way to the outside world,

Think of an impulse as beginning as a single, unified energy which is then split into different pathways to bring it more easily under control—to alter it, evaluate it, direct it toward an objective, or perhaps inhibit it. We can say that one way of splitting this basic life-energy into parts is by sending some of it into feeling and thought (psychic energy) and some of it simultaneously into muscular energy (somatic energy). One cannot exist without the other, although a psychotic character may exhibit a complete blockage of one or the other.

Within the human body, you see how the muscular structure translates this splitting of energy into two parts in yet another way: one energy pathway runs along the *back* of the body, another along the *front*. Because the muscles of the back are so large and hard, the rear pathway usually carries our aggressive and sexual energies; the muscles and tissues in the front of the body are softer and more accessible or vulnerable, so that the front pathway usually carries our "tender" and sensory feelings.

Besides the split between front and back, you must also consider whether an impulse runs *upward* or *downward*. If you consider the outline of the body, you will see two narrow places, at the neck and the waist. You can think of these narrow places as "dams" or "conduits." As energy which has been stored in the larger reservoirs of the chest and pelvis flows outward, it passes through these narrow places and—as you would expect —it is at these points that blockage or control of the energy is most likely to occur. If the energy moves upward through the neck, the energy from the rear and the front pathways is reunited in the face, leaving the eyes or the mouth as a single gesture or discharge. If, on the other hand, the energy moves downward through the waist, the rear and frontal flows are reunited in the genitals or anus, leaving as a single gesture or discharge.

Finally, you must consider the nature of the energy itself. Is it a *high charge,* or a *low charge*? Is it primarily *deep* within the body, using those deep muscles and organs which are involved with our unconscious drives, or is it primarily a *surface* or *peripheral* impulse of which we tend to be more conscious and ego-involved?

The exact quality of any gesture, we see, is the product of an interior flow of energy which can be described in five primary ways:

1. Is the energy charge *great* or *little*?
2. Is it deeply *interior* or on the *surface*?
3. Does it flow *upward* toward the face, or *downward* toward the genitals?
4. Is it predominantly along the *rear* of the body (aggressive, pleasure-seeking, sexual, muscular) or along the *front* of the body (tender, vulnerable, reality-seeking, sensory)?
5. Is the energy *constricted* along the way, especially at the waist or neck?

While these qualities can describe any specific gesture, you can also see how a chronic tendency to respond one way or another will eventually establish habitual mannerisms. In this way the quality of the movement of the body is deeply expressive of the person's psychological orientation to the world and to himself. Consider, as one fundamental example of this fact, a person's *walk*. An insecure person, with a weak sense of self-identity, tends to be unstable. We speak of such a person as a "pushover," someone who "won't stand on his own two feet." In the opposite extreme is the "pushy" person who carries his weight on the balls of his feet and whose energy flows up his back into the aggressive stance of a fighter. The "flighty" person is disconnected, light on his feet; the ponderous or chronically depressed person is nowadays called a "downer" or a "bring-down."

A person's energy structure, then, functions within and also helps to determine the configuration of the body itself. The body soon comes to announce the nature of the energy which inhabits it. The Elizabethan idea of reading character in the body ("this is the forehead of a murderer," etc.) was crude but entirely accurate in principle.

BODY ALIGNMENT AND CHARACTER

Just as dramatic characters tend to be abnormally centered, so abnormal centering is always accompanied by a distortion of natural body alignment. One school of psychiatry, in fact, believes that it is possible to match various basic personality types with certain basic bodily alignments. A habitual bodily alignment must be understood as more than a posture, however, although posture is a crucial factor. It involves a characteristic way of moving and—especially—the chronic ways in which movement is inhibited and areas of the body withheld from movement. As Alexander Lowen, a psychoanalyst who works in the field he calls bioenergetics, puts it: "[T]he muscles can hold back movements as well as execute them. . . .

Consider the case of an individual who is charged with rage and yet must hold back the impulse to strike. His fists are clenched, his arms are tense and his shoulders are drawn and held back to restrain the impulse."[18] If such a temporary, conscious suppression of rage becomes a chronic and eventually unconscious repression, the muscular tension in the hands, arms, and upper back also becomes chronic. Eventually, the muscles and other tissues in these areas actually harden, losing their flexibility and sensitivity. The rigidity of these areas will affect the person's posture and movement, and a trained observer can diagnose the psychological pattern captured in the musculature. For this reason, the configuration of the body and its movement pattern are, interestingly for the actor, called the *character structure.*

The repression of emotion is not the only way character structure is created. The influence of heredity, the infant's mimicry of his parents' bodily types, and patterns of social response (like the teenager's slouching) can all become "built into" the body. Such a bodily configuration actually alters the tendons, cartilage, tissue, and bone until it becomes, as some therapists call it, an *armor.* In earlier exercises you examined your armor and began working to remove it so that you would be left free to adopt the bodily configuration most appropriate to your character.

You attempt to do this not only because it can help you to a more full and vivid participation in the life of your character, but also because your bodily configuration is a powerful communicator of experience and understanding of character to your audience. In everyday life, we have many vivid (albeit usually unconscious) responses to the body alignment of those around us. We also tend unconsciously to imitate, to a slight degree, the body alignment of a person with whom we are relating, so that the dominant feeling expressed by his bodily type is empathically aroused in us. Figure 24b exhibits in profile six basic bodily alignments and briefly states the personality traits usually connected with each.

There is a further system that deals not with body *alignment* but with physiological *type:* this system recognizes three main body types, the mesomorphic, the ectomorphic, and the endomorphic, which correspond roughly to the muscular body, the thin and nervous body, and the fat and jolly body. However, since there is little (short of wearing padding or girdles) that the actor can do about his own basic bodily *type,* we will pay greatest attention to *alignment* which *can* be altered during the creation of a role. Moreover, any one of the three body types may adopt any of the basic alignments and still produce a vivid result, so variation in your

---

[18]Alexander Lowen, *The Language of the Body* (New York: Collier, 1971), p. 32. While this is a very technical book, every serious student of the relationship of bodily and psychological expression should be familiar with it.

alignment will service you as an actor regardless of your basic bodily type. Examine figure 24b; try "putting on" some of these alignments and see what attitudes are aroused in you. Next, think of specific dramatic characters and explore body alignment for each. Can you pick Willy Loman from among the bodies pictured? Which alignment might Jerry in *The Zoo Story* have? Which Falstaff? Which Hotspur?

Do you see how a *change* in a character's alignment in the course of a play can signal a profound change in his personality? The Willy Loman we see at the beginning of the play may not be the same Willy we see in his better days during the flashbacks. Likewise, imagine Lear at the beginning of his play, and again after his ordeal in the storm, when his daughter has to help him to walk. Do you see how such changes express not merely physical conditions but psychological and even spiritual conditions?

QUALITIES OF GESTURE AND CHARACTER

Whatever energy-center and bodily alignment you may develop for a given character, the character's way of moving and gesturing may still fall within a wide range of expressive qualities. We will explore six basic aspects of gesture: altitude, strength, tempo, direction, flow, and integration.

Altitude: the character's energy-center will cause him to emphasize an altitude of gesture related to that center. A stomach person, for example, will tend to gesture within that general area, and his voice will likewise tend to be a "stomach" voice. Figure 24a charts the altitudes related to the five primary character centers.

Strength: the character's gestures may be typically strong or weak.

Tempo: the character's gestures may be typically fast or slow.

Direction: his gestures may be typically aimed *directly* at people or objects, or *indirectly* in a more diffuse, broad, or even evasive manner.

Flow: the character's energy may flow easily outward in a continuous stream, or it may be "bound in."

Integration: the character's energy flow may be sporadic, and his body may be broken into disassociated parts. (Such disassociation of the parts of the body is typical of schizoid characters.)

These categories actually work in combination to produce the quality of gesture appropriate to the character. We can examine the character's way of gesturing, however, by using each of these categories for analysis; each sets a parameter within which the character functions in response to specific situations. A person whose basic tempo is slow may, in a specific situation, gesture or move very quickly, but it will be a different quickness than that exhibited in the same situation by a character whose dominant

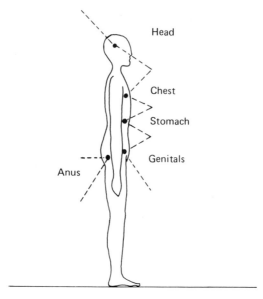

FIGURE 24A   Primary character centers and their corresponding gestural altitudes.

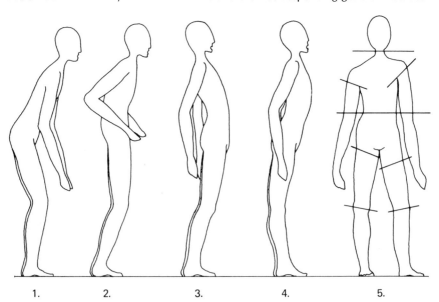

1.   2.   3.   4.   5.

FIGURE 24B   Basic body alignments. (1) *Head-centered.* Flighty or off-balance, always "ahead of himself." Poorly grounded, sex impulses withheld. Tends toward the schizoid character in (5). Energy fritters off in all directions at once. (2) *Shoulders rounded, swayed back.* When this structure is based upon a head orientation and a weak energy level in the lower body, it is called the *oral* body. The chest is collapsed, the arms express yearning. The legs are weak, making the body unstable and poorly grounded. Aggressive energies at the rear are blocked, and a great deal of grief is held in the front of the body. When this structure (with the pelvis not so thrust forward) is based upon a high energy level and a dominance of aggressive energy up the rear of the body, it is called *masochistic.* The shoulders are rounded because of the overdevelopment of the muscles in the upper body, giving a gorilla-like hulking aspect. The bound-in aggressions of this type are turned inward upon the self; notice that the energy pathway along the back begins to approach a circle. (3) *Belly-centered.* This "heavy" character responds with great equanimity and could be called the "aw shucks" body. We usually think of such characters as unaggressive (the sway back blocks the aggressive energies of the rear body) but jolly and sentimental (as the preponderance of the frontal energies would indicate). The lack of aggressiveness limits the sexuality of this type—all sexuality must have a large aggression component (which is not at all identical with violence)—so increased oral activity often compensates, in turn increasing and softening the belly. (4) *Rigid.* Sometimes called the militaristic character because it resembles the stance of a soldier at attention, this is the most hostile of all alignments. The shoulders are thrown back and an enormous amount of anger is stored in the rigid area between the shoulder blades and in a tight chest front—the result of holding the arms back from striking. Firmly rooted but so rigid in response that grace gives way to mechanicalness. The rear of the body is in complete charge (as opposed to the previous type) so that phallic narcissism is frequent in men of this type. In any case, unconsciously aggressive energies dominate and the tender areas of the body and feelings are made hard. Small wonder that we train soldiers to stand this way, and not to think for themselves. (5) *Schizoid.* Here the parts of the body at all the major joints are disassociated so that the person is literally "in pieces." The head is often cocked in a birdlike way. Very unstable and poorly grounded; lacks grace in movement. *Note:* If the first four alignments are performed in one unbroken sequence, they produce a wavelike pattern taught by French mime Jacques LeCoq. These bodily types are variations of those identified by bioenergetic therapy. For a more complete discussion of items (2), (4), and (5), see Alexander Lowen, *The Language of the Body.*

tempo is quick to begin with. Notice too that these qualities may exist in surprising combinations; one does not absolutely determine any of the others.

Exercise 24   Body center, energy structure, alignment, gesture, and character

This complex exercise is of tremendous importance. It can sensitize you to the components of physical characterization and extend your range of choice in each area. Take as much time as you can with the exercise, and repeat it a number of times, each time making a new set of choices and exploring a new set of combinations; work with each set until a unified experience results.

A. Randomly select one of the five bodily centers from figure 25a and begin to move and speak from it.

B. Feel the energy flowing from this center; trace its pathway through the body:

1. Is the energy charge great or little?
2. Is it deeply interior or on the surface?
3. Does it flow upward or downward?
4. Is it predominantly along the rear or the front of the body?
5. Is it blocked or altered at some point?

C. Discover the *walk* that results from these energy-choices. What is your orientation toward the ground?

D. As you move, and then come to rest, see if you begin to fall into one of the basic body alignments in figure 25b. Adopt it fully; check yourself in a mirror if possible.

E. Using numbers, letters of the alphabet, or gibberish as your "dialogue," relate with a partner using and exploring all the different gestures (physical and vocal) available within each range:

1. from different centers and altitudes
2. weak and strong
3. slow and fast
4. direct and indirect
5. free-flowing or bound in
6. integrated or disassociated

F. Select a specific dramatic character you know well and repeat this exercise while creating the physical aspects of his personality. What feelings are inspired in you?

This entire system of categorizing bodily alignments, character centers, and qualities of gesture is compiled from the work of four people: Wilhelm Reich, a psychiatrist who pioneered the analysis of character through bodily alignment; François Delsarte, a nineteenth-century acting theorist who first formalized a system of centers for the actor; Etienne Decroux, a great mime and teacher of mime; and Rudolf Laban, whose pioneering studies in effort-shape have been of monumental importance in the dance.

We use this system not as a *formula* for creating a role, but as a methodical way of *sensitizing* ourselves to the potential range of bodily expression and its relationship to character. There may, of course, be times when you will find these ideas helpful in creating a character, or at least as a source of stimulation to your imagination as you work.

Many actors like to hit upon a quality of gesture that "triggers" a sense of the character in them. It is said that Alec Guinness sometimes uses the *walk* of the character as a trigger; the great acting teacher Michael Chekhov suggested finding a single *psychological gesture* that sums up your understanding and feeling for a character. Remember, however, that all such gestural "touchstones," whatever their form, must be the *result* of a process of exploration, *never a substitute for it!*

THE ACTOR'S USE OF PHYSICAL CHARACTERIZATION

The main question about the actor's creation of externals is whether they should be treated *as* externals and approached "from the outside," or viewed as the necessary result of an inner state and approached "from the inside." Different schools of acting adopt an emphasis on one or another, but rarely is one point of view taken to the complete exclusion of the other.

Even a ridgidly "external" approach, as in the Kabuki theatre of Japan, takes into account the significance of inward states. Earle Ernst, in his book *The Kabuki Theatre,* describes the oriental actor's attitude toward his character this way: "The approach of the Kabuki actor to the character is summed up in this practice: in the small room at the end of the *hanimichi,* there is a large mirror; when the actor is fully prepared for his entrance, he sits before the mirror and studies his figure so that he can absorb the nature of the character he is to play by concentration on its external appearance." But the Kabuki actor's job is only half done if he is satisfied with simple externals. Although the Kabuki actor does not "base the character on something within himself," he *does* derive "from the visual image an inward significance." In doing so, he follows the theory and practice of Japanese art. The poet Basho's advice to his pupils was "feel like the pine when you look at the pine, like the bamboo when you look at the bamboo." In other words, "Truthful, artistic expression can arise only with the complete surrender of the artist to the nature of the object before him, a surrender uninhibited by the artist's intellect or emotions."[19]

Seemingly opposite to this point of view is the type of acting that emphasizes the actor's use of his own emotions in his creation. Even though we think of Stanislavski as representing this point of view, he also emphasized this idea of the actor's surrender to his character. The Kabuki actor achieves it by working from the "outside" to the "inward significance"; Stanislavski achieved it by working from the "inside" of the character to the "outside," by helping the actor to establish a true inner feeling that generated his external behavior. Nevertheless, we often overlook the importance Stanislavski himself placed on the externals; like the Kabuki actor, he himself liked to stand in full costume and makeup before a mirror, fully realizing his own externals before he considered his own characterizations complete.

Both approaches, reasonably used, are pathways to the same objective: *aesthetic control over external form supported by a vital involvement in the "inward significance" of the character.* External form, no matter how precise, is empty unless filled with the real experience of the actor, while the actor's inner experience is useless without a precise external form in which it may be communicated. In order to achieve both, we must discipline ourselves to avoid imposing aspects of our real-life behavior on our character, either in terms of bodily or vocal mannerisms, or in terms of attitudes of thought or emotion. Instead we must reach out to the new form of behavior and thought required by the character, then allow our own real energies to flow into that new form.

The two exercises that follow will give you experience with both approaches, beginning with a predetermined set of externals that you must "fill" with inward significance by working "from the outside in."

Exercise 25   Putting yourself in the scene

Take the hostess-guest scene and recreate it on the stage as faithfully as you can. What you are doing is not much different

[19]Earle Ernst, *The Kabuki Theatre* (New York: Grove Press, 1956), p. 193. Used by permission of Oxford University Press.

from playing a scene in which a playwright has provided extensive stage directions for the actor. After experiencing the scene fully, review it: isolate aspects of the character's behavior in the scene that were different from your real-life behavior. Did performing these actions give you special insight into the character? Did these modifications in your own behavior give you new insights into yourself? Examine those aspects of your real-life behavior that happened to fit the scene, and those aspects that were most different from your real-life self. Which contributed most to the scene and your understanding? To improve the scene, on which would you have to work further?

Having had this experience of working "from the outside in," you will now experiment with working "from the inside out."

Exercise 26   Gesture communication scene

A. With a partner, decide on some important message to be communicated between you, and a reply. It should be about something of *vital* concern to both of you in whatever imagined relationship you establish. When you are both clear about the message, the reply, and the imagined relationship, and when you have allowed for the possibility of communication that extends beyond the predetermined message and reply, begin to work out a dance-like scene in which you communicate the message and reply using only physical gestures and nonverbal noises.

Do not limit yourself to realistic movements or noises, and do not treat the scene as a charade. Your objective is *not* to make the message and reply clear to the audience; a few words would do that job much better. The gestures and noises are here not merely a substitute for words, but a means of profound emotional communication between you and your partner. Your objective, then, is to communicate fully *with each other* using only the vehicle of gesture and noise; the information communicated to a spectator is of secondary importance and should not be a conscious part of this experience.

B. When you feel that honest communication has taken place in this scene (usually you will have been led beyond the original give and take to a further scene), present it to your audience and ask them to guess at the nature of the original message. (Keep the experience alive—don't falsify it by playing it "to" the audience!) Though the accuracy of their guesses is unimportant, their

FIGURE 25   Three illustrations of gesture communication exercises.

comments will be revealing about the quality of your communication. What did they find most "real"?

Review the experience of these two exercises: do you see how each has its own virtues and limitations? Do you see how each involved a different kind of creativity and that both kinds of creativity are necessary and fulfilling for the actor? Did the end result of the two exercises "feel" very different to you? If so, why? Do you see how each *could* be a complete experience, and that both ways of working are necessary in the creation of a role, even though you may gravitate toward one or the other as your dominant personal methodology?

THE MASK OF PERSONALITY

In the hostess/guest scene (exercise 25), you "put on" the externals of a person's behavior in a social situation almost as if they were parts of a costume. Did some of the person's attitudes and feelings grow within you? Did your participation in these externals develop greater empathy ("in-feeling") for you with the person you were playing?

The feelings you had as the person in the hostess/guest scene were necessarily drawn from your own awareness and experience; you were responding not to *his* feelings, but to *your* feelings as they would be *if you were in his place.*

Having put yourself physically in his place, some of his experience is yours; what new insights did you gain? Did you begin to feel the character's inner state? Did the exercise *extend you* into a new experience of yourself to some degree?

When you adopted the externals of the character in this exercise, it was much like putting on a *mask*. If you put on the mask of a fat, happy person, you *look* fat and happy, regardless of how you feel. However, if you concentrate on your own appearance in the mask (like the Kabuki actor before his mirror) and begin to behave appropriately to your appearance, you will soon begin to *feel* fat and happy. Twenty-five centuries ago Plato observed that imitations of human behavior soon cease to be imitations and tend to become reality for the imitator.

The word *personality* is derived from the Greek word *persona,* which literally means both *mask* and *through sound.* Your personality is the "mask" or external image as well as the "sound mask" that you attempt to present to the outside world. Your "mask of personality" consists mainly of the gestures (in our broad sense of external physical and vocal signs of feeling) that are characteristic of your social self. Though your personality also consists of inner attitudes and feelings that lie "behind" the mask, these "hidden" feelings usually seep out from behind the mask in many ways, or may even "explode" through the mask upon occasion.

The actor began, according to one theory, as a priest wearing a mask. He wore it as an act of worship, believing that by wearing the mask of the god he assumed some of the power and identity of the god. Man still wears "masks" of various types and for the same purpose: owning a Cadillac makes us feel rich, even if we're not; smoking a pipe makes us feel mature, even if we're not; waving the flag makes us feel patriotic, even if we're not.

So it is for the actor. Putting on the mask of the character's personality —if we honestly surrender to the demands that the mask makes upon us, rather than attempting to reshape the mask to fit us—will help us to feel like the character, to extend ourselves into new realms of experience, that is, to experience ourselves in new forms.

Remember, however, that an actor's mask is not merely an object, nor is it merely an outward appearance; it is a *pattern of behavior, a mask of actions* motivated by thoughts and feelings.

Exercise 27 Masks

Buy or make some masks. Select one and wear it for a time, looking in a mirror. Move about with it on and try to behave totally as the mask demands, *allowing sound to be a continuous part of the process.*

A. Checking yourself frequently in a full-length mirror, create a complete body composition inspired by the mask. Cover each of the following points, making vivid, specific choices.

1. Is your *center* in your
   a. genitals?
   b. anus?
   c. stomach?
   d. chest?
   e. head?
   Explore each center and select one; this becomes the area of the body from which the character's energy tends to flow.
2. How much do you *weigh?* Are you light or heavy?
3. Is your *tempo* fast or slow?
4. Is your *rhythm* regular or erratic?
5. Do you *move* through a heavy or a light atmosphere? (Try unusual combinations like heavy/fast/regular/light atmosphere, or light/slow/erratic/heavy atmosphere.)

6. Are you *angular* or *curvy?*
7. Are your movements *through space* angular or curvy?
8. Is your main energy flow *vertical* or *horizontal?*
9. Are you *symmetrical* or *asymmetrical?*
10. Are you *hard* or *soft?*
11. Are you *aggressive* or *recessive?*
12. Develop an expressive *silhouette* based upon one of the basic body alignments.

B. When the bodily composition is complete and natural to you, check the types of bodily gesture used by your character:

1. Are your gestures *weak* or *strong?*
2. Are they *slow* or *fast?*
3. Are they *direct* or *indirect?*
4. What is your characteristic *altitude* of gesture? How does your altitude relate to your character center?
5. Are your gestures integrated or disassociated?

C. After further exploration, can you sum your experience of the character up in a single *psychological gesture?*

D. Enter into improvised relationships with other mask characters within the group. Add simple props and costume pieces (if available) to your mask-character.

This exercise can take many days to complete, and there are many further exercises you can explore using your mask-characters. The basis for this work was developed by Michel St. Denis, a great director and teacher of acting; it is most useful in reawakening that beautiful childhood impulse to assume characters (even characters of *things,* like locomotives) easily and joyfully. This *mimetic instinct* seems fundamental to man and is surely at the very root of acting and of the theatre itself. Find this joy of being someone or something else, which you had as a child, and recapture it—for it is the very essence of the actor's art. Look back on your mask work: did you truly *enjoy* it? Were your choices timid, within a narrow expressive range? What has "growing up" done to your mimetic instinct? Share your experiences with your fellow students.

In the last exercise, your mask-character was your own creation. The next exercise will give you experience in adopting a form created by someone else and filling it with your own energies, thereby letting it serve as the source of new experience for you.

Exercise 28   Doppelgängers

Working with a partner, and using the same mask-characters created in the previous exercise, develop a relationship and some shared activity between your two mask-characters.

Begin gradually to *trade identities,* literally, piece by piece, quality by quality. This will take some time. You "direct" each other as you go so that eventually you, having put on your partner's mask and character, are now directing your partner in the playing of your original character, and vice versa.

Review this exercise: critique each other's performances of the adopted characters. What kinds of "directions" were the most useful to you? Did you gain insights into some of the problems of directors as they try to help actors realize a characterization? What did you learn about *your own original character* by directing your partner in it?

TYPES

While masks often have unique properties of their own, they usually represent some general *type* of character. The idea of "type" is today in disfavor; we prefer to regard each individual and each dramatic character as unique, and the idea of a "type" on stage today is often synonymous with bad acting.

However, there *is* such a thing as "typical" behavior, and each of us to some extent shares in sets of typical traits and aspects of behavior that are common in our culture. We also, of course, possess unique individual qualities in combination with these more typical traits. The trouble with a "type" on the stage is that it tends to disregard these unique aspects of behavior, and the results are a generalized caricature that is as unbelievable as it is dishonest.

Unfortunately, the reaction against "types" in our theatre has been so strong that we have practically banned typicality from our stages. We tend to think, for example, that if your Stanley Kowalski isn't a completely unique character with a set of idiosyncratic gestures never before used by another actor, you are somehow less of an "artist." The fact that Tennessee Williams meant Stanley Kowalski to be typical of a large segment of American heterosexual society therefore may be subordinated to the individuality of your performance.

It has always been a purpose of art to reveal significant common patterns of human experience at the same time that it embodies these typical qualities in a creation possessing its own unique properties. *Typicality* and *uniqueness* are *both* essential to a dramatic character; typicality provides comprehensibility and relevance, while uniqueness provides vitality. This same principle applies equally to stage gesture.

The language of gestures *is* a language in the sense that some kinds of gestures are typical within a cultural group, but just as we all have unique qualities of speech, so do we all have a unique way of using gestural language. Your performance will be based upon what the playwright has supplied, but its unique quality will be finally determined more by the way you use your own energies in creating your own role. Underlying the uniqueness of your performance, however, you must not lose sight of the typicality of your character, since it provides the "universality" that permits each spectator to say, "Yes, I've done that, or felt like that myself," or at least, "I know people like that."

Group Exercise 7 Types

Make two sets of slips of paper. On one set, write a number of personality "types" (for example, timid soul, bully, business tycoon, spinster, and so on). On the other slips, write emotions (for example, fear, jealousy, joy, and so on). Pick one slip from each pile without showing it to anyone else. Without time to think about it, perform the following pantomime, attempting to manifest both the type and the emotion: walk into the room, sit down in a chair at a table and eat and drink for a few moments, then rise and leave the room.

In discussion with the group, see what agreement there was about the physical type and the emotion portrayed. Try to isolate which aspects of the performer's behavior communicated each of the impressions received by his audience. For example, "We knew you were a spinster by the way in which you sat up so straight on the edge of the chair with your knees tight together," or "I knew you were a successful man because when you walked into the room you didn't bother to look where you were going." Examine the symbolic meaning of each of the physical details that led to these impressions. In the first example, "spinsterliness" was communicated by the knees being held close together, because of the modesty, the frigidity, or the sexual fear implied by that posture. Also, the fact that you sat on the edge of the chair with a stiff back showed that you weren't willing to conform to your environment (in this case the chair), and that your behavior remained constant no matter what your situation so that you were literally a "rigid" person. The stiffness of your movements implied not only the stiffness of age but the intellectual stiffness of someone very set in her ways.

In the second example, the fact that the tycoon walked firmly and without looking where he was going showed that he was used to having his own way and did not stoop to make many accommodations in his behavior for the sake of his environment; he more or less expected things to stay out of his way. What attitude toward life did he manifest in the way he ate and drank?

Pay special attention to the expressiveness of the eating and drinking you performed in this exercise. Just as breathing is a way in which we take the outside world into ourselves, so is eating; your pattern of eating and drinking can be extremely expressive of the way you feel about life. The tycoon might tear at his food animalistically, "getting the most" out of life by taking what he wants forcibly; the spinster, on the other hand, might cut the food into tiny pieces, placing each in her mouth and thoroughly chewing it, showing that she prefers to take her experience neat and in easily manageable portions. She doesn't want to "strain" her responsive system too much.

Of course, not all women who sit up rigid on the edge of their chairs are spinsters, nor do all spinsters behave exactly this way, since their inflexibility may manifest itself variously. If we were to depend in the creation of our performance on such erroneous thinking, then we would be guilty of caricature; but as such behavior arises *in context*, it communicates because of its typicality and provides you with a *starting point* for further exploration and development of more subtle, more unique qualities of character.

PHYSICAL CHARACTERIZATION IN THE TEXT

Playwrights are extremely sensitive to the bodily behavior of their characters. Notice in *The Zoo Story* how specific Albee is about the ritualistic patterns of Jerry's behavior in the way he paces; see what his attitude toward food and drink is within the play. Peter also maintains a characteristic posture and pattern of movement that has been carefully determined by the playwright. In these physical aspects, *The Zoo Story* is almost a *pas de deux,* a dance for two people. *King Lear* also presents a beautifully balanced set of contrasts of gesture; for example, the hesitant, slight Cordelia and the husky, aggressive Goneril and Regan, and the constant contrasting of the disability of age with the vigor of youth.

Playwrights have always used the "silent language." The entrance of the blind Oedipus speaks more than all the words of the messenger who describes his blinding. Shakespeare's plays are filled with examples: Falstaff's fatness as an expression of his incontinent spirit; Hotspur's stuttering as an expression of his impulsive nature, which prefers action to words; the mad Lear and the blinded Gloucester coming together at the end of the storm, showing us one picture of both the mental and physical agony of man in their two beings. The language of gesture is one of the most eloquent spoken by great playwrights.

Group Exercise 8   Physical characteristics

As a group, select one character from a play you have all studied. Now, individually, make lists of all the clues to his bodily characteristics and physical behavior you can find; check the author's preface, stage directions, things said by other characters, and characteristics strongly implied by his background, situation, or behavior.

Now each make a second list that represents your extensions of the character's psychology based upon his physical traits; in the way an archaeologist might reconstruct a whole animal from only a few bones, try to construct a whole personality from the given physical characteristics.

Then compare your lists; did you each find all the physical information there was to find in the play? How much agreement was there among your second lists, your psychological extensions from the physical traits? Do you see how each spectator at a play tends to make the same sort of imaginative deduction and extensions about a character's personality from his physical traits and mode of gesture?

The next time you go to the theatre, pay special attention to the physical choices the actors have made and the nature of your responses to them. See how each actor has used himself, making (hopefully) the most of his own energies in the creation of the character without imposing falsely upon it. See also how the *vocal* aspects of the character are organic to the *physical* aspects; it is to the vocal level of the performance as an organic part of the whole physiological and psychological makeup of the character that we will now turn our attention.

Lesson 6

Vocal Gesture

Speech is more than sound: it is at once verbal and nonverbal. Speech may be viewed as primarily expressive movement, "gestured meaning," or in the most limited sense, mouth gesture. . . . When speech is expressing ideas, we are content to accept it as symbolic, but when speech is understood as an expression of the *whole* personality, we must recognize the importance of the mimetic features that are essentially nonverbal.[20]

The great emphasis our culture places on words as a way of imparting information makes us forget that the voice, apart from the speaking of words, is an integral part of our whole expressive mechanism. While articulated speech is probably a socially learned ability, vocal expressiveness is instinctive; in fact, the beginnings of speech have recently been observed in two-month-old infants, so it is possible that speech itself is more instinctive than we have previously thought. In any case, we tend in everyday life to be much more consciously aware of formal speech than of natural vocal noises. Actors suffer especially from this dictatorship of words and are usually reticent to embellish their speaking of the author's dialogue with even the modicum of expressive nonverbal sound we use in daily life. This is unfortunate, since vocal sounds are an important type of gesture, highly expressive of personality.

Vocal gesture is a symbolic, but nonverbal, expression of personality and emotion. Margaret Schlauch points out in *The Gift of Language* that

we use these nonlinguistic means of conveying ideas, all of us, as an accompaniment to speech. A cry, a tonal inflection, a gesture, are means of communication far more universal than language as we understand it. They

[20]Bacon and Breen, *Literature as Experience*, p. 298.

are, in fact, universal enough to be conveyed to animals as well as other human beings.[21]

The "universal" appeal of all gesture, vocal and physical, makes it of great importance to the actor. Even when our vocal sounds are articulated as speech, we should regard this not as a separate activity, but only a further extension of our expressive behavior. In the next lesson, we will discuss the articulation of words as a special category of "gestured meaning"; in this lesson, however, you will begin to explore the wide range of vocal but nonverbal behavior that surrounds and supports the speaking of words. Some theorists believe that these nonverbal sounds are in fact the source from which our spoken language evolved and are still used to express those deep feelings that are "beyond speaking of."

VOICE AS AN ORGANIC FUNCTION

When we examine the physical process by which we produce sound, a rather surprising fact comes to light. As linguist Edward Sapir points out, "There are properly speaking no organs of speech. There are only organs that are incidentally useful in the production of speech sounds."[22] All the organs directly concerned in the production of speech first evolved for some other, more "basic" purpose. For this reason, speech is called an "overlaid function," a sort of "double duty" performed by organs and muscles that evolved originally for breathing, eating, or both. The diaphragm and lungs evolved for breathing, the larynx for swallowing, the tongue, the teeth, and the lips for chewing, the palate and tongue for tasting. We have already explored the intimate way in which breathing and eating are related to the expression of emotion, and we can see that the voice is, in its physiological genesis, integrally connected with these most basic expressive functions. Because of the vast complex of muscles involved in producing the voice, and the vital nature of these muscles, emotion is immediately and automatically reflected in the voice, *if* this natural process is not blocked in some way.

The network of overlaid functions that produce speech are complex and far-reaching. Each of the organs used for speech depends upon a complex

---

[21]From *The Gift of Language* by Margaret Schlauch, Dover Publications, Inc., New York, 1955, p. 3. Reprinted through permission of the publisher.
[22]Edward Sapir, *Language* (New York: Harcourt, Brace & World, Inc., 1949), pp. 8–9.

set of muscles for its operation so that the production of speech ultimately involves the participation of the entire body. Radio actors were good examples of this fact: though their audiences could not see them, they did not decrease the extent of their physical activity while performing. Quite the opposite. Since the audience was depending solely on the sound of their voice to create in the mind's eye a visual picture of what was happening, they usually overemphasized the movement of their bodies while performing, so that the voice, coming out of a massive muscular involvement of the body, would "sound right."

Exercise 29   Radio shows

A. Select an extreme physical posture; while the rest of the class have their eyes shut, use vocal noise (not words) to communicate to them, strictly by the sound of your voice, the position of your body. As they listen, they mimic your sound and try to duplicate your physical position. *NOTE:* Do *not* use intellectual devices or suggestions in this exercise; simply produce sound *from your center* and become very aware of the *pathway* that the sound-energy must follow as it passes through your physical composition. *Allow* your voice to take on the natural characteristics demanded by this posture; *do not force* it to "sound" any particular way!

B. Repeat this exercise with a repeated movement pattern (like lifting a box, or lying down) and again *allow* your voice to reflect your activity while the class attempt to find it for themselves through mimicry.

C. With a partner, select a simple action that may pass between two people and, as above, communicate this repeated action to the class.

Group Exercise 9   A radio spectacular

Form a group of at least four persons, select some big event that requires very little dialogue (like an Indian attack on a wagon train, or a machine blowing up), and prepare a "radio show" of the event for the rest of the class who, of course, keep their eyes shut as they listen. The only restriction is that you can use only the sounds you can make or mimic with your body, without words.

VOCAL GESTURE AS "OVERFLOW"

You saw earlier that your natural impulse is to externalize your sensations and emotions, and that these externalizations are, in fact, an *integral part* of sensation. According to Sapir:

> . . . the sound of pain or the sound of joy does not, as such, indicate the emotion, it does not stand aloof, as it were, and announce that such and such an emotion is being felt. What it does is to serve as a more or less automatic overflow of the emotional energy: in a sense, it is part and parcel of the emotion itself.[23]

There are two important ideas here: first, that nonvocal and vocal gestures result as an "overflow," a sort of safety-valve action; second, that such externalizations of our inner feelings are part and parcel of the feelings themselves.

Exercise 30   Overflow

This is an exercise in experiencing the "overflow" or "safety-valve" action of vocal and physical gesture. Using a speech expressing a violent emotion, read aloud with full concentration, suppressing all vocal and physical gesture. Repeat it several times over; feel how the demand for physical and vocal gesture grows in you as an increasing tension; force yourself to the point where physical and vocal movement must erupt as the natural result of these tensions. When it has erupted, explore the gestures fully; push them to an extreme. Examine how you feel and how you sound.

There is an old story about a highly mannered, flamboyant actress who gestured so indiscriminately that her movements ceased to have any organic relationship to the scene she was performing. The director tied her hands together with a string. "When your impulse to move is so strong that you must break the string," he said, "then you can." This is a necessary caution that your gestures must grow immediately out of the demands of your scene. Our aim in these exercises is to lift inhibitions toward physical and vocal gesture, so that you can respond *freely* and *fully* to your text, but always with a sense of *necessity* and *economy*.

[23]Ibid., p. 5.

In the course of rehearsing a part, you should go as far as you can in exploring the possibilities of gesture and movement. Later on, the essential details should be identified and the performance economized. Unfortunately, beginning actors rarely go far enough in their exploration; assuming that you properly analyze your text and respond fully and freely to it, the overflow of your response should provide you with a wealth of sound and movement from which to shape your performance.

VOCAL GESTURE AS MIMETIC BEHAVIOR

Some vocal gestures have consistent and communicable meanings in our culture, and form a sort of "subvocabulary." These are sounds that communicate thoughts and attitudes by symbolically mimicking an appropriate physical act; or we may use a sound associated with an appropriate situation or sensation, or a sound that is abstractly "symbolic," like the suspended tone of the "vocalized pause" ("It's . . . ah . . . a question of . . . ah. . . ."), which symbolically asks the listener to "hold on now, I'll get it in a moment, in the meantime I'll make this noise to hold your attention while I think." Most of our mimetic speech sounds, however, symbolically imitate larger physical actions.

As with physical gestures, it is the common construction of our bodies that makes these mimetic sounds communicative. You will remember Charles Darwin's explanation of physical gesture as a vestige of animal behavior; he also believed that many vocal gestures were symbolic of general bodily functions, as explained here by Robert Breen:

> Darwin pointed to the primitive practice of children who expressed their dislike for someone or something by sticking out their tongues and making a sound something like a bleating sheep. Sticking out the tongue was for Darwin a primitive reflex of vomiting or rejecting something distasteful; so, too, was the sound, which got its peculiar vocal quality from the extremely open throat through which it came. The open throat was, of course, a feature of the regurgitation, or vomiting, reflex. It is interesting that the civilized adult will show his contempt or distaste in much the same fashion, though much repressed. We are all familiar with the tone of voice which we recognized as "superior" or "contemptuous" because it has that "open throat" quality.[24]

Exercise 31   Vocal emotion

Observe real-life conversation, looking for vocal gesture. List three types: those that have consistent meaning in various situations;

[24]Bacon and Breen, *Literature as Experience,* p. 286.

those that are expressive of individual personality traits; and those most influenced by emotion, situation, and age.

Using your lists and observation of someone's vocal behavior while experiencing strong emotion, create for yourself a vocal portrait of an emotion expressed in a certain situation by a person of a certain type and age. Now "put on" your portrait and perform it until the vocal action spreads to the entire body and the emotion becomes self-generating.

Concentrate your awareness upon the sound of the exercise. What is the relationship between the internal feelings evoked by the scene and their externalization in sound? How does the act of externalization in sound itself further the completeness of the inner sensations? How is character expressed by vocal gesture?

VOCAL GESTURE AS "OFFSTAGE" BEHAVIOR

Just as physical gesture can express suppressed feelings that situations force us to conceal and that are contrary to the surface meaning of what we are saying and doing, so too can vocal gestures express such "offstage" attitudes. Though the dictionary meaning of the words you speak imparts information of a factual nature, the *way* in which you speak them is far more expressive of the way you feel. The tone of voice usually recognized as *sarcastic* is one obvious example of your conscious use of vocal gesture to express a feeling contrary to the meaning of the words being spoken, but there are many examples from your unconscious behavior as well.

If, for example, I am attempting to convince you that I feel strongly about what I am saying, I may increase the loudness of my voice, elevate my pitch slightly, and enunciate sharply, hitting the hard consonants as a sort of vocal "pounding-on-the-table." But when I interrupt my speech to take a breath, the breath turns out to be a sigh that is very close to a yawn. I have unwittingly revealed that I am actually bored with what I am saying, and probably with you, as well. There is a kind of perverse honesty in people, which causes them to betray themselves in these small ways. It is like the child who crosses his fingers while telling a lie: because the deception isn't perfect, we have satisfied our private need for honesty. The actor can make good use of this fact by bringing normally offstage vocal behavior within the realm of his conscious control.

Exercise 32   "Offstage" vocal behavior

A. Examine real-life conversation to discover examples of offstage vocal behavior. Attempt to analyze the logic behind such behavior. What makes it expressive?

B. Try out some of the gestures you have observed by selecting a speech from a play and performing it so as to communicate the opposite meaning and emotional tone from what was originally intended. Do this by manipulating your vocal gestures.

C. Try the speech as if it were delivered by someone of a different age, sex, or physical type from the original, using vocal gesture to make this substitution clear.

As you delivered the speech with changed meaning, feeling, age, and so on, how much of the original text's richness was sacrificed? How much did the text resist your substitutions? From this exercise, you begin to see how vocal gesture is a submerged part of a playwright's verbal design.

In fact, you can begin to see how the words of the dialogue may not always mean what they *seem* to mean and that just as in real life, stage characters often say one thing when they are feeling and meaning another. It is part of a great playwright's genius that he is able to use these *implied* meanings (sometimes called "subtext" because they lie *below* the apparent surface of the dialogue) and still make the true meaning clear within the given situation and characterization. It is part of your job as an actor to recognize these hidden meanings and to retain them in your performance. We will examine the question of subtext again in lesson 8; for now, you can see that things are not always exactly what they "seem" to be onstage, and that it is mainly the nonverbal aspects of your performance that will retain these submerged meanings.

Think back to the hostess/guest scene as in exercise 25; it presents a splendid example of subtext in action.

Exercise 33 Subtext

A. Recreate the hostess/guest scene; this time focus your attention on the vocal sounds and the nonverbal aspects in and around the dialogue; how do inflection, emphasis, tonal quality, and vocal noises help communicate the hidden attitudes of the two characters?

B. Perform the scene twice: once focus full attention on the surface meanings, *ignoring* the subtext; then again, use physical and vocal gesture to bring the subtext entirely to the surface, so that the characters actually "act out" their true feelings.

Discuss the two different versions of the scene; was one more interesting or dramatically accurate than the other? You will probably decide that it is unwise to reveal subtextual meanings too completely, just as it is equally unwise to ignore their presence. If you ignore them, the scene is flat and misinterpreted; if you let too much that ought to remain submerged come to the surface, the scene loses texture and tension. Your job, then, is not to *explain* your character's behavior by exposing all his secrets, but rather to *enact* that behavior with complete integrity, experiencing what he hides as well as what he reveals, what he does *not* say or do as well as what he *does* say or do.

As an actor, you must recognize the presence of submerged meanings and feelings and retain them in your performance, thus allowing them to "feed" your performance with hidden sources of energy; to bring them to the surface of the scene would rob the performance of an important source of texture, reduce dramatic tension, distort the characterization, and deprive your audience of the fun of "figuring things out for themselves." The psychologically realistic playwriting of the past few decades encouraged a kind of acting devoted to the revelation of motivation; and yet such revelation (unless specifically demanded by the play) removes a certain element of mystery vital to the drama. Many contemporary writers have rebelled against this emphasis on the revelation of character motivation and have returned to what they see as a more "classical" emphasis on events and action. As Harold Pinter puts it:

> A character on the stage who can present no convincing argument or information as to his past experience, his present behaviour or his aspirations, nor give a comprehensive analysis of his motives, is as legitimate and as worthy of attention as one who, alarmingly, can do all these things. The more acute the experience the less articulate its expression.[25]

The important thing is to recognize the presence of subtextual meanings in almost all good dramatic writing and learn to incorporate them into your enactment *while retaining whatever degree of obviousness or obscurity intended for those meanings by the playwright.* In short, your job is not to *explain,* but faithfully to *relive* your character's actions with a full understanding of the source, form, and dramatic purpose of those actions. The words of the text are your main guide in this endeavor, but it will be the nonverbal elements of your performance that will eventually carry the fullest weight of your understanding of what your character does and does not do, and why.

Exercise 34   Interior monologue

Using the hostess/guest scene, create an "interior monologue" for your character; that is, provide a verbalized, continuous stream of thought that moves him or her through the scene. Perform the scene

---

[25]Quoted by Martin Esslin in *The Theatre of the Absurd* (New York: Doubleday & Company, Inc., 1961), p. 206.

twice: once, using your interior monologue as if it were the actual dialogue; again, using your interior monologue silently "in your own head" while speaking the original dialogue.

This exercise forces you to examine the continuous line of your character's thought and to see how he moves from idea to idea, from feeling to feeling. Since part of your job as an actor is to make the private consciousness of your character public, you must be sure that you have adequately traced your character's thought throughout his stage life. This technique is not much different from a reality of everyday life explored in the next exercise.

Exercise 35   Talking to yourself

Become aware that there is often (though not always) an interior monologue running inside your own head, that you spend a good deal of time privately "talking to yourself."

Once you have identified this inner voice, gradually begin to whisper what it is saying; after a period of time, you may be able to exteriorize this inner monologue completely and speak it at normal volume.

The ability to "talk to yourself," that is, to exteriorize easily an interior verbal process, will be useful to you as an actor. You may find this exercise surprisingly difficult, however, and if it becomes threatening in any way it should be discontinued with no regret—your ability to exteriorize your *own* private inner world is not synonymous with your ability to do the same thing for a fictitious character.

The interior monologue device is a useful way of checking yourself to insure that you have traced the continuous line of your character's thought throughout a scene, and to be sure that you *relive* this thinking *every time* you perform the scene.

VOCAL GESTURE AS THE ORIGIN OF LANGUAGE

We now turn from vocal gesture to noise shaped into the symbolic sounds (words) that make up our language. Several theories about how language developed suggest that the conventional word-language evolved out of man's early vocal expressiveness. According to philosopher Ernst Cassirer:

> . . . when we seek to follow language back to its earliest beginnings, it seems to be not merely a representative sign for ideas, but also an

emotional sign for sensuous drives and stimuli. The ancients knew this derivation of language from emotion from the *pathos* of sensation, pleasure, and pain. In the opinion of Epicurus, it is to this final source which is common to man and beast and hence truly "natural" that we must return, in order to understand the origin of language. Language is not the product of mere convention or arbitrary decree; it is as necessary and natural as immediate sensation itself. Sight, hearing, and the feelings of pleasure and pain are characteristic of man from the very first, and so likewise is the expression of our sensations and emotions.[26]

Early theorists supposed that as our *mimetic* cries and grunts became "standardized," speech resulted. Although a great deal of mimetic speech behavior persists even in today's language, recent studies point out that the development of symbolic speech cannot be entirely explained in this way, and is a complex *social* process involving a continuing interaction between people that exceeds mimetic self-expression. "Gestures and cries," said philosopher John Dewey, "are modes of organic behavior as much as are locomotion, seizing, and crunching. Language, signs and significance, come into existence not by intent and mind but by overflow, by-products in gestures and sounds. The story of language is the story of the use made of these occurrences."[27]

In any case, the articulation of vocal sounds into symbolic speech is a highly expressive activity involving our total organism. The actor should remember that speech is a *physical* process whereby thoughts find their expression in the muscular activity that produces articulated sound. As such, it is a type of gesture (an external sign of an inward state). This highly physical aspect of speech is especially important to the actor, since the *written* language of the text is only a representation of the *spoken* language envisioned by the playwright.

SPEECH AS DECISION MAKING

As we form our thoughts into the physical activity called speech, we perforce make a great many decisions that are expressive of our feelings and personality. The communal nature of our shared language determines to some extent the way in which we express ourselves and (since language is one of the principal vehicles of thought) the way in which we think.

---

[26]Ernst Cassirer, *The Philosophy of Symbolic Forms*, trans. Ralph Manheim (New Haven, Conn.: Yale University Press, 1953), p. 148.
[27]John Dewey, *Experience and Nature* (La Salle, Ill.: Open Court Publishing Company, 1925), pp. 175–76.

Therefore, the process of verbalization also expresses the way in which we react to our social environment.

This *active* nature of the process of verbalization is of prime importance to the actor. If you deliver your lines merely as memorized words, you deprive your audience of the living process by which those words came to be. The character's impulse to express himself begins in some felt need or reaction; as the words that he utters are chosen, as he shapes them into phrases and sentences, he is constantly making decisions about emphasis, emotional tone, and so on. These decisions reveal what is really important to him and how he feels about it, and it is this living quality of speech "coming to be" that you must communicate to your audience.

This, of course, does *not* require halting speech, slow tempo, long pauses, or muttering and mumbling, all of which are too often used as easy substitutes for an honest participation in the process of verbalization. The playwright will have given sufficient indications of the quality of the process in the case of each character.

The style of the play will also suggest a characteristic verbal process: the ornate witticisms of Restoration comedy are formed by a quick, graceful process, a sort of verbal fencing match, while some modern plays tear chunks of speech out of experience in a clumsy, painful manner. "Stammering," said Eugene O'Neill, "is the native eloquence of us fog people."

One of your primary responsibilities toward speech on the stage is to recreate the living process of verbalization in the way demanded by the psychological nature of your character and the style of his play. The script is both your starting point and your final judge; it is a finished verbal product, which you take apart in rehearsal in order to rediscover the process of its creation; then, by embodying this process in your performance, you arrive once again at a living expression of the text.

Exercise 36   Slow-motion verbalization

Choose a short speech and, after memorizing it thoroughly, perform it so as to expose the process of verbalization. Begin by physically portraying it in full dance-like movement, accompanied by full vocal sounds expressing the *impulse* to speak (though not yet actual speech); then, again portrayed in full movement and sound, allow the words of the speech to evolve gradually out of your movement and sound like a picture coming into focus. Do this with each phrase or sentence, after finding the germinal thought expressed by that group of words. "Search" for each word, letting it be formed out of the need to communicate an exact idea. Let your voice and movement also express your searching for, and finding, of words.

Does a sense of character begin to emerge as you understand the choices that are being made during the process of verbalization?

The "process of verbalization" that you explored in this exercise is usually described by the term *diction,* which refers to the selection of specific words to express our thoughts. As you shall see in lesson 8, the playwright's choice of words for each character reflects his entire concept of that character. Your ability to revitalize the process by which the selection of words was made is crucial to your understanding and creation of the character.

First, however, you must examine something more of the physical process by which articulated speech is produced.

Lesson 7

Voice Production and Articulation

The articulation of vocal sound into English speech has evolved in a surprisingly rigid manner. Out of the vast range of sounds of which our bodies are capable, only a limited number are utilized for speech. For example, all the sounds of our language are "expiratory," produced by outgoing breath. "Inspiratory" sounds are entirely in the realm of nonverbal vocal gesture for us (though some of the world's other languages do use them for speech, along with clicking, whistling, and so on).

Your speech begins with outgoing breath, and it is with the breath that you begin to study it. You have already experienced moving and sounding from center, so that you know the integral connection between your activity, your emotion, your breath, and the voice which is "vibrating breath." The aim of our breath study is to enhance this organic unity of action, emotion, breath, and voice, while at the same time extending, strengthening, and making more responsive the massive, deep, muscle involvement in breath support.

BREATH SUPPORT

The system of diaphragm, lungs, and bronchial tubes acts as a "bellows" and influences the voice by supporting basic speech sound as well as accent, stress, and changes in volume. As the force of the breath stream increases, there are concomitant changes in resonance as well. The actor must develop this system of breath supply. You rarely utilize, in real life, even half of your potential reservoir of air, nor do the demands of everyday speech cause you to develop the muscles that activate this bellows system to anywhere near their full potential.

This "bellows" operates simply: as the diaphragm (see figure 26) pulls downward in the chest cavity, air is drawn into the lungs. As it pushes upward, the air is driven through the bronchial tubes and trachea, through the pharynx and then into the throat, mouth, and nasal chambers. There

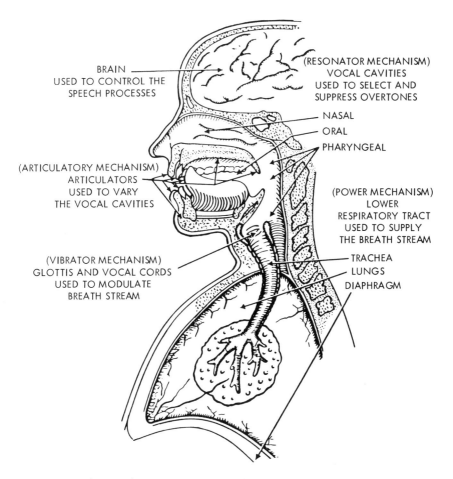

FIGURE 26   The vocal apparatus.

is a "zero" point at which your diaphragm is at rest; from this resting position you may *push out* additional air, or *pull in* additional air. *Pushing out* sends you into the "negative," with a deficit of air, and merely *relaxing* will cause you to breathe in until you have again reached "zero." *Pulling in* sends you into the "positive," with a surplus of air, and merely relaxing will cause you to breathe out until you reach zero. This sort of breathing *by relaxation* requires no effort and is usually the way we wish to breathe on stage. Feel this process in yourself: find your "zero" point and feel the action of "negative" and "positive" breathing as the diaphragm moves up down down from its restful position.

The relative distance that the diaphragm travels and its responsiveness relate directly to your ability to "project" your voice, though several other factors are equally important. The actor must be prepared to project effortlessly in even the largest auditorium; in many theatres, scenes that are supposed to be quiet and intimate must be practically bellowed. Only the actor who can effortlessly provide the necessary minimum volume will be able to supply an illusion of quietness at the same time. Since there are a vast number of muscles involved in supporting the breath system, only massive, long-range, and continuous exercise can develop you properly. Here is a simple exercise that can help you begin your development.

Exercise 37   Breath and sound

In a standing position, place yourself at rest and in alignment. Produce a continuous vocalized tone, and explore the variations in that tone that are possible principally through manipulation of the breath supply. Observe how the resonance of the tone is affected by changes in the force of the breath stream. Observe the different qualities of starting and stopping made possible in the tone by the manner in which you stop and start, by controlling the movement of the diaphragm. Place your hand on your stomach (the center area just *above* your waist) and feel the movement of the diaphragm. How full and precise is it? Is it unduly tense, causing its movement to be limited and erratic? Concentrate on eliminating tension here. Check also the areas at the sides of the lower back; are you breathing and responding 360° around your abdomen?

The regular program exercises outlined earlier will help you to increase the volume of your reservoir of air; also concentrate on developing the stamina and flexibility of the muscles that control that reservoir of air. Timing how long you can produce a sustained tone is one way of judging your development.

The breath supply is utilized by the body just as it would be by any wind instrument. The outpouring column of air causes vibration as it passes through an aperture (the vocal cords) designed for the purpose. The vibration sets the column of air in motion. Thus, the vibration is amplified, and by being resonated and changed in quality (articulated), it finally emerges as the tone characteristic of the instrument that produced it. You experienced this in exercise 29, when you allowed various bodily compositions to produce different vocal sounds as the breath found its pathway through your bodily configuration. This natural process, unless you resist or block it for some reason, will automatically insure the organic unity of breath and activity.

Exercise 38   Breath and activity

A. Select a simple speech and a simple but strenuous physical activity (e.g., running in place). Perform the activity for a few moments, and while continuing the activity, begin speaking. As in the radio show exercise, *allow* your activity to affect your voice.

B. Now stand still, but let your muscles "remember" your activity internally; "relive" the feeling of the activity without actually doing it. When the experience is vivid, again begin speaking, allowing your muscular memories to affect your voice.

You see (or rather hear) in this exercise that just as external activity affects the voice, so does the *internal dynamic* of the body (to a lesser, but more suggestive, degree), even in the absence of actual movement.

This fact is crucial, for it is your internal dynamic condition that is most (and always) involved with emotion and a sense of stage action, even when external movement is at a minimum. The actor, we may say, is *in motion even when he is not moving*—and this "interior motion" or *bodily dynamic* affects his breath, his voice, and his total consciousness. Explore this for yourself, and observe it in everyday life.

We turn next to the point at which the breath is vibrated and becomes sound, which happens when the breath stream passes through the aperture of the vocal cords and causes them to vibrate.

TONE PRODUCTION

Without *both* an adequate breath supply and efficient breath utilization, you will be adversely limited in expressing the speech rhythms, phrase lengths, and expressive vocal tones demanded by your characterization. Unnecessary tension in the vocal cords and failure to utilize fully our amplifying and resonating chambers wastes our breath supply, no matter how fully we may develop it.

When we consider how the vocal cords operate, we see that they are capable of four basic types of movement:

1. When they are closed and tensed, the air stream is forced through them, and they vibrate like reeds in the wind, producing tone. By increasing or decreasing their tension, we increase or decrease pitch.
2. When the vocal cords are drawn fully apart so that the air stream is permitted to pass through them unhindered, we produce the quality of speech called "voicelessness."

3. By a quick closing, the vocal cords can interrupt the breath stream suddenly and entirely, resulting in "glottal stop."
4. There is also a stage somewhere between the first and second that produces a semivoiced tone called "stage whisper."

Unnecessary tension in the throat area will adversely influence the operation of the vocal cords and unnecessarily restrict the flow of breath. Under these circumstances, speech becomes an exhausting task; no undesirable muscular tension is communicated as quickly to an audience as tense throat. Actors have been known to perform with a painfully sprained ankle with no one in the audience being the wiser; but a tense throat on stage results instantly in a wave of coughing from the audience. This fact demonstrates the strong communicativeness of our vocal quality.

The vocal cords are most involved in articulation by either "voicing" the breath stream or allowing it to pass freely as a "voiceless" sound. For example, *p* is a voiceless sound, while *b* is voiced; otherwise, these two sounds are articulated in the same manner. Surprisingly, it requires more effort to produce voiceless sounds than voiced ones. Drawing the vocal cords fully apart is more difficult than allowing them to remain partly together, which is their normal position. You may have noticed that as you relax entirely just before sleeping, you sometimes produce a soft vocal tone as the breath flows through the relaxed vocal cords.

Exercise 39   Voiced and voiceless sound

Using the summary table of consonant sounds (figure 27), explore the voiced and voiceless sounds. Do not move any part of the jaw, the tongue, or the palate while producing each pair of sounds. Make the change only by drawing the vocal cords apart or by allowing them to remain together. Hold a finger over your pharynx (your Adam's apple) and feel it change.

You have experienced the first way in which you articulate, by producing voiced or unvoiced sounds. As the breath stream, whether voiced or not, passes beyond the pharynx, it encounters three further forms of articulation. Next, the soft palate may raise or lower to direct the breath either into the nasal or the oral areas; then, if the breath flows into the mouth, it is either impeded, or allowed to pass freely; finally, if it is impeded, the location of the point at which it is impeded produces a particular sound. The entire list of articulation of the breath stream is:

FRONT VOWELS	MIDDLE VOWELS	BACK VOWELS	DIPHTHONGS *(Glides from one vowel sound to another in a single syllable)*
W_E_	U_P_	CH_A_RLES	M_AY_
W_I_LL	FURTH_E_R	W_A_NTS	_I_
M_A_KE	F_U_RTHER	_A_LL	J_OI_N
TH_E_M		_O_LD	Y_OU_
M_A_D		B_OO_KS	N_OW_
F_A_ST		T_OO_	J_OE_

FIGURE 27   Summary table of vowel sounds. Arranged from front to back in the mouth as you read down and across. Note that all vowels and diphthongs are voiced. Adapted from Evangeline Machlin, *Speech for the Stage* (Theatre Arts Books, 1966).

1. Is the breath voiced or unvoiced?
2. Does the breath pass into the nasal or oral chamber?
3. If the oral chamber, is the breath impeded?
4. If impeded, at what point is it interrupted?

We will proceed to examine each of these points in turn.

NASAL SOUNDS

The first point beyond the vocal cords at which the breath stream is articulated is at the soft palate near the rear of the mouth. As this soft palate lowers or raises, it opens or closes the pathway by which the air stream may pass into the nasal cavity where it is resonated. In English we have only three basic sounds that depend upon nasal resonance: *m, n,* and *ng* (as in si*ng*).

Nasal resonance plays an important part in causing the subtle variations of tone that produce the individual quality of our speech. Some regional dialects, as well as some speech defects, spring from the incorrect use of nasal resonance. As you perform these exercises, you may find defects or regional vocal mannerisms; you should do all you can to eliminate these inhibiting patterns of vocal behavior. If you have such a problem, seek out specialized training to help solve it. Few things can be as limiting to an actor as adverse vocal traits that remain uncorrected.

Exercise 40   Nasal sounds

A. While producing a continuous open tone (for example *a* as in *fa-*
ther), open and close the soft palate (turning the sound of *a* into
ng), and concentrate your awareness on the vibrations produced in
your throat, mouth, and in the area of your face surrounding your
nose. Try this with a number of different sounds. While nasalizing,
attempt to project the tone into the triangular area around the nose
with such force that the surface vibrations in this area can be easily
felt with the fingertips.

   B. While producing nonnasal tones (such as a vowel sound), see
how much resonance the nasal cavity can contribute *without altering*
the basic quality of the tone. Check this by snapping the nostrils
open and shut between your fingers. Projecting the tone toward the
front of the face, producing strong vibrations in the nose and mouth
area (or "mask") provides maximum resonance in this area of critical
articulation.

ORAL SOUNDS: VOWELS AND DIPHTHONGS

The most complex acts of articulation take place in the mouth. The breath
stream, voiced or unvoiced, may be either allowed to pass freely or is
impeded in some way; if it passes freely, it may be "shaped" by the
positioning of the mouth's movable parts (mainly the jaw, tongue, and
lips). The sounds produced in this "open" fashion are, generally speaking,
the vowels. The vowel sounds actually used in English far exceed the
simple list, *a, e, i, o,* and *u.* (See figure 27.) The four categories of vowels
include those produced by shaping the mouth at the front (involving
mainly the lips), the middle (using mainly tongue and lips), or back (using
mainly the tongue and jaw), and those combined sounds called "diphthongs," which are unbroken glides from one vowel sound to another.

Exercise 41   Vowels and diphthongs

A. Place yourself at rest and in alignment, and using the summary
table of vowel sounds (figure 27), make each sound in turn,
concentrating on developing the fullest resonance possible and on
efficiently using the breath supply. Are you getting maximum
volume and resonance for minimum expenditure of air?

   B. Exaggerate the "shape" of the mouth in producing each sound.
Read the lists in order, concentrating on the movement from front

to rear in the mouth, and on the increasing "size," as more and more space is created within the mouth.

C. Speak the diphthongs in slow motion for a time to explore the gliding motion from one sound to another. Do you produce a clearly distinguishable sound for each type? As in your earlier vocalization exercises, a tape recording of your voice will be extremely useful in spotting any inefficiencies or peculiarities in your articulation.

ORAL SOUNDS: CONSONANTS

When the breath stream is impeded or interrupted in the mouth, the resulting sounds are the consonants. The consonants are necessarily less resonant and more incisive than the vowels. The word *consonant* originally meant "sounding with," indicating that these sounds alone cannot comprise a syllable; they must be combined *with* a vowel. While there are subtle exceptions to this rule, the consonants do serve, by virtue of their shorter duration and sharper tonal quality, as punctuation for the beginning or ending of vowel sounds, thus forming syllables.

When we consider the articulation of consonants, there are two principal questions: first, at what *position* in the mouth is the breath stream altered, and second, to what *extent* is it altered? In considering the first of these questions, we see that there are four principal positions within the mouth at which articulation may occur (see figure 28).

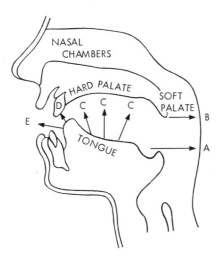

FIGURE 28   The points of articulation in the mouth: (A) guttural, (B) soft palate opens or closes nasal chambers, (C) palatal, (D) dental, (E) labial.

1. *Guttural:* the rear of the tongue may rise up to make contact with the soft palate to make sounds like "*g*un."
2. *Palatal:* a slightly higher sound may be produced by the middle of the tongue rising up to contact the roof of the mouth as in "*k*ey."
3. *Dental:* here the tongue is used in conjunction with either the bony ridge directly behind the upper teeth (as in the sound "*t*ea") or the teeth themselves (as in the sound "*th*ese").
4. *Labial:* the lips may be involved either by contacting the lower lip with the upper teeth (as in "*f*riend") or by having the lips contact each other (as in "*b*oy").

Notice that in each position different sounds are produced by either voicing or unvoicing the tone without any other alteration.

When we next consider the *extent* to which the breath stream is altered, there are two main questions: is the breath stream entirely interrupted, or is it only impeded? When the breath stream is entirely interrupted, the result is called a "stop," since such a sound cannot be produced except for a short moment (*b*oy). "Stops" are also called "plosive," since they are produced by closing the breath stream off at some point in the mouth and then letting it "explode" suddenly. On the other hand, an impeded but continuous breath stream produces continuants, so called because these sounds can be held out over a period of time (b*oy*).

We now have two broad categories of consonants, *stops* and *continuants.* Within the general category of *continuants,* there are several subcategories:

1. *Nasals* (*m, n, ng*) have already been discussed.
2. *Fricatives* are produced by forcing the breath stream through a narrow passageway (*f*riend). Some (but not all) of these sounds have a hissing quality and are also called "spirants" or "sibilants" (*s*orry).
3. *Blends* are combined sounds produced by a plosive palatal sound that blends immediately into a soft fricative or "hushing" sound. Examples are "*ch*oice, *J*oyce."
4. *Glides* are momentary (and relatively slight) constrictions of the breath stream, which immediately "glide" into a full vowel sound. Or, if the vowel precedes the glide, we "glide" into the constricted position. These are the "smoothest" of the consonant sounds and share some qualities of the vowels. Some of these sounds, like "*l*ove*l*y," are called "laterals" because the breath stream is blocked in the center of the mouth but allowed to flow around the sides of the tongue, or "laterally." Others, like "*r*at," are called "liquids," because there is only a slight constriction of the breath stream involved.

POSITION IN THE MOUTH	STOPS		CONTINUANTS					
	Voiced	Unvoiced	Nasals (Voiced)	Fricatives Voiced	Fricatives Unvoiced	Blends Voiced	Blends Unvoiced	Glides (Voiced)
Labial	_B_oy	_P_ony	_M_oney	_V_ERY	_F_UNNY	——	——	_W_O_W_
Dental	_D_OG	_T_OY	_NO_NE	_TH_ESE _Z_OO (SIBILAN_T_S)	_TH_INK _S_ORRY	——	——	_L_OVE_L_Y
Palatal	_G_EEK	_K_EY	CA_NY_ON	PLEA_S_URE	_SH_E	_J_OYCE	_CH_OICE	_R_AT _Y_ES
Guttural	_G_UN	_C_UT	SI_NG_	——	_H_OT	——	——	——

FIGURE 29   Summary table of consonant sounds.

The summary table of consonant sounds in figure 29 lists examples of each; notice that nasals and liquids are always voiced, while fricatives and blends are either voiced or unvoiced.

Exercise 42   Consonants

Using the summary table of consonant sounds (figure 29), explore the relationships between sounds. Exaggerating the motion or position involved, read in slow motion:

1. All labial sounds;
2. All dental sounds;
3. All palatal sounds;
4. All guttural sounds;
5. All nasals and glides;
6. All voiced and unvoiced pairs in the other categories.

Are you producing a distinctly different sound for each? Are regional peculiarities or bad speech habits affecting any of the sounds? Is the breath supply efficiently used for each? Are you getting maximum resonance from each?

Adequate vocal projection is not only a matter of strong breath support and efficient vocalization; it also depends greatly upon efficient articulation. Many young actors think that being heard is a matter of speaking _loudly_; it is much more a matter of speaking _clearly_. The most common vocal shortcoming in the theatre, in fact, is the actor who can be easily _heard_ but not easily _understood_. Psychotherapists have often noted how vocal projection relates directly to a person's sense of self-esteem and assertiveness. Nothing reduces the effectiveness of the human voice more than a lack of commitment or understanding; even when we speak loudly, insecurity causes our voices to "hide" in unintelligibility. It has been my experience that actors with even modest voices can be heard in the largest auditorium when they fully understand and are fully focused upon their action as it is reflected in their speech.

You have probably experienced the shock connected with hearing a recording of your voice. Besides the fact that we do not hear ourselves accurately "from the inside," our disembodied voices frighten us because there is a tremendously strong sense of personal identity connected with the voice. It is interesting that we generally have much less trouble orienting ourselves to the way we look than to the way we sound. The word *personality*, in fact, comes from two roots: one is the ancient Greek word for *mask*, and the other is the literal (and older) translation of *per sona*, *through sound*. For this reason our study of dramatic language and of the voice must bring us to a concern for the voice's ability to express *character*.

ARTICULATION AND CHARACTER

As important as it is that you be able to speak "correctly," our study of articulation is really aimed at developing your voice as a *flexible instrument*, responsive to the demands of *character* and *style*. To achieve this flexibility and to be able to escape when necessary the speech habits of your everyday life, the muscles that control articulation (like any other muscles) need exercise and disciplined development.

Along with the development of your technical control of articulation, however, you must also develop your "ear," your ability to hear the expressive aspects of articulation in real life.

Exercise 43   Articulation and character in life

A. Observe around you the articulation habits of all sorts of people: how are laziness, timidity, audaciousness, and the host of other personality traits expressed in articulation?

B. What effect do a person's physical "type" and his dominant personality trait have upon his articulation?

C. What effect do various emotions have upon articulation?

D. Try to recreate articulatory patterns you have observed, and examine your feelings when you speak in various ways.

Situation has an enormous impact upon articulation. Since articulation is the muscular means by which you verbally present yourself in society, it is extremely expressive of your feelings regarding that social situation. The emphasizing of hard, biting sounds may indicate one attitude, while the elongation and softening of open vowel sounds may indicate another. An evenness of accent and pitch may indicate timidity or a sense of repression, while the voice of uninhibited joy may be extremely active in both range and dynamics. The host of expressive possibilities is subtle and complex, and deserves considerable exploration and study.

Exercise 44   Articulation and character on stage

Here is a prose speech from *King Lear.* Forget for a moment the actual meaning and function of this speech in that play and the character who speaks it, and use it for the following experiments. A tape recording will help you immeasurably.

These last eclipses in the sun and moon portend no good to us. 'Though the wisdom of nature can reason it thus and thus, yet nature finds itself scourged by the sequent effects. Love cools, friendship falls off, brothers divide. In cities, mutinies; in countries, discord; in palaces, treason; and the bond cracked 'twixt son and father. This villain of mine comes under the prediction, there's son against father; the king falls from bias of nature, there's father against child. We have seen the best of our time. Machinations, hollowness, treachery, and all ruinous disorders follow us disquietly to our graves.

A. Read the speech for "perfect" articulation. Exaggerate the sounds until your articulation is painfully precise. Read it as if this were not a sequence of meaningful words but only a sequence of sounds.
B. Read the speech again to express various emotions. What effect does anger have upon the articulation of these sounds? What sounds have been provided by the playwright to assist you in expressing anger? Likewise, consider the expression of fear and sorrow in the speech. Since all three of these emotions are present simultaneously in the speech as it occurs in the play, you will be discovering the sounds that the playwright provided as a means for the muscular expression of this compound emotion.
C. Read the speech as expressive of various dominant personality traits. What effect would timidity have upon the articulation of these sounds? Laziness? Pompousness? Stupidity?

D. What effect would situation have upon the articulation of these sounds? Read the speech as if it is a secret being communicated to a friend, then as a public statement being made before an immense crowd. Besides simple changes in volume, what other changes are there in your articulation in these contrasting situations?

Articulation, you see, is the muscular connection between *what* you say, and *how* you say it, since articulation is itself a *complex gesture.*

Articulation of the sounds selected by the playwright is the first step in your muscular involvement in his play. From this involvement comes your sense of rhythm, vocal gesture, physical gesture, and all the aspects of the physicalized performance. As you shall see in the next lessons, playwrights, in their choice of words, create what might be viewed as a musical score filled with rhythms, sounds, dynamic markings, implied gestures— much of what you need in performance.

Playwrights write for the human voice; the human voice is deeply involved in the body's musculature; the body's musculature is deeply involved in your emotional life and thought. The playwright's words and implied actions provide, then, a direct route to a fully living, vivid, and appropriate stage experience that will fill your performance with the richness of your deepest energies.

OTHER IMPORTANT SKILLS

We have dealt in this first part only with the most basic expressive skills of the actor. Advanced training in voice, speech, and movement goes far beyond what has been suggested here; and yet these basic skills and exercises will continue to challenge and benefit you for the rest of your acting life.

Seek out every opportunity to explore related training in such skills as mime, singing, dancing, clowning, fencing, Tai Chi Chu'an, karate, tumbling, and meditation. Each contributes in its way to useful acting skills and, more importantly perhaps, to your contact and control of the body, voice, and spirit. It is the practice of the physical and vocal *discipline,* presented in basic form here, honed and extended by advanced work and work in related fields, that liberates the actor's creativity. This practice disciplines his mind, his emotions, and his imagination simultaneously with its effect on his body and voice. These skills are not only meant to make you more able to express character and meaning to your audience; they are equally useful in helping you to realize a full, living experience on the stage. Just as most religions involve physical discipline as a pathway to spiritual experience, so your technical discipline can become the mechanism of your "spiritual" development as an actor.

PART TWO

The Actor's Blueprint

THE AIMS OF TEXTUAL ANALYSIS

"Language," said Edward Sapir, "is the medium of literature as marble or bronze or clay are the materials of the sculptor." In order really to understand a dramatic text, then, you need first to study the language, the words, which are the building blocks of the play. But since you are an actor and not a literary scholar, your reason for this study, and your approach to it, will be different from that of the English student. While he analyzes the text for its own sake as literature, you analyze it in order to solve the problems of "bringing it back to life" on the stage. This idea of *rejuvenation* of your text will be at the heart of your study of plays.

THE TEXT AS A RESIDUE OF A LIVING VISION

The playwright begins by developing a living experience or idea, which we will call his *vision*. It is this vision that moves him to create a specific play, and each character in that play comes to life in the writer's consciousness as part of a whole mechanism that expresses the central vision or purpose of the play.

Unlike the novelist, the playwright cannot usually speak directly to us to describe or qualify a character; the character must speak for himself. Ultimately, the words spoken by the character will be all that is left (except for a few stage directions) of the fullness of the author's visualization. For you as an actor, then, the text is the *residue* of a much larger conception of the character. It is your job to give life to this residue in your own way.

You study the text in order to get back to the vision of which it is a residue. Remember, though, that this vision is not the same thing as the specific feelings and thoughts of the author. The good playwright transforms himself, submerging himself in his characters just as the actor must. The written text is an accurate record of this transformation and should be accepted as such.

The vision that underlies the text is something we can all share if we develop the ability to reach for it through the text. It is more basic than words: it is the power behind the words, a preverbal germ of communication.

REACHING FOR THE VISION

Since the vision drove the playwright to select and combine certain words in certain ways, to create certain characters in certain situations, and to structure the whole in a certain style, you can reach back to the vision best by analyzing these details, thus reversing the process by which the play was constructed. This is a more reliable and fruitful approach than simply trusting your own intuition or generalized response to the play.

Many actors simply read a play and get a very strong feeling or intuition about it, which they then convince themselves is the vision behind the play. There is a great danger in working this way. While you certainly need to respond vigorously to plays, you must be careful to guide and correct your response by an informed and minute study of the details of the script; otherwise, you have no guarantee that your response is really to the play itself and not merely to the personal feelings it may trigger in you. All sensitive readers have a personal relationship to a good play, but the actor has the greater responsibility of presenting a public performance of it. You owe it to your playwright, to your audience, and to yourself to present the play for what it really is, and not simply as a vehicle for your own feelings about it.

SEEING THE WHOLE PLAY

Your analysis must take the entire play into account. Dramatic characters are not meant to be met as individuals; they are each created for a specific purpose as part of a total structure, and they must interrelate properly if the mechanism of the play's structure is to work as it should. We cannot understand our characters if we don't recognize the way they fit into the total picture.

Too many actors wear "blinders" and never see beyond their individual roles. They behave as if they were spokesmen for their own characters at the expense of a total interpretation. This is a kind of selfishness that is deadly to the team effort required by good theatre. You must respect the whole play, not just your part in it.

This requires *reading* and *studying* the whole play. Though this seems self-evident, many acting students work on scenes from plays that they have only scanned. This kind of laziness is encouraged by the fact that most acting classes work only on individual scenes or speeches. Also, beginning actors usually concentrate more on fulfilling each moment than on the shaping of a whole role. Yet each word, each speech, each scene can be properly understood *only* in relation to the whole play. If you fail to make this connection from the outset, you may become the kind of actor who has difficulty forming a meaningfully shaped and purposeful overall performance.

So, although the following lessons begin with work on individual speeches and progress to scenes, be sure you study the whole play carefully before you start work. Since you have no director, develop your own basic interpretation of the play. Ask your instructor, or read commentaries on the play, to assist you in interpretation. Of course you will make many discoveries about the whole play as you work on each part (and in fact the only complete interpretation of any play is based upon such detailed study), but a good grasp of the play's outlines and a basic interpretation are possible and necessary at the outset.

Later, as you work in productions, your director will help you and your fellow actors to agree upon an interpretation for the entire ensemble, because even if everyone involved analyzes the play carefully, there will still be some disagreement about the exact interpretation. This is because a truly great play has many levels of meaning; *King Lear* might be viewed as a play about old age, the responsibilities of kingship, the bond of love between parents and children, social injustice, or many other things. Even if you all agree that each of these interpretations is *part* of the play's total meaning, you must come to some mutual agreement about the point of view or "focus" of your particular production. This focusing demands that each of your performances, as well as the setting, the costumes, and all the other aspects of the production, work effectively toward the total import of the production.

The focusing of interpretation is the director's province. Even if your personal preference might be for a different interpretation or emphasis, it is still your job to work effectively within the director's production concept. If he has decided, for example, to do *The Merchant of Venice* so as to make Shylock the hero, then it is your job to perform within his interpretation, even if you disagree with it. Remember that he is attempting to interpret the text in the way he feels will be most meaningful to your audience and will take the best advantage of the actors and facilities available. Thus, the responsibility for basic interpretation is his. But, within the bounds of a basic interpretation, you must minutely examine your role in relation to the whole and grasp all that the playwright has provided.

THE ACTOR'S BLUEPRINT

Just as there are several layers of meaning in a play that operate simultaneously, there are also several levels upon which we can approach the analysis of the play. They may be described as:

1. *Diction:* the words themselves as units of meaning;
2. *Melody:* the sounds and rhythms of the words;
3. *Imagery:* the sensations imparted by the words;
4. *Figurative language:* the patterning of words to achieve special meaning and feeling;
5. *Dialogue* and *scene structure:* the patterning of speeches into units of action;
6. *Plot:* the linking of units of action into one basic movement, and the importance of the action to characterization.

We shall examine each of these aspects of the text in the following lessons, but as we do so, remember that each is only a different point of view toward the same whole; a play cannot actually be broken into parts. In analysis we take the play apart to see what makes it tick; eventually we must reassemble it in our performance and make it run again "under its own power."

In other words, we must *synthesize* what we learn from analysis in a unified and congruous performance. Just as the carpenter or machinist reads in his blueprint a detailed instruction for making an object, the well-trained actor can read in a play specific clues about rhythms, inflections, emphases, and all sorts of characteristics needed to begin creating his role if he learns the techniques of analysis and applies them carefully and diligently. It is for this reason that we call the text the "actor's blueprint."

POLARIZATION EXERCISES AND SAMPLE ANALYSES

As each lesson introduces a new aspect of text analysis, a brief sample analysis of speeches from *King Lear* and *The Zoo Story* will be given. Both these plays should be read carefully before continuing. These analyses exemplify, in a brief way, the principles outlined in the lesson; your analysis of a speech for performance would be much more thorough. The speeches to which all these sample analyses refer will be found on pages 263 and 264.

As we study each aspect of text analysis, you will be presented with an exercise *polarizing* that element of the text, an experimental exercise that concentrates *exclusively* on some single aspect of the text. It will be especially interesting if you select a single solo speech, of one to three minutes duration, and use it for all six of the polarization exercises that follow. A speech from a great play with a strongly "poetic" content (whether it is in prose or poetry) would be the best choice. It should be thoroughly memorized *before* attempting the exercises, since they demand full concentration and complete freedom of movement.

In part 3 you will begin *scene* work, so your speech should be taken from a two-character scene or scene-segment that can be performed in less than five minutes. You may then carry the work on your speech into your scene work in part 3.

These exercises are *not* meant to be performances, but rather experiences for yourself. Each is a chance to take what you have learned from analysis of some aspect of the text and turn it into movement and sound. In this way, your analysis does not remain coldly intellectual, but can be a meaningfully alive experience. Your objective in each, then, should be to find a pattern of movement and sound, based on qualities of the text, that will fully involve as many of your muscles as possible. Give the *entire* body a chance to participate. Never tie yourself to "realistic" movement, or even to the movement you might really use in performance. Rather, extend yourself to as active and as large a pattern of movement as possible.

While these exercises may sometimes resemble modern dance with vocal noises added, our interest is quite different from the dancer's. He creates movement for its own sake; you create it in order to provide yourself with a muscular experience, which brings some aspect of the text alive.

Don't let this personal nature of the exercises make you think that careful preparation is unnecessary, or that clarity and energy should be lacking. Think of them as a sort of interpretive gymnastics. Though you might never move this way if you were performing the same speech, it is important to let your body experience the fullest possible response to the text. The impulses to move that the body will remember will enrich your performances later, even when extensive movement is not actually involved.

As you work on them, remember that you are *abstracting,* or removing from its original context, one aspect or another of the speech. It may help you to begin work on each exercise using the actual words of the speech, then "boiling it down" to rhythm, melody, or whichever aspect is the aim of the exercise. Of course, many of the exercises also use the words of the original; follow the instructions in each case.

Advanced or more adventurous students may wish to select a two-minute segment from a two-character scene to use in these exercises, sharing the analyses in each case with their partners.

In any case, remember that each polarization exercise still follows the scenario, or specific shape and sequence, of the original scene or speech. The character speaking is still trying *to do something* (or is having something done to him) within a particular situation. Keep the *essence* of the scene action in your exercises, but allow the *form* to be very free and extended, so that each exercise *sensitizes* you to a different aspect of the text without losing a sense of the meaning and shape of the original scene action.

If you can begin to feel the essential qualities underlying the scene as you focus on one aspect of it after another, you will begin to understand that your preparation as an actor is not a matter of creating a rigid and unchanging external form that you simply repeat in performance after performance (although the basic outlines and fundamental qualities of your performance must, for the sake of your fellow actors, be somewhat stable). You will find instead that true preparation is the grasping of a specific set of principles and impulses that shape the scene and from which you will make adjustments (albeit subtle ones) as the scene or speech is relived in each and every rehearsal and performance.

You should therefore prepare your exercises thoroughly by trying to experience what is essential in them and by trying to feel the underlying qualities and form that best express that essence; then *relive* those impulses and find that form "anew" each time. Never merely "perform your rehearsal"; have a living experience within the boundaries you established in your preparation each time you rehearse or perform.

Note: You will find it useful to prepare four triple-spaced copies of your speech (or one for each partner in a scene) to be used in the exercises that follow. You will also use the entire *scene* from which the speech is taken for your work in part 3.

Lesson 8

Analyzing the Speech: Diction

The vision of a great play is inextricably bound up with the exact words of the text. One of the things that makes a play great is language that has been so expertly used it becomes a part of the vision itself. As Sapir puts it, "In great art there is the illusion of absolute freedom. The formal restraints imposed by the material . . . are not perceived. . . . The artist has intuitively surrendered to the inescapable tyranny of the material, made its brute nature fuse easily with his conception."[28] If you doubt the truth of this, try taking a speech from a great play and rephrasing it in your own words; even if, individually, the words have the same meaning as the original, the whole speech will not communicate the same meaning or feeling. In a great play, the words themselves become *part* of the vision. For this reason, we begin a study of our role by studying the words themselves, the play's *diction.*

The term *diction* is sometimes used to mean "enunciation, or manner of speaking aloud," but this is only its secondary definition. Its primary meaning, in the sense of *"diction*ary," is "choice of words to express ideas: mode of expression in language." The process of verbalization, which we examined at the end of part 1, is the sequence of decisions that results in word-choice. Understanding diction is one of an actor's primary obligations, not only because it is a characterizational device, but also because we have a responsibility to our author and our audience to communicate the meaning of our lines accurately.

Remember Sapir's statement, "Language is the medium of literature as marble or bronze or clay are the materials of the sculptor." Words, however, are basically different from the sculptor's clay or the painter's pigment; words have a prior meaning of their own, which is not completely determined by the way the artisan shapes or patterns them. Though the writer exercises considerable control over subtle shadings of meaning and emotional values of words, they present him with basic meanings of their

[28]Sapir, *Language,* p. 221.

131

own, which he must take into account. This basic dictionary meaning is called *denotation*. The emotional values that the words may generate are called *connotations*.

Until you have considered these two aspects of diction, the literal meaning and also the emotional colorings of the words of your role, you are not in a position to recreate the expressive process of word-choice or to proceed to a more detailed analysis of your text.

DENOTATION

It is surprising how many actors think they can get along on their intuition of the exact meaning of the words they speak. This is true of the actor who meets an unfamiliar or archaic word and "figures out" what it might mean from its context, and also of the actor who takes it for granted that he knows the meaning of words that "seem" familiar to him. When this happens, he may commit himself to a partially or completely erroneous line-reading without even suspecting that anything is amiss.

Meaning is not a static thing. There may be several possible definitions for a word; also, the meaning of even common words in popular usage often changes. Topical and colloquial speech may change its meaning very quickly, and doing a play only ten years old may require some investigation of the meaning of words and expressions. You must be sure that the meaning you take for granted today is not a distortion of the playwright's original intention.

Juliet, coming out on her balcony (Romeo is hiding somewhere in the garden below) says, "O Romeo, Romeo? Wherefore art thou Romeo?" and many young actresses deliver the line as if Juliet were wishing that Romeo were there, in the sense of "Romeo, where are you?" But knowing that *wherefore* originally meant *why*, we see that she really is saying, "Why are you named Romeo, member of a family hated by my parents?" Such obsolete meanings are labelled "archaic" in the dictionary, and the intentional use of an obsolete word by a playwright is called an *archaism*.

Another common way in which playwrights manipulate denotation is by *punning*. Though puns have been called "the lowest form of humor," they are used by great writers for both serious and comic effect. A pun depends on placing a word that has more than one denotation in a context in which both meanings could be applied. A "mark," for example, might be a marking, a bruise, or a kind of money. In Shakespeare's *Comedy of Errors*, a play literally filled with puns, one of the heroes has entrusted his money to his servant and later meets his servant's twin brother, who knows nothing about the money:

MASTER: Where is the thousand marks thou hadst of me?
SECOND SERVANT: I have some marks of yours upon my pate,
Some of my mistress' marks upon my shoulders,
But not a thousand marks between you both.
If I should pay your worship those again,
Perchance you will not bear them patiently.

From a modern source, we see the same delight in the possibilities of diction when we examine the names of Beckett's characters in *Endgame:* Hamm (ham), the decaying and impure meat and Clov (clove), the spice traditionally used with ham for flavor and preservation; ham is a meat that comes from an animal with a *clov*en hoof, and Clov is indeed the "feet" of Hamm; Hamm actor, the tragedian, and Clov (clown), who together are the two masks of drama and the two faces of mankind; Nell (nail), Clov (*clou* means "nail" in French), and Nagg (*Nagel* means "nail" in German) are pounded down by the overbearing Hamm (hammer). All these meanings, wonderfully appropriate to the play, are incorporated through puns.

CONNOTATION

The connotative possibilities of words are variable, unlike denotation, which is much more clearly determined by common usage. Therefore, you need to consider *context* in order to determine which of the connotative possibilities of a word are appropriate. In rich, skillful language, words will be selected so as to utilize more than one of their connotations, thereby supplying various levels of emotional impact.

Just as do persons in real life, dramatic characters use connotation as a way of revealing their attitudes and feelings toward something or someone; connotation is therefore closely tied to the emotional life of the character. If a character describes someone as "swilling and gnawing and hulking," we understand not only her attitude toward the other person, but also something about the character herself, because of the way she has chosen to express her attitude.

As in the preceding example, the sensations that words evoke make up an important part of connotation and demand from the actor a strongly physical response. The physical qualities of "swilling," and so on, should be forcefully suggested by the line delivery and will heighten the emotional expression. When you understand your character's attitudes and feelings as they are revealed in connotation, you will possess a source of vivid physicalization of his emotional life.

PARAPHRASE

The problems of diction in old or modern plays are not restricted to puns, archaisms, or colloquialisms. They encompass your whole understanding of what you are saying in its historical, social, and psychological context. As you consider the words you speak, you must answer each of these questions: 1) *What were the meanings of the words when the play was written?* 2) *What do they mean when used by the kind of character we are playing?* 3) *What "hidden" meanings or references might there be in them?* 4) *How might any or all of these meanings operate in this context?*

One very good way to be sure you have asked yourself the proper questions about diction is to *paraphrase*. This is the practice of restating the meaning of your lines in your own words. Going carefully over your lines, word by word and sentence by sentence, try to reword what the author has given you. Obviously, much of the emotional tone, the connotations and mood, and the poetic richness of the original will be destroyed; but even this will make you appreciate the subtleties of the author's language, and you will at least have made sure that you have considered seriously the possible meanings of each word you speak.

Good dictionaries will help you to be sure about diction. For modern plays, the Merriam-Webster dictionaries based on either their second or third unabridged editions as well as a dictionary of slang will be useful. For old (English) plays, the *Oxford English Dictionary* (the *O.E.D.*) lists the changing meanings of words with the dates of their currency. There are carefully noted editions of great classical plays with glossaries, or with a "running gloss." There are *variorum* editions of Shakespeare's plays, with explanatory notes and excerpts from important critical commentary, line by line.

Exercise 45   Paraphrase on four levels

Using your speech or scene, write a paraphrase of it on each of the following levels:

A. For literal denotation;
B. For connotation and emotional attitude;
C. To express simply the germinal *idea* behind each sentence;
D. To express the subtextual, submerged meanings or feelings carried by the speech or scene (this last paraphrase may be much longer than the original, of course, and the entire play must be taken into account when interpreting subtext).

Save these paraphrases for use in the diction polarization exercise to follow.

A paraphrase, especially of poetry, will usually be much longer than the original. Your aim is to make the *implied* meanings *explicit*. The words of the original have been compacted until their meaning is distilled or intensified. To be sure you aren't missing anything, expand the speech into more prosaic language. This will also help you to realize the economy of the original, the "rightness" of every word in every place.

You will probably find it difficult to paraphrase the words of a contemporary play, at least for the first level of literal meaning; however, you will probably find that the subtextual level of realistic plays is of great importance since the revelation of character psychology was one of the aims of most realistic playwrights. This fourth level of paraphrase for realistic plays will be quite extensive.

SYNTAX

Syntax refers to "the due arrangement of word forms to show their *mutual relation* in the sentence." This idea of "mutual relation" is expressed in an old theatrical maxim that a good delivery of a line will "throw away" or de-emphasize 80 percent of the words in order to give the proper emphasis to the remaining 20 percent in which the meaning is crystallized. This is only to say that the intelligibility of our speech depends more on the "shape," patterning, or mutual relation of words than on the meaning of individual words.

It is the nature of our language that "idea units" (sentences or independent phrases) have, to some extent, a conventional structure that provides unity and focus. Playwrights may also achieve unusual effects by departing from traditional structures and employing inverted or other unusual syntax. The emphasis that is directed to certain elements of the sentence, either by traditional or unusual structure, must be reflected in our delivery if we are to be faithful to the *phraseology* of the author.

In music, instrumentalists are often told by their teachers, "Don't play the notes, play the music!" This means understanding the shape and sense of a whole phrase, or section, as a unit and not simply as a succession of individual notes. The actor's problem in the delivery of lines is like the musician's problem of phraseology; it is from the shaping of the larger thought units, of phrases, sentences, and paragraphs, that meaning best emerges. There are two basic types of syntax: *periodic* and *nonperiodic*.

In periodic structures, the sense of the idea unit is suspended throughout its length. The various elements "pile up" upon each other until the fullness of meaning is revealed at the end. This structure is particularly appropriate to the painting of word-pictures, where the total effect is achieved through a "funding" or combining of a number of descriptive elements. An excellent example of periodic structure, especially in its ability to create a funded verbal picture, comes from this description of Cleopatra's barge as it sails down the Nile in *Antony and Cleopatra:*

> The barge she sat in, like a burnish'd throne,
> Burn'd on the water. The poop was beaten gold;
> Purple the sails, and so perfumed that
> The winds were love-sick with them; the oars were silver,
> Which to the tune of flutes kept stroke, and made
> The water which they beat to follow faster,
> As amorous of their strokes.

Do you *feel* the way the images of this speech begin to form one total picture?

Nonperiodic structures are less formal, more "conversational." One form of nonperiodic structure is the *balanced* sentence. Here, relatively self-sufficient elements of the sentence are juxtaposed, and meaning is revealed by contrast. The contrasted elements need not be opposite to one another, only different. You can see this sort of structure at work in this famous speech by Marc Antony from *Julius Caesar:*

> Friends, Romans, countrymen, lend me your ears;
> I come to bury Caesar, not to praise him.
> The evil that men do lives after them;
> The good is oft interred with their bones;
> So let it be with Caesar. The noble Brutus
> Hath told you Caesar was ambitious.
> If it were so, it was a grievous fault;
> And grievously hath Caesar answer'd it.

Do you *feel* the balancing of contrasted ideas in this speech?

SAMPLE DICTION ANALYSES

(Refer to sample speeches, pages 263 and 264).

King Lear. The periodic syntax of the first four lines develops a vivid cumulative picture of poverty. *Poor* in the first line is not simply a term of pity but refers literally to those who suffer poverty. The theme of the speech is economic and social injustice; the plight of the poor is made vivid by highly physical connotations. *Wretch* originally referred to an exile who had been driven out of his native country, so *wretches* are not only unfortunate persons but also those who are helpless and alone. The poor are, in this sense, disenfranchised as well as miserable. To *bide* or "abide" connotes not only endurance but a sense of expectation, the poor waiting to be lifted out of their misery. The *pitiless* storm in which Lear finds himself also comes to signify the pitilessness of society toward the poor. Lear makes it clear that he refers not only to his own actual storm, but to the pitiless storm of human life in general when he says "wheresoe'er you are" (whether you are in *my* storm or not). *Pity* also connotes *piety* or moral rightness, a quality therefore lacking in Lear's society. *Loop'd and window'd raggedness* depicts the holes in the clothing of the poor and refers us to *naked.*

The physical connotations of all these words develop a feeling of defenselessness, exposure to the elements, and helplessness, as well as a sense of spiritual desolation. In line 6, he suggests the remedy: *Take physic, pomp. Pomp* refers to the vain splendor of the rich, and *Take physic* connotes that this concentration of riches is a disease that must be cured. *Physic* in the sense of *physician* refers to healing and especially the giving of purges or enemas. The image of *pomp* taking *physic* graphically reveals how Lear feels about the rich as well as the way in which wealth needs to be dislodged and allowed to flow freely to all levels of society. This image is supported by *shake the superflux to them,* which means "scatter your surplus wealth to the poor." *Shake* also gives the physical connotation of shaking a tree so that the ripe fruit fall out of it to be eaten.

In the last line, Lear suggests that *heaven* would seem to be more *just* if man treated man humanely.

A paraphrase of this speech might look like this:

1. Poverty-stricken, defenseless, and helpless people, whether you are in this actual storm or not,
2. Who are awaiting the end of this inhuman and unjust misery,
3. How will you be able, without adequate shelter and food,
4. With your tattered clothing, to withstand
5. This incessant deprivation? I was once rich, a king, in a position to help,
6. And I was blind to your plight. The splendor of the rich must be dislodged;
7. The wealthy must open their hearts to the suffering of the poor,
8. And redistribute the excess wealth now in the hands of the few,
9. And thereby make the universe appear fairer than it does now.

The Zoo Story. "Realistic" prose is often less compact than poetry, but none the less rich. At the beginning of this speech, the diction is almost severe in its stark, straightforward simplicity. Around line 14, however, Jerry has "tuned in," and his thoughts begin flowing in longer phrases, an outpouring of pent-up frustrations, the connotations becoming richer and more physical.

In lines 1–3, he is trying to get started, searching for a way of explaining his problem. In line 4, he begins enumerating the things he has tried to relate to, and he is soon describing his world, the world of his rooming house and apartment. The theme of *coping,* of "dealing" with things recurs, and the connotations of most of the words reflect a sense of basic physical inhibition, which relates to the search for identity through contact with others. The important thing about the pornographic playing cards in line 13 is that they are associated with an *unlocked* strongbox (they are a form of sexual contact that is accessible). In the next phrases, *love* triggers a sequence of *vomiting* (symbolic rejection of nourishing contact with life), *crying* (a vocal gesture of frustration in this context), *fury* over the disappointment of the realities of sex, the exaltation of the love act as transcendent of the circumstances in which it occurs, and *howling because you're alive* as the ambivalent awareness of the pain of existence (compare Lear's "Howl, howl, howl, howl").

Finally, God, who symbolizes for Jerry contact between people, is connected to *A COLORED QUEEN* (a black homosexual), who, as a symbol of unreal sexual contact, is preoccupied with maintaining a false illusion of femininity by plucking his eyebrows, and *A WOMAN WHO CRIES WITH DETERMINATION,* whose sorrow has become the only possible aggressive, *determined,* self-expressive gesture toward life behind *HER CLOSED DOOR.* Jerry's inability to open his door to human contact will lead him to his final, desperate act, a physical and strongly sexual contact through the knife.

Exercise 46   Diction polarization

Using your four-level paraphrase as a basis, do each of the following exercises:

A. Deliver the speech or scene slowly in its original language, using descriptive and other gestures to make the *denotations* (as in the first-level paraphrase) and the germinal *ideas* (as in the third-level paraphrase) perfectly clear.

B. Do the speech again, without words, using free-flowing dancelike movements and emphatic gestures to make the connotations and feelings of the speech (as in the second-level paraphrase) as vivid as possible *for yourself* as a real experience of those feelings and attitudes.

C. Perform your first-level paraphrase as if it were the speech; feel what is lost when you depart from the specific language selected by the playwright.

D. Finally, perform the speech or scene in a "normal" fashion, but use your subtextual (fourth-level) paraphrase as an *interior monologue* (refer to exercise 34). Keep the interior monologue running through your mind as you trace your character's thoughts and feelings through the actual words of the text.

Whether you are performing a solo speech or a scene with a partner, remember that this exercise is designed to sensitize you to the meanings, feelings, and attitudes carried by the language of your text; it is *not* meant to encourage you to work entirely "inside your head," as if the words your character speaks are merely the result of something going on inside of you. Remember that *acting is reacting* and that you have not understood the whole process by which your character comes to speak until you have connected it to the action/reaction chain that moves through the entire scene and play. Your skill as a *listener* and a *reactor* is an essential aspect of your ability to bring your text and character to life.

Lesson 9

Analyzing the Speech: Rhythm

Rhythm is not just a matter of the tempo of the speech (fast or slow) or the basic rhythm or "beat" of the speech, but also the variation of tempo and beat that provides *emphasis.* In good writing, rhythm has been carefully controlled to provide a many-leveled or "contrapuntal" texture. Rhythm provides emphasis by *contrast;* the variations from the basic rhythm of a speech provide emphasis and focus on certain words, images, or other elements of the speech and therefore contribute to the communication of meaning.

Besides supporting meaning through emphasis, rhythm is also expressive of personality. The blustery, pompous man has a rhythm of speech much different from the thoughtful, introspective man. Even nationality and social background affect rhythm: the Irish tend to speak each thought on one long exhalation of breath, imparting an unmistakable rhythm to their speech. While in real life there are many exceptions to these stereotypes, playwrights nevertheless supply built-in rhythms that are appropriate to a character's personality and emotion, and your analysis of those rhythms will aid you in forming your characterization.

Many emotions have recognizable rhythmic qualities. All emotion causes measurable changes in the tension of our muscles, and this tensing of the muscles has a direct effect on our speech. Take anger as an example: as anger rises in us, the body becomes tense, especially in the deep center, where the largest muscles mobilize themselves for action. Tension in the interior muscles is communicated directly to the diaphragm, limiting its movement and forcing us to take shallow breaths. Since we need to oxygenate the muscles for defense purposes, however, we compensate by taking more rapid breaths. This causes us to break our speech up into shorter breath-phrases and to increase its tempo. Tension, spreading to the pharynx, causes an elevation of pitch, and coupled with the increased pressure of the breath stream, this results in a "punching" delivery and increased volume. The vestigial biting and tearing of the jaw related to anger encourages us to emphasize hard consonant sounds, and our speech may become, in rage, similar to the snapping and growling of the angry animal.

This very basic example will remind you that both tone and rhythm are tied to our emotional state by the muscles that produce speech. By understanding the rhythms and tones your playwright has supplied for you and by experiencing them in your own muscles as you pronounce them, you will have a better chance of recreating the feelings they express.

The next lesson will deal with tone, and it is rhythm and tone *together* that make the music of speech. For now, however, we study rhythm separately for two reasons: to help us understand and support the meaning of our lines through the proper placement of emphasis, and to give us yet another tool for entering into the feelings of our character.

RHYTHM IN POETRY: SCANSION

We will turn first to the analysis of rhythm in poetry, since it is more formal than prose rhythm, and analyzing it requires various special techniques. The heightened patterning of rhythm in poetry is both a hindrance and a help to us: on the one hand, it makes our analysis and delivery of the speech more complex, but on the other hand, it allows our analysis to be more orderly and specific than an analysis of prose rhythms can be. Nevertheless, rhythm is as carefully structured by good prose writers as it is by poets, and most of the *principles* of poetry analysis are also applicable to prose. The general term for the patterning of poetic elements is *prosody,* and the name for analyzing rhythm syllable by syllable is *scansion.*

Any word is made up of syllables, some of which are emphasized or *stressed* and some of which are relatively unstressed. When these words are joined into a poetic line, their stressed and unstressed syllables work together to form an overall rhythmic pattern for that line. The first step in scanning a line is to identify the stressed and unstressed syllables. Take this famous line from *Romeo and Juliet* as an example:

But soft! What light through yonder window breaks?

We know, first of all, that the pronunciation of multi-syllabled words determines the placement of some stresses, and we put a line called a *machron* (−) over the stressed syllables and a semicircle called a *breve* (⌣) over the unstressed ones.

But soft! What light through yōndĕr wīndŏw breaks?

Filling in the rest, we see this pattern emerge as we place other stresses demanded by meaning and syntax:

Bŭt sōft! Whăt līght thrŏugh yōndĕr wīndŏw brēaks?

Though we have marked syllables as either stressed or unstressed, these are only very general categories, and there is actually a great deal of variation within each. If we were to read all stressed syllables one way and all unstressed another, the result would be a monotonous singsong. Only a few of the stresses in each line are actually *major* stresses. In this line, for example, we would probably read only *soft!*, *light*, and *breaks* as major stresses. At the same time, an unstressed syllable like *What* certainly receives more emphasis than another unstressed syllable like *der.* Nevertheless, a general pattern of alternating stressed and unstressed syllables can be recognized; remember that stress is *relative* to *adjoining syllables,* and that not all stressed syllables nor all unstressed syllables are equal to one another.

The rhythmic pattern of this line can be identified by using the most common system of English scansion, *foot scansion.* To use foot scansion, one arranges the stressed and unstressed syllables into units called "feet." There are a limited number of these arrangements of stressed and unstressed syllables established by tradition, and they work very much like measures in music. If I write | ♩♩♩ |, you recognize it as a measure of waltz time. The same is true of our arrangment of syllables. If I write | Bŭt, sōft! |, it is recognized as a *foot* called an *iamb.* The traditional feet used in English verse are six in number and look like this:

⌣⌣|⌣–|–⌣|⌣⌣–|–⌣⌣|––|
 P   I   T   A   D   S

You can remember their names by remembering the nonsense word PITADS. The first letter of PITADS, *P,* stands for the weakest and smallest foot, the *pyrrhic,* which has only two unstressed syllables |⌣⌣|. The second letter, *I,* stands for the most common foot, the *iambic,* which has an unstressed syllable followed by a stressed one | ⌣– |. The third letter, *T,* stands for *trochaic,* the opposite of the *iambic* |–⌣ |. *A* is for *anapestic,* which is different because it has three syllables, two unstressed and one stressed |⌣⌣–|. D is for *dactylic,* the opposite of the anapestic |–⌣⌣|. Finally, *S* is for *spondaic,* the strongest foot of all, with two stresses |––|. If we look again at our line from *Romeo and Juliet,* we see that it divides regularly into iambic feet:

Bŭt, so͞ft!│Whăt li͞ght│thro͝ugh yŏn│dĕr wi͞n│do͝w bre͞aks?│

Notice that the division of feet does not necessarily coincide with the division of words, and this is the first source of the contrapuntal quality of poetic meter. The *basic rhythm* or *meter* of alternating stressed and unstressed syllables goes against the natural pauses between words in some cases. This creates a contrapuntal tension, and there is usually a reason for this: some particular part of the line, image, or idea is emphasized by the irregularity.

In this example, a series of words are tied together; by de-emphasizing the pauses between the words *through, yonder,* and *window,* the poet encourages us to speed over this section of the line. This helps shape the meaning of the whole by leaving more time for the key words *soft, light,* and *breaks.* Notice that you could say these three words alone in such a way as to communicate the sense of the entire original line.

We now know that our line is comprised of iambic feet, and we see that there are five feet in all. We can name this meter "iambic five-meter," or *iambic pentameter.* If there had been more or fewer than five feet, we would have named it dimeter (2), trimeter (3), tetrameter (4), hexameter (6), or heptameter (7). We identify the meter *by combining the name of the predominant kind of foot with the average number of feet per line.* Trochaic tetrameter, for example, would be a meter that *generally* had four trochaic feet in each line.

The iambic line has a momentum that flows from the unstressed syllables to the stressed ones and is called *rising meter.* A trochaic line has the opposite tendency and is called *falling* meter. It is sometimes used to express sadness, as when King Lear, with his dead daughter in his arms, says:

She'll come no more,
Ne͞vĕr,│ ne͞vĕr,│ ne͞vĕr,│ ne͞vĕr,│ ne͞vĕr.│

Iambic pentameter is the most common English meter. When it does not rhyme, iambic pentameter is called *blank verse.*

A word of caution: *basic rhythm, in either prose or poetry, is not the same thing as the tempo of the speech.* Just as waltz time can be played quickly or slowly and still be ¾ time, a passage of prose or iambic pentameter can be read with any tempo. The basic meter establishes internal relationships or *proportions* of one syllable to other syllables, while tempo is determined by the meaning, overall patterning, emotion, and character.

METRICAL VARIATIONS

We name poetry by the *dominant* kind of meter it possesses, expecting that there will be many variations. For example, we call Shakespeare's poetry "blank verse" or "iambic pentameter," even though there are some lines with less or more than ten syllables, and there are many feet that are not iambic.

Some variations are more common than others. In *Romeo and Juliet,* Juliet exclaims:

Gallop apace, you fiery-footed steeds!

If we scan for pronunciation and meaning, we get:

Gallop apace, you fiery-footed steeds!

When we divide this into feet, we get:

$$-\,\smile\,|\,\smile\,-\,|\,\smile\,-\,|\,\smile\,\smile\,-\,|\,\smile\,-\,|$$

Two irregularities are immediately obvious. The first foot is not iambic, it is trochaic; this is an *inverted first foot* (since a trochee is an inverted iamb) and is a common variation. (It is also fairly common to find a spondee in the first foot.) The fourth foot is also not iambic, but anapestic. There is a great deal of argument about whether three-syllable feet (the anapest and dactyl) are "proper" in English poetry. Most critics feel that they are not, and that the poet wanted the line read to conform to the two-syllable pattern demanded by convention. Nevertheless, we ought to determine each case on its own merits, not by an all-inclusive rule.

If you pronounce all three syllables in *fiery,* you find that it stands out somewhat from the dominant meter. Your impulse is to speed up the word and compact these two syllables into the time taken by one of the other unstressed syllables, thereby keeping the basic beat of the line regular. This speed is certainly appropriate to the meaning of "fiery" and the image of which the word is a part, and this analysis might be a good argument for "leaving in" the extra syllable. If we do, the line has one syllable more than the basic ten syllable pattern and is called *hypermetrical.*

On the other hand, many scholars would say that this extra syllable should be "taken out" so that the line becomes regular. This can be done by the process of *elision.* You *elide* a syllable by slurring or gliding over it as you speak it, so that it is *minimized* or eliminated altogether. You can see that it is quite easy to glide over the middle syllable of *fiery* and say the word as if it had only two syllables, *fi-ry*. If you do this, the meter of the line becomes regular. One of the best arguments in favor of such an elision is that hypermetrical lines usually contain words that are easy to elide, and so must have been chosen for this purpose by the poet. Theatrical tradition is also in favor of making these elisions.

Elision is sometimes marked by the printer, and sometimes not. When you see a word printed "Heav'n" it may or may not be a proper elision. Only your own analysis will tell you, because these typographical markings were rarely made by the playwright himself.

SHAPING OF POETIC LINES

We have now identified sources of contrapuntal levels of poetic rhythm that involve individual syllables and words. There is a larger rhythmic pattern, however, one that the poet establishes by the overall shaping of poetic lines.

One way poets achieve extra rhythmic effect in the shaping of their lines is by breaking up the flow of the line. A strong pause that interrupts a poetic line is called a *caesura.* It may be marked by a comma (though not all commas are caesuras), a semicolon, colon, or period. Often it is unmarked by punctuation but is only implied by syntax and sense.

Poor na | ked wre | tches, where | soe'er | you are, |

As you see in this example, the caesura (marked by an arrow) may interrupt the foot division. Though this caesura is in the middle of the line, it could occur anywhere, and there may be more than one in a line:

Too lit | tle care | of this. | Take phy | sic, pomp; |

Another way poets shape lines is by grouping them into rhythmic units. Lines may end on either stressed or unstressed syllables; most common are those ending on stresses, which are called *masculine* endings. An unstressed syllable at the end of a line is a *feminine* ending. Often such a final syllable will be hypermetrical and was not meant to be elided:

He was | a thing | of blood | whose ev | ery mo | tion
Was timed | with dy | ing cries. | Alone | he en | ter'd

Thĕ mōr│tăl gāte│ŏf thĕ' cī│tў, whīch│hĕ pāin│ tĕd
                    ꜛ
Wĭth shūn│lĕss dēs│tĭnў;│

In these lines from *Coriolanus,* we feel the effect of the extra last "feminine" syllable driving us on into the next line, supporting the vigor and
determination of what is being described. When lines, like these, "run on"
into each other, they are called *enjambed* lines. *Enjambed* lines are the
opposite of *end-stopped* lines. Several lines may be enjambed to form a
larger rhythmic unit.

Just as in prose, poetic lines form sentences, and these sentences form
verse paragraphs. These are larger rhythmic patterns, which we must manifest in our delivery to give the proper shaping to the development of the
ideas in our speeches. These larger patterns can be analyzed just as if they
were prose.

We have seen that the various levels or layers of poetic rhythm exist
simultaneously, and their interaction produces a contrapuntal richness,
which provides emphasis and texture. We can list these layers of rhythm
from those producing the smallest patterns to those producing the largest:

1. The arrangement of stressed and unstressed syllables;
2. The division of these syllable patterns into feet, and the tension
   between word division and foot division;
3. Variations within the basic foot pattern;
4. The placement of caesura within the line;
5. The manipulation of line-endings to form larger patterns;
6. The grouping of several lines into a verse paragraph.

PROSE RHYTHMS

A skillful writer utilizes rhythm purposefully, whether he is writing prose
or poetry. Prose rhythms are usually not as heightened or formalized as
those of poetry, but they operate on much the same principle of *variety
within regularity.*

The basic rhythm of prose, like that of poetry, is established by the
alternation of stressed and unstressed syllables as they fall into characteristic rhythmic units. While they are not identifiable by tradition or a system
of nomenclature, the sensitive reader will quickly sense the "beat" underlying a prose speech. The rhythmic layers of prose we will call *cadences,* and
this basic rhythm established by the flow of syllables is the *syllabic cadence.*

Next in the hierarchy of cadences is the *breath cadence.* The evolution of our written language was greatly influenced by the way we speak, and we still tend to break our sentences up into smaller units that can easily be said in one breath. These breath cadences are sometimes marked by commas, semicolons, or colons (in music, the comma is still used specifically as a breath mark). Playwrights, since they are writing specifically for the human voice and not for the eye, manipulate breath cadences to guide the actor into a pattern of breathing, and we have already seen how the rhythm of breath is a primary factor in the generation of emotion. The sample analysis of the speech from *The Zoo Story* will deal particularly with this use of breath cadence. Note that breath cadences are also important in poetry, often coinciding with caesuras and end-stopped lines, and influence our breathing in the same way.

A still larger rhythmic pattern is developed by the length of sentences and independent phrases, the ends of which are marked by a strong pause symbolized by a period, question mark, or exclamation point. This is called the *terminal cadence.* In longer speeches, especially, it is helpful to organize the thoughts of the speech into coherent groupings according to terminal cadences. Radical changes in the terminal cadence are usually our best indicators of changes in tempo; shorter terminal cadences usually indicate a faster tempo, longer ones a slower tempo—though this is by no means a hard-and-fast rule. Terminal cadences are also of great importance in poetry as organizing factors and tempo indicators.

Finally, in extremely long speeches, there may be a *paragraph* cadence, with the end of the paragraph symbolizing a major change in thought and therefore a major pause. In most dialogue, however, the speeches by the individual characters themselves act as paragraphs. We get a good impression of the tempo of a scene by looking at the density of the printed script. A mass of long speeches suggests a different approach to tempo than, for example, the extremely short back-and-forth exchange of some farce, and we can call this the *dialogue cadence.*

A summary of these cadences—which apply as well to poetry as to prose —running from the smallest rhythmic units to the largest looks like this:

1. syllabic cadence
2. breath cadence
3. terminal cadence
4. paragraph or dialogue cadence

YOUR BASIS FOR ANALYSIS

Remember that the rhythm of speech does not absolutely determine meaning or even emotion; as you begin to analyze rhythm, you will see many possibilities, and you will probably be puzzled about how to select one or another of them. Your choice must be based upon your understanding of the meaning of the line and your evaluation of the relative importance of its various elements, taking into account the demands of character, situation, and emotion as well.

Nevertheless, a detailed analysis of rhythm, if it only reveals the possibilities to you (and it will usually do much more), should begin to impart to you the sense of the personality of the speaker. In our social, everyday life, we all have an intuitive and highly developed sense of the communicative value of sound and rhythm. It is what gives our speech its color and individual flavor, and it helps us to catch implications, sarcasm, and all sorts of connotative values that round out our daily speech and make it fully human. In any good writing, these aspects of melody have been incorporated into the structure of the lines in a carefully selected and heightened way. Through careful and informed analysis, you can unlock these inherent values of tone and rhythm, and by surrendering yourself to experience the muscular actions required to produce tone and rhythm, you can bring them back to life for your audience.

SAMPLE RHYTHM ANALYSES

1. Poor nā | kĕd wrēt | chĕs, whēre | sŏe'ēr | yŏu āre,

2. Thăt bīde | thĕ pēl | tĭng ōf | thĭs pīt | ĭlĕss stŏrm,

3. Hōw shăll | yŏur hōuse | lĕss hēads | ănd ŭn | fĕd sīdes,

4. Yŏur lōop'd | ănd wīn | dŏw'd răg | gĕdnēss, | dĕfĕnd | yŏu

5. Frŏm sēa | sŏns sūch | ăs thēse? | Ō! Ī | hăve tā'en

6. Tōo lĭt | tlĕ cāre | ŏf thīs. | Tăke phy̆ | sĭc, pŏmp;

7. Ĕxpōse | thy̆sēlf | tŏ fēel | whăt wrēt | chĕs fēel,

8. Thăt thōu | măy̆st shāke | thĕ sŭ | pĕrflūx | tŏ thĕm,

9. Ănd shōw | thĕ hēa | vĕns ⎯⎯ (—)|(⌣) ⌣ ⎯ |(⌣) ⎯
      mŏre   jŭst.

King Lear. Examine the above sample scansion for metrical variation. Notice especially the use of spondees in the first feet of lines 1, 3, and 6. There is also a pair of spondees in the fourth feet of lines 5 and 6. The speech has a strongly emphatic quality, and the heaviness of these stresses contributes to the strongly determined comparsion Lear expresses in this speech.

In line 2, we follow custom by eliding *pitiless.* The fact that we "mispronounce" the word when making the elision helps call attention to the aspect of justice it represents.

Line 4 appears to have a hypermetrical feminine ending, with the final *you* being the extra syllable. There are two reasons for this: first, the leftover beat moves us on strongly into the next line, and this is one of only two run-on lines in the speech; second, the word *you,* which appears in some form in lines 1, 3, and 4, shows Lear's concern for others. At the beginning of the play, he was self-concerned, but through his suffering he learns concern for others. His realization of his past lack of compassion is crystallized in this speech.

The elision of *taken* into *ta'en* in line 5 is marked by the printer. Nevertheless, we might argue with it; there are only two run-on lines in the speech, lines 4 and 5; line 4, directly preceding, uses a hypermetrical feminine ending to move us over the line-ending and into the next line. Therefore, it might be consistent to utilize the same device in line 5 and leave *taken* as a hypermetrical feminine ending. It is further true that feminine endings usually appear *in groups* in Shakespeare's writing. The decision, however, is yours and your director's. This may seem like a ridiculously small point, but crucial meanings sometimes turn on such minute detail.

The terminal cadences and placement of caesura in this speech are intriguing. The first four lines and three feet are one long and cohesive sentence. There follows the short sentence, *O! I have ta'en / too little care of this,* which, though it is broken up by the line endings, reads as one line of iambic pentameter formed between the caesuras in lines 5 and 6. There then follows the short phrase *Take physic, pomp,* which is itself broken by a caesura. The remainder of the speech is one sentence, which flows smoothly until we come to the last line. The terminal cadences break the speech into three units of thought and emotion: in the first four lines, Lear's attention is on the *poor.* In line 5, he realizes his own guilty share of things with *O! I have ta'en / Too little care of this.* In the remaining lines, Lear turns his attention again to others, those who are rich as he himself once was, and he prays that they will act as he did not.

The last line is particularly interesting. *Heaven* could be elided to *Heav'n* —a common Shakespearean elision, though it is difficult to pronounce— and the line could scan as regular iambic trimeter:

And show|the *heavens*|more just.

This seems terribly weak, however; the shortening of this line seems to suggest that Shakespeare wanted it sustained to fill the time usually taken by a full five feet. I have therefore scanned the speech to used implied pauses, which produce an iambic line.

$$\smile \quad — \;\big|\; \smile \quad — \;\big|\; \smile \quad (—) \;\big|\; (\smile) \quad — \;\big|\; (\smile) \quad —$$
And show | the heav | ens $(—)$ | $(\smile)$ more | $(\smile)$ just.

This results in a reading that emphasizes the concept of justice, provides a strong rhythmic finish for this crucial speech, and makes positive use of the line's irregularity. Again, however, there is no absolute rule about such matters.

Accepting this scansion, we see a beautiful shaping of the whole speech. Since caesuras give the effect, in reading, of "false" line endings, and strong run-on lines obscure actual line endings, we could print and read the speech like this:

Poor naked wretches,
Wheresoe'er you are,
That bide the pelting of this pitless storm,
How shall your houseless heads and unfed sides,
Your loop'd and window'd raggedness,
defend you from seasons such as these?
O!
I have ta'en too little care of this.
Take physic,
pomp;
Expose thyself to feel what wretches feel,
That thou mayst shake the superflux to them,
And show the heavens
more
just.

As it is printed here each line represents a breath cadence. Read it aloud, taking a breath for each line, and see what effect this has on your tempo, and what emotion begins to result. Do you see which ideas and feelings are emphasized by this shaping of the whole?

The Zoo Story. As in the speech from *King Lear,* cadences play a crucial role in shaping here. The syllabic cadence is heavily stressed, since the preponderance of words are of one syllable. The effect is emphatic. The hard consonant and fricative sounds combine with this rhythm to produce a staccato effect, like sharp tapping on a snare drum. As the speech progresses, however, the beat and tones change, deepen, and quicken, until they are like a prolonged tympani roll.

The breath cadence is probably the most crucial rhythmic level in this speech. The pauses, which Albee his indicated by three dots, form a pattern of breath reminiscent of orgasm, beginning short and fragmentary as Jerry searches for words to describe his feelings; then, as his thoughts begin to flow, the breath cadences begin to lengthen and swell, reaching a prolonged climax in lines 18–20, then dying away in a few final gasps, finishing with a heavy sigh. The use of capital letters as volume and emphasis markings supports this pattern.

Imagine the speech printed *as if it were modern poetry.* Where would you break the lines? Try marking the breath cadences, and imagine the speech printed the way the speech from *Lear* is printed above. Read it aloud as if each breath cadence were a line of poetry, and see what tempos result.

The terminal cadence supports this pattern; if you mark the major punctuation, a pattern like this emerges:

Just as in the speech from *King Lear*, certain ideas are emphasized by being isolated as short units surrounded by longer cadences. The long, continuous terminal cadence, which begins in line 10, runs until the semicolon in line 17 and is followed by the two words, *with God.* The question of God, then, is the culmination of Jerry's verbal searching during the first part of the speech. Once he has crystallized his feelings in this concept, the full outburst, the section in capital letters, is unleashed. Then, his energy spent, he says *"with God who, I'm told, turned his back on the whole thing some time ago ... ,"* he returns to his starting point, people.

Exercise 47   Rhythm polarization

Since the speech you have chosen for the polarization exercises is highly poetic, scan it very carefully. Then analyze its various rhythmic levels. Typing several carbon copies of the speech will enable you to use markings, colored pencils, and so on, to help visualize the rhythmic patterning. Now, *without using the actual words of the original:*

1. Using very overt movements, hand clapping or other devices, perform the speech to exaggerate the *basic* rhythmic pattern. Then do it again, emphasizing as many of the *variations* as you can. Finally, do a full movement expression of what you consider the important *basic* rhythmic qualities of the speech, without trying to recreate every specific rhythm. Move always from your deep center, involving your breath.
2. Now do this basic rhythmic expression of the scene, allowing the movement to produce noises that are the natural outgrowth of the body's activity. Does your vocal sound come freely, or have you not yet integrated vocal activity with all the other forms of muscular activity? How much of the meaning and emotion of the original is retained, or extended, in this performance?
3. Immediately perform the speech in its original form; how much of your body's memory of steps 1 and 2 carries over to enrich the speech in its traditional form?

In the course of these polarizations, have you discovered inflectional patterns, pitch ranges, perhaps even postures, types of walking and move-ment, or other physical qualities that have helped create a full experience of the speech for your whole body? If you haven't, you are probably failing to analyze carefully enough or, more likely, failing to involve your muscles fully in the polarization exercises. Has part of your body been unavailable during the exercises? Have you avoided the fullest possible movement, with the excuse that it isn't "real" or "believable," or that you just "don't know what kinds of movement to use"? Remember that these are *training exercises, not* performance or even rehearsal techniques. The aim is to create a full, organic experience *for yourself,* based upon the important qualities of text, which you have identified through careful analysis. As such, the completeness and commitment of your movement and noises is far more important than their "correctness" in terms of a performance. Don't evade the experience; move! Make noise! Involve your center! Breathe!

In this and the other polarization exercises that follow, you are creating an extended *visceral* experience that renders the rhythm, tone, imagery, or configuration of your character's language into *real* bodily experiences. The body will "remember" much of these experiences far better than could the mind. In Stanislavski's terms, you are creating *sense memories* based upon the qualities and associations embodied in the text. Later, as you rehearse and perform the text in a "normal" way, these bodily memories will automatically enrich your performance *without conscious effort*—for your mind, in performance, must be totally free to concentrate on *what* you are doing, not *how.*

The athlete drills himself in the component skills of his sport. Then, when he focuses his attention completely on his immediate task, his preparation makes all his component skills flow together "intuitively" into his one activity. So, too, your rehearsal preparation gives you many component skills in the playing of a role that are then swept into your single focus on your stage objective, on *what* you are doing. Experience this by repeating your speech or scene in a "normal" way immediately after each of the polarization exercises: how much does your body carry with it? Trust the body to remember the really important things, and let the rest fall away!

This lesson on rhythm has been long and complicated because it is difficult to describe such a profound organismic phenomenon as rhythm. Remember the work you did on rhythm in part 1, in which you learned to experience rhythm as *the shaping of your energy through time.* Now that you have learned how to *recognize* and, in the polarization exercise, to *experience* the playwright's use of rhythm in the language he has given your character, you have begun to master one of your most valuable stage tools. Allow the rhythm of your speeches to penetrate deeply into your center where it can affect your breathing, muscle tone, and bodily rhythms; you will discover a wealth of understanding and feeling available in no other way. All the terms and techniques covered in this lesson are meant only to assist you in creating such an experience.

Lesson 10

Analyzing the Speech: Vocal Melody

There is a story about the famous Italian actress Eleanora Duse, who moved a New York audience to tears by reading the Manhattan telephone book in Italian. Since the audience didn't understand Italian, her speech was communicative strictly as gesture, as a *vocal melody.*

Any good actor develops great expressiveness in the use of the sounds of speech, apart from the dictionary meaning of those sounds as words. This applies not only to moans and sighs and other noises we make that are not words, but to the sounds that make up words themselves.

Usually, as actors, we are not speaking meaningless sounds or words of our own invention, but words that have been chosen and arranged by a playwright. Any good playwright has selected these words, not only because of what they mean (for there are often many words that could produce roughly the same meaning), but also because of the way they *sound.* Our use of vocal melody on the stage should be controlled by the author's use of it in his text.

THE VOCO-SENSORY THEORY

There have been attempts to develop systems that will decode vocal melody and attach certain emotional meanings to certain sounds. The most famous of these was the *Roback Voco-Sensory Theory.* Experimental subjects were asked to tell which of several three-letter nonsense syllables, like *mil* and *mal,* made them think of larger or smaller objects. As you probably guessed, *mal* seemed "bigger" than *mil.* The theory explains this by pointing out that the physical act of saying *mal* requires opening the mouth more than does saying *mil.* The "big" space in the mouth causes the sensation of bigness associated with *mal,* while the reverse is true for *mil.* The theory goes on to suggest that much of language was formed by this sort of translation of physical sensations into appropriate sounds, hence the name *voco-sensory* theory. "Rough" words *sound* rough, "smooth" words *sound* smooth, for example. Indeed, they often do, just as *rushing* rushes, *explode* explodes, and so on.

This is an interesting view of language for the actor, since it provides a relationship between physical sensation and the meanings of words. However, it has become obsolete, since many words do *not* seem to relate to physical sensations, and because of the many exceptions to the rule. *Small* is made of "big" sounds, while *big* is "small." Let us suggest for our purposes that the physical sensations of words are often more important to their *connotation* than to their *denotation*.

If we examine a sentence like "the ghost wind howled a scream," we can see how many sensations appropriate to the mood are contained in the windiness of *wind,* the howling of *howled,* and the scream of *scream.* We can also see that the organ-like open vowel tones of *ghost* and *howled* alternate with the thin sounds of *wind* and *scream,* providing an ebb and flow, a rising and falling like the "ghost wind" itself. But all these qualities of the sentence's melody can be analyzed only *after* we have understood its meaning and emotional intention. With exactly the same sounds in the same arrangement, for example, we can also say, "the Post-Six Bowling Team."

Although the voco-sensory theory can thus be disproved, we can still learn a great deal from it. It awakens us to the importance of speech melody as it provides a physical manifestation of appropriate connotations. A good playwright will have selected words whose sounds can be useful to us in supporting the meaning and emotional tone of our speech. As long as we remember that meaning is not *determined* by sound, but is *supported* by it, we will be able to find the physical aspects of pronouncing the speech that will generate and communicate appropriate emotions.

ONOMATOPOEIA AND ALLITERATION

There are a few technical terms we should learn to describe the patterning of sounds in our speeches, remembering that our *use* of these patterns is the important thing. The first is *onomatopoeia.* This refers to words whose sound resembles the thing they describe. Even if there is no specific use of onomatopoeia, a good writer will have supplied us with sounds that we can emphasize to heighten the effect of a line. When Juliet says "Gallop apace, you fiery-footed steeds," we recognize that *gallop* can be pronounced so as to sound like a horse galloping and is onomatopoeic. But *fiery,* although there is no particular sound connected with fieriness, lends itself to being spoken in a fiery manner. The quick explosion of air from between our lips on the *fi* sound can be the sort of aggressive, bold attack we connect with fieriness.

Notice how the poet has reinforced the onomatopoeia of *gallop* by repeating the key sounds in other words: "Gallo*p* a*p*ace" not only sounds like galloping, but because the sounds are repeated in close proximity, and the rhythm is arranged to move quickly, it sounds like *fast* galloping, which is exactly appropriate to the sense of the line. Likewise, the repetition of the *f* sound in "*f*iery-*f*ooted" helps reinforce the effect of fieriness and also relates fieriness to the feet of the horses, thus referring us to a quality of their galloping.

This repetition of similar initial sounds of words in close juxtaposition is called *alliteration.* We can use the term broadly to refer to all closely repeated sounds that form melodic patterns, being equally interested in repeated vowel and consonant sounds whether they occur as *initial* sounds or *within* the words. As in the case of onomatopoeia, the actor should be liberal in his application of this principle.

Though alliteration formally applies to sounds that are quite close together, we will also be interested in types of sounds that recur within a speech or even within a role. While individual cases of alliteration or onomatopoeia can be used for emphasis of particular points, the overall patterning of sounds on a larger scale produces an effect that good writers will use to help distinguish one role from another, one mood from another, or the changing of emotional states within a role.

You might find, for example, that the sounds of your speeches make a particular pitch range and inflectional pattern more comfortable than others, and that this pitch and pattern will be psychologically and physically appropriate to your role. The melody of your speeches suggests vocal qualities of delivery, which in turn suggest aspects of characterization.

MELODY AND CHARACTERIZATION

We cannot, unfortunately, go into an intensive study of the effect of age and social background on voice, or of dialects and the other complexities of vocal characterization. Such an advanced study demands considerable skill. But even on a beginning level, the effect of voice on total characterization is apparent.

One of the most important functions of speech-melody is that it serves as a link between the words of our written text and our total physical performance. Any skillful playwright has incorporated in the words of his play a wealth of vocal actions that can lead the sensitive actor to a full involvement with his character. Stanislavski, in *Building a Character,* put it this way:

Letters, syllables, words—these are the musical notes of speech, out of which we fashion measures, arias, whole symphonies. There is good reason to describe beautiful speech as musical. . . . Even if we do not understand the meaning of words, their sounds affect us through their tempo-rhythms. . . . There is an indissoluble interdependence, interaction and bond between tempo-rhythms. . . . The correctly established tempo-rhythm of a role can, of itself, intuitively (on occasion automatically) take hold of the feelings of an actor and arouse in him a true sense of living his part.[29]

When we fully revitalize the melody of a speech, we find that the sounds help to make the feelings and meaning more vivid and more immediate. We should not merely "act out" the sounds, but we should treat them as "sound effects" that are an integral part of the speech's meaning. We usually see dance accompanied by music; the physical aspects of our stage performance are likewise accompanied by the melody of speech. But in a great dance, the music does not simply accompany; the movements and music have been synthesized into an indivisible expressive whole. Such is the case of the great stage performance as well.

SAMPLE MELODY ANALYSES

King Lear. The melody of poetry is carefully patterned, and it is often useful to chart graphically the recurrent sounds, by underlining, coloring, or some other device.

In line 1, the falling vowel sound of *Poor* followed by the hard, almost cruel sound of *naked* set the mood. These sounds, of course, are not *of themselves* hard or soft but can be *used* to physicalize the meaning of each word. As you say *Poor,* the full weight of poverty and all that it means must be present. *Naked* must likewise be delivered with a vivid sense of nakedness. The pronouncing of these words demands certain vocal and physical gestures, which must be full enough to achieve the appropriate intensity of meaning and feeling.

Wretches is a somewhat onomatopoeic word; its sound is bitter and regurgitative as in "retching." *Wretches, wheresoe'er* is alliteration of the *w* sounds, extending the effect. *Wheresoe'er you are* is a triple repetition of *r* sounds.

[29]From Constantin Stanislavski, *Building a Character* (New York: Theatre Arts Books, 1949), pp. 218–36.

In line 2, *bide, pelting* and *pitiless* alliterate, tying these three aspects of the condition of the poor together. *Pelting* is onomatopoeic, and the physical and vocal gestures required to pronounce it peltingly carry a sense of physical cruelty over to *pitiless,* which contains roughly the same sounds, turning it into an especially ruthless and active lack of compassion and morality. Try continuing the analysis for yourself for lines 3–6.

In line 7, *Expose* is a sound that begins small and opens, "exposing" the mouth, and this quality can be extended to our whole body and attitude, so that Lear does physically expose himself here *to feel what wretches feel,* the alliteration emphasizing the important point *to feel,* to have compassion, to *not* be pitiless. Lear calls this speech a *prayer* earlier, and a gesture of exposure from a prayerful attitude might be to throw the arms open into a pose reminiscent of the crucifixion, the pose of another man who exposed himself *to feel what wretches feel.*

The thought in lines 8 and 9 is emphasized by the balancing of the *sh* sounds in *shake* and *show.* Other qualities of these lines were discussed earlier.

The Zoo Story. At the beginning of the speech, the sounds are clipped and mostly consonant, emphasizing the halting quality of Jerry's thought here. But as the speech progresses and his associations begin to pour out, the sounds likewise begin to elongate, until lines 18 and 19 are one prolonged tonal outcry.

There are strong onomatopoeic words in the latter half of the speech, and their qualities reflect the quality of Jerry's emotion: *bleeding, hard, oily-wet, wisp, vomiting, crying, fury, howling,* and so on. There is a surprising amount of alliteration as well, *wisp of smoke, pornographic playing, pretty little ladies aren't pretty little ladies, making money, COLORED QUEEN . . . KIMONO . . . PLUCKS.*

As we noted earlier, the description of Jerry's world is a strong theme in this speech. The kinds of sounds we have listed, and the gestures they demand, should be used to make Jerry's response to that world vivid, as well as making that world itself, with its illusions (*wisps of smoke; pretty little ladies aren't . . .*), its pain (*vomiting, crying, fury, howling*), and its futile efforts at meaningful contact (*pornographic playing, COLORED QUEEN*) as real to us as possible.

Exercise 48 Melody polarization

Using the speech you have selected for all the polarization exercises, analyze it for its patterning of sound; then:

1. Recite it in monotone. Feel your impulse to break out of the monotone into melody. Where is this impulse the strongest?
2. Sing it as if it were pure music. Forget that the sounds have any verbal meaning; invent a melody that stresses the sounds you have decided are most important.
3. Now repeat your rhythm polarization, but replace the "accidental" sounds that grew spontaneously from your muscular activity then with the specific sound patterns (not necessarily all the actual words) that you think are of basic significance in the speech. What do you discover about the interrelationship of sound, rhythm, and muscular activity? Retain any words of the original that are of special sound value, but treat them as pure *sound* rather than for their meaning as words.
4. Now perform your speech or scene in a "normal" way: how much is carried over from your polarizations?

The melody and rhythm of your stage language are powerful sources of a sense of character. Remember your work on vocal gesture in part 1 and the profound relationship among sound, breath, energy, and character. As we pointed out then, personality has a root meaning of *per-sona, through sound.* Synthesize the techniques of analysis you have experienced in these two lessons and allow them to extend your intuitive participation in your character's sound and through it, in his personality as well.

Lesson 11

Analyzing the Speech:
Imagery and Figurative Language

The skillful playwright gets an extra measure of expressiveness from his language by utilizing the sensory potential of certain words and arranging words in special combinations that produce heightened meanings. In this way words can be used not only to communicate meaning and connotated feelings, but to create sensations. The creation of sensation by words is *imagery,* and heightened meaning achieved by special combinations of words is *figurative language.*

SENSE IMAGERY

Imagery is often subtle or even hidden beneath the surface of seemingly ordinary speech. For this reason, we cannot trust to intuition but must carefully analyze and internalize the imagery of our speeches. In its most literal sense, "imagery" refers to "something imagined," the painting of word-pictures. But the general category of imagery encompasses many more types of images than just "word-painting." Images can appeal to *any* of our senses. This speech from Shakespeare's *Antony and Cleopatra* describes Cleopatra's royal barge sailing down the Nile in the night, and it is filled with imagery:

> The barge she sat in, like a burnish'd throne,
> Burn'd on the water. The poop was beaten gold;
> Purple the sails, and so perfumed that
> The winds were love-sick with them; the oars were silver,
> Which to the tune of flutes kept stroke, and made
> The water which they beat to follow faster,
> As amorous of their strokes. For her own person,
> It beggar'd all description. She did lie
> In her pavilion, cloth-of-gold, of tissue,
> O'erpicturing that Venus where we see

The fancy out-work nature. On each side of her
Stood pretty dimpled boys, like smiling Cupids,
With divers-colour'd fans, whose wind did seem
To glow the delicate cheeks which they did cool,
And what they undid did.

The picture of the barge drawn by these words is so vivid that we can "see" it in the mind's eye. This "word-painting" aspect of the speech is called *visual imagery*. But we can find examples of almost every other type of sense imagery in this speech as well. The image of the silver oars "which to the tune of flutes kept stroke" appeals to our *hearing* and is an *aural* image. The image of the "perfumed" sails which made the winds "lovesick" appeals to our sense of *smell* and is an *olfactory* image. The humorous reference to the water chasing the oars, as if the oars' strokes were lovers' caresses, and the smoothness of the fabric of Cleopatra's pavilion awaken our sense of *touch* and *texture,* and are *tactile* imagery. The cooling breeze of the fans and the flowing warmth of Cleopatra's cheeks are contrasted *thermal* images. If only Cleopatra were (as she might well have been) dining upon some exotic delicacy, we might have been treated to some tasty *gustatory* imagery.

Throughout the description of the barge, we have a sense of its slow, gliding movement on the water, of the softly billowing sails, of the rhythmic stroking of the oars. Such senses of movement and physical states are categorized in two types of imagery. *Kinetic* imagery refers to our sense of actual movement (like the barge's sailing). *Kinesthetic* imagery refers to our sense of physical states that do not necessarily involve movement, such as our sense of Cleopatra's relaxation upon her cushions.

Kinesthetic imagery often serves as a physical "background," a general physical state that underlies other sensations. If, for example, we put ourselves completely in the place of the speaker here and attempt to relive all his original responses, we would have to be aware of the feeling of the openness of the night air stretching out over the dark water, and the cool breeze upon our face. This generalized kinesthetic response helps us to recreate a scene as vividly as possible by imaginatively "putting us in the picture."

The vividness of our response to images, our ability to recreate the sensations as if they were happening for the first time, is the crucial factor in communicating the images to the audience. By fully physicalizing our own response we are in the best position to inspire a similar response in the audience. In this way we do not simply ask our audience to respond to us: we have helped them to visualize and respond to the scene for themselves.

SAMPLE IMAGERY ANALYSES

King Lear. The context of this speech gives us a clear idea of its kinesthetic background—Lear using a lull in the storm to adopt a prayerful attitude. Notice how the words that melody and rhythm have already emphasized are also rich in images. The speech is about the poor, and the visual images make the poor vivid to the mind's eye: *naked wretches, houseless heads, unfed sides,* and so on, and the periodic syntax of the first four lines causes these images to "fund" into a single impact. As you examine each visual image, you find that they also have strong kinesthetic content: *naked, houseless, unfed,* and so on. Lear not only makes us *see* the poor, he makes us *feel* what it is to be poor as well, as he himself does at this moment. Supporting this is the strong tactile image, the *pelting* of the storm. Continue the analysis yourself, recognizing each of the many sensations contained in the speech and identifying the way each supports and heightens meaning.

The Zoo Story. This speech is filled with a host of images. The visual images are preponderant and, again, the sound, rhythm, and our diction study have already picked out the key ones. As in Lear's prayer, Albee has provided a clear kinesthetic context for the speech, both in the situation and in the stage directions. Jerry, growing more and more tense, is heading for an explosion; the climax of this speech is one of the minor climaxes leading up to his death.

Besides the obvious visual images, there are a good many other types. The touch of things seems important to Jerry, and most of the visual images have a tactile impact as well. Textures are contrasted in *oily-wet* and *wisp of smoke.* The sequence of kinesthetic and partly kinetic images— *vomiting, crying, fury, making money with your body, act of love, howling,* WEARS A KIMONO, PLUCKS HIS EYEBROWS, CRIES WITH DETER-MINATION, *turned his back*—has already been discussed as diction, but here the uniquely physical imagistic content makes us aware of a sequential increase in the violence of the physical associations of the speech. There is then a falling gentleness at the end of the speech that relates to Jerry's physical responses to his world and to his psychological condition.

In both these speeches, the physical vividness of images supports meaning and emotion. These speeches also demonstrate how important the interaction of types of images is, and how a single word often has several imagistic values.

Exercise 49   Imagery polarization

A. Again perform a word-dance of your speech in slow motion, but this time exaggerate in your physical responses the sensory impact of each image. Treat each image individually and fully explore it, attempting to relive the sensation of each. Then speed your dance up to normal tempo, and concentrate on the flow of your physical responses to the images. How does this sensory content relate to the meaning and emotion of the speech? *Be sure to involve the articulation of the words directly in your physical actions in all the remaining exercises.*

B. Immediately perform the speech in a "normal" way; do the sensations you experienced remain alive?

FIGURATIVE LANGUAGE

Figurative language—the use of "figures of speech"—stands in contrast to *literal language*. When we speak *literally*, words can be taken at their face value. But when we speak *figuratively*, we combine words (place them into a *configuration*) to make them express more than their face value, producing new levels of meaning and reference. We will divide the figures of speech into four categories: (1) *sound* figures, which depend upon the patterning of sounds; (2) *diction* figures, which require the selection and manipulation of specific word meanings; (3) *structural* figures, which are products of syntax; and (4) types of *metaphor*, which combine disparate elements to create new meanings.

1. *Sound figures.* You are already familiar with several figures of speech. The sound figures, for example, are alliteration and onomatopoeia.

2. *Diction figures.* You also know two of the diction figures, puns and archaisms. Another common diction figure is *allusion*, a brief reference to a person, place, or thing which the writer assumes will be known to the audience, who will then "fill in" the reference from their own knowledge. When Juliet, looking at the sky, says "Gallop apace, you fiery-footed steeds," Shakespeare assumes that the audience will know that she is alluding to the chariot of Apollo, which, according to myth, carries the sun across the heavens. Since she wants Apollo's horses to hurry, we understand that she wants night to fall as soon as possible, because then Romeo will come.

The last of the diction figures we will cover is *hyperbole,* the use of conscious exaggeration for either comic or serious effect. Lear says, "Had I your tongues and eyes I'd use 'em so heaven's vault should crack," which is an exaggeration expressive of the magnitude of his grief.

3. *Structural figures.* Structural figures achieve their meaning by arranging elements of a line or speech so that they are contrasted or compared. These figures are helpful in suggesting line readings, since we must emphasize the comparisons being made through our use of pitch and emphasis. Even physical gesture will be involved in a full response to the shaping of structural figures.

We have already met one structural figure in the last line of the description of Cleopatra's barge. Boys are standing beside Cleopatra fanning her, and the wind from the fans "did seem to glow the delicate cheeks which they did cool,/And what they *undid did.*" This is a *paradox,* a seemingly impossible combination of words which turns out to have a coherent meaning. In this case the motion of the fans, instead of cooling Cleopatra, acts like a bellows on a fire, causing her to glow like a burning ember. Since they are trying to "undo" her heat but in fact are making her hotter, we can say that "what they undid" they "did." This is a marvelous way of expressing the torrid quality of the sensuous Cleopatra.

Another important structural figure for the actor, and one of Shakespeare's favorite devices, is *antithesis,* which places two halves of a line or speech in contrast. The two sections will have a similar syntax, but different meanings. In this speech from *Romeo and Juliet,* Juliet has just learned that Romeo has killed her cousin Tybalt in a fight. Naturally, she is torn between her love for Romeo and abhorrence of what he has done. This ambivalence manifests itself in a series of antitheses:

> *O serpent heart,* hid with a *flowering face!*
> Did ever *dragon* keep so *fair* a cave?
> *Beautiful tyrant! fiend angelical!*
> *Dove-feathered raven! Wolvish-ravening lamb!*
> *Despised substance of divinest show!*
> *Just opposite* to what thou *justly seem'st,*
> A *damned saint,* an *honorable villain!*

The compared elements in each line are in italics; as you read them aloud, you will find yourself naturally physicalizing this balanced structure in inflection, pitch, gesture, and so on.

Notice the combination of some words with opposite meanings and connotations in a single phrase, like *damned saint* and *honorable villain.* This immediate juxtaposing of opposite sensations or meanings within a single phrase is called *oxymoron.* If we look at the structure of one of the lines that uses both antithesis and oxymoron, we see

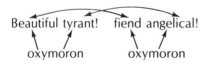

a pattern demanding the utmost skill from the actor in the use of inflection, emphasis, pitch, and supportive gesture.

4. *Varieties of metaphor.* This is the broadest and most complex category

of figurative language. While a *metaphor* is a certain kind of figure of speech, the metaphorical *process* or *principle* is common to many related figures. All types of metaphor have one thing in common: they take disparate things or ideas, and "combine" them in order to reveal a new meaning. Imagine the superimposition of two images in a movie; the two images combine to make a new image with a meaning of its own, a meaning that transcends the individual meanings of the two previously separate images. In this same way, metaphorical combinations of words crystallize a wealth of meaning in a single image.

When we say *he's a rat,* we have taken two different kinds of things and put them together, at least verbally, in such a way as to make them seem identical. *He* (man) is one kind of thing; *rat* is another kind. *He is a rat* implies by its construction that man and rat are identical. It is obvious that man and rat are not identical in *all* ways, so the metaphor refers only to certain qualities that might be shared by both. "Man" and "rat" may share qualities like cowardice, dirtiness, guile, meanness, and so on. We project these qualities of rat-ness upon the object of our metaphor. The object of the metaphor (here, *man*) is called the *tenor;* the metaphorical word (here, *rat*) is the *vehicle* because it "carries" the meaning of the metaphor.

We value metaphor because it can achieve new and often startling meanings through the combination of otherwise commonplace words. The more startling the combination, the greater the insight it may give us, and the best metaphors combine extremely dissimilar ideas. In *Othello,* for example, Iago sums up his moral code with a tremendous metaphor that combines the lowliest of real and perishable objects with the highest of abstract concepts: "Virtue? A fig!" Similarly, Falstaff comically dismisses "Honor" as "a mere scutcheon," a scutcheon (escutcheon) being part of the coat-of-arms. Our delivery should make the surprise of the combination vivid by giving each of the two words its full individual value, thereby heightening their dissimilarity rather than diminishing it.

Besides pure metaphor, in which dissimilar things are used as if they were identical, there are several more moderate forms of metaphor. The mildest form is *simile.* Here the elements are not directly combined but only compared, shown to be *similar,* not *identical.* The comparison is usually expressed by a word such as "like" or "as." In the Cleopatra scene, the "pretty dimpled boys" who fan the queen are compared to mythological figures, "like smiling Cupids." In paintings of Venus, goddess of love, cupids were often shown hovering near her. The picture of Cleopatra lying on her pillows with cupids about her is a simile combined with an allusion referring to Cleopatra's superhuman beauty.

Several other types of metaphors have been given their own names. *Personification* occurs when an inanimate object or abstract idea is described as if it were alive, as when Macbeth describes his own greed as "vaulting ambition, which o'erleaps itself. . . ." And if the abstract or inanimate thing is not merely described, but is spoken to as it if were alive, we have an *apostrophe*. Edmund in *King Lear* apostrophizes, "Nature, thou art my goddess!"

5. *Clustering of images and figures of speech.* Figures of speech and images form an important element of a play's whole structure when they appear in clusters, or when they recur throughout a role or play as *motifs,* such as the recurrent references to nature in various forms in *King Lear,* or the recurring references to eating and drinking in *The Zoo Story.* Such clusters and motifs can be indications of dominant attitudes in a character, or of important thematic content in a role. Often these motifs will not simply recur, but will change and develop within a play, providing concrete "touchstones" for the actor as his character develops. In *Lear,* for example, Lear's religious references at the beginning of the play are ornate allusions to pagan gods, and his images are of regal splendor. During his madness, his images become bestial, sexual, and scatalogical. By the end of the play they are simple and human; he no longer speaks of "Hecate" and "Juno" but simply of "God." He no longer speaks of himself as a "dragon and his wrath" but as a "fond, foolish, old man." These clustered images and figurative motifs, when carefully examined and physicalized by the actor, help him to manifest many important changes in his character.

SAMPLE ANALYSES OF FIGURATIVE LANGUAGE

King Lear. The entire speech is an apostrophe to the *poor* (lines 1–5) and to the *rich* (lines 6–9). In apostrophe, we must direct our concentration to the imagined object of our speech, here visualizing clearly the lowly poor, then the exalted rich. This gives the speech two sections, separated by Lear's awareness of himself in lines 5 and 6, and this suggests to the actor the posibility of a physical change to delineate the sections.

The sound and diction figures have already been mentioned, except for what could be considered a hyperbole in the last line—Lear's characteristic scope of thought in showing the heavens themselves *more just.*

The Zoo Story. The speech revolves around the central metaphor concerning God in lines 18–20. Earlier there are two "submerged" metaphors. The first is in line 9, where *toilet paper* "is" a *mirror.* The usual mirror is one in which we see our face, where the world enters us in breathing and eating; toilet paper is a mirror of the orifice through which the world leaves us as excrement, and occasionally, appropriately to Jerry's torment, as blood. The second submerged metaphor is the *strongbox . . . WITHOUT A LOCK* in lines 14–15, a metaphor for accessibility, for the possibility of being "open," just as the woman's *CLOSED DOOR* is an antithetical image. Also, a strongbox that cannot be locked is useless, unable (like Jerry) to fulfill the purpose for which it was created.

Finally, the central metaphor is that *GOD* is *A COLORED QUEEN* and *A WOMAN WHO CRIES*. God, the fulfillment of all human aspirations, of all possibilities of goodness and perfection, is, for Jerry, the choice between illusory, perverted sexual relationships on the one hand, and complete isolation and determined sorrow on the other.

Exercise 50   Figurative language polarization

A. Find ways to physicalize each figure of speech in your selection, so as to communicate its structure and its meaning to your audience. Don't be tied to a realistic delivery; *your aim is to make the figurative language as literal as possible in your performance,* to "release" the wealth of meaning that has been condensed in each figure of speech. Again, remember to involve the physical act of articulating the words of the speech directly in your overall activity. Do *not* separate the words and the actions, but emphasize their interrelationship. The audience should *hear* the effect of your actions on your voice and *see* the effect of your voice on your actions.

B. Again, perform the selection in a "normal" way to allow your body's memory of the polarization to influence the performance.

Like the lesson on rhythm, this brief sojourn into the world of imagery and figurative language has been filled with technical terms and labels. It matters not, however, if you can correctly identify a kinesthetic image or a metaphor if you cannot *experience* it in your whole organism and allow this experience to generate feeling and understanding of the character. Remember that the kinds of sensations which are carried within the character's speech, and the way in which he uses words to achieve meaning through figuration, are profoundly revealing of his way of thinking and feeling. None of this, in other words, is "literary," it is all alive!

Lesson 12

Dramatic Action and Play Structure

So far we have been analyzing the words that are the "building blocks" of the play. Now we are ready to examine the larger pattern of experience they form.

The largest pattern we can perceive in a play is the pattern of its overall shape, the way in which all the elements that make up the play have been combined into an artistically unified whole. This quality of artistic unity, this overall patterning, we will call the play's structure or *organization*.

Although many works of art of the same generic type (for example, Classical tragedy or Restoration comedy) share similar structural conventions, every successful work of art also has its own unique structural identity. The actor, his director, the designers, the technicians, all strive to contribute to a fulfillment of the play's structural unity in an appropriately unified stage production. Therefore, a clear view of the whole play and a clear sense of how your character contributes to the whole must be the foundation of your creation. This is what Stanislavski called your *super-objective:*

> We use the word super-objective to characterize the essential idea, the core, which provided the impetus for the writing of a play. . . . In a play the whole stream of individual minor objectives, all the imaginative thoughts, feelings, and actions of an actor should converge to carry out this super-objective. . . . Also this impetus toward the super-objective must be continuous throughout the whole play.[30]

---

[30]From *An Actor's Handbook* by Constantin Stanislavski, edited and translated by Elizabeth Reynolds Hapgood. Copyright © 1936, 1961, 1963 by Elizabeth Reynolds Hapgood. Used with the permission of the publishers, Theatre Arts Books, New York.

MAIN ACTION AND PLAY STRUCTURE

The arts are distinguished from each other by the materials they use. Any organization of sounds may be music; any organization of words may be literature; any organization of line, mass, and color on a ground may be painting or other graphic art, and so on. The material that distinguishes drama is *human action*; therefore, any organization of human actions may be drama.

Human action is the foundation of all drama. We must remember, though, that *action*, as we use the term, does not refer exclusively to *events*. The great theatrical theorist Francis Fergusson described dramatic action this way:

> The word "action"—praxis—as Aristotle uses it in the *Poetics,* does not mean outward deeds or events, but something much more like "purpose" or "aim." Perhaps our word "motive" suggests most of its meaning. . . .
>
> I remarked that action is not outward deeds or events; but on the other hand, there can be no action without resulting deeds. We guess at a man's action by way of what he does, his outward and visible deeds. We are aware that our own action, or motive, produces deeds of some sort as soon as it exists. Now the plot of a play is the arrangement of outward deeds or incidents, and the dramatist uses it, as Aristotle tells us, as the first means of imitating the action. He arranges a set of incidents which point to the action or motive from which they spring. You may say that the action is the spiritual content of the tragedy—the playwright's inspiration—and the plot defines its existence as an intelligible *play*. Thus, you can never have a play without both plot and action; yet the distinction between plot and action is as fundamental as that between form and matter. The action is the matter; the plot is the "first form," or, as Aristotle puts it, the "soul" of the tragedy.
>
> The dramatist imitates the action he has in mind, first by means of the plot, then in the characters, and finally in the media of language, music, and spectacle. In a well-written play, if we understood it thoroughly, we should perceive that plot, character, diction, and the rest spring from the same source, or, in other words, realize the same action or motive. . . . [31]

The central or *main action* of the entire play, then, is the source from which all else springs, and you must strive to perceive your character as

[31]Francis Fergusson, "*Macbeth* as the Imitation of an Action," *The Art of the Theatre,* eds. Robert W. Corrigan and James L. Rosenberg (New York: Chandler Publishing Co., 1964), pp. 200–201.

an organic part of this main action and the way in which the playwright has organized the action in his play.

It is rarely easy to state the main action of a play in words, for it lives within the entire structure of the drama and was meant to be *experienced*, not *described*. The actor and his director strive to capture the experience of the play's action and should not be unduly concerned if they cannot provide a verbal description of the feeling they are searching for. It will help, however, to remember that in Western drama the main action of a play will usually be embodied in the *central conflict* of the play; identifying this conflict and the way in which it is *resolved* will help us to understand the action it expresses.

CONFLICT AND ACTION

The fundamental shape of a dramatic action, then, is often expressed as a basic conflict that in the course of the play is resolved. In *Oedipus Rex,* for example, we see that famine and plague have descended upon the city; as king, it is the responsibility of Oedipus to find the cause of this misfortune and to alleviate it. We learn that the source of the famine is an unpunished crime, the slaying of the old King Laius. Oedipus now begins to investigate, and the apparent action of the plot is *to purify the city by finding and punishing the guilty man.* In the course of his investigation, however, Oedipus discovers that *he* is the guilty man, that he has unwittingly killed his own father and has married his own mother. We discover that in a deeper sense the main action or "soul" of the play is really man's attempt, as embodied by Oedipus' story, *to know himself.*

The need to know who we are is the deepest conflict and source of action of *Oedipus Rex:* the plot, the characters, the thoughts and feelings, the sounds, and the sights of the play all spring from it. Thus defined, the action of a play is a *source of energy* or *dramatic tension*; it may exist as the tension that *precedes* an event, or even tension that might potentially *become* an event. There are many contemporary plays with few "events" in the traditional sense (Beckett's *Waiting for Godot,* Pinter's *The Collection,* Ionesco's *Victims of Duty,* to name a few), and yet these plays are rich in the dynamic tensions that provide a strong sense of dramatic action.

Every actor in a cast must strive to contact the main action of the play, whatever its form, for it is the deepest and truest source of energy motivating and shaping the life of his character. Further, the actors and their director must strive to realize, *in experience,* the specific quality and shape of the action of the entire play, for only thus can the true meaning of the play be expressed.

ACTION AND MEANING

We will call the specific underlying idea of a play the *theme* of the play. A play's *thematic content* is simply what the playwright was trying to say, and this can take many forms.

For example, the underlying premise or theme of Brecht's *Mother Courage* is the effect of the need to "get along" by "doing business" upon the human character. In Ibsen's *An Enemy of the People,* the central theme is that one man's conscience may be more important than the will of the majority, because the truth is not always determined by majority vote. These are themes in the traditional sense of "message" or *thesis.*

But a *theme* is not always a *thesis,* since not all plays have a "message." A theme, as the underlying premise of the plot of a play, may simply be a situation; the typical Restoration comedy, for example, is based upon the "sex chase" of boy-wants-girl/girl-wants-boy/but-there-are-obstacles-to-overcome, and the entire play is motivated by this premise. In many modern plays, the theme may be only a mood or anxiety; the underlying premise of *Waiting for Godot* is, appropriately, *waiting,* without the possibility of action or knowledge beyond the necessity to wait.

A play may have more than one basic theme, though a director will usually focus his interpretation on one. We have already pointed out that *King Lear* could be viewed as a play about kingship, about the generation gap, about justice, about the development of humanism, as an allegory of judgment day, and so on. With the help of the director, the creative ensemble must focus on a view of the theme or themes of the play and see how each element of the play contributes to it.

One word of caution: the meaning of a great play cannot be stated simply. When we discussed the themes of several plays just now, we were only stating in oversimplified terms one aspect of each play's structure. The true meaning of a play lives only in the *experience* of it as a theatrical event, and the play's dynamism, as we have seen, springs from a main action expressed through a central conflict.

The nature of a play's conflict is related to the play's thematic content. A Shaw play may achieve its sense of conflict through the interplay of *ideas* represented by various characters; a Beckett play may use the attempts of the characters to cope with their *situation* as the basic conflict; in an O'Neill play, the conflict may arise from the *psychology* of the characters themselves. Whatever its source, the play's conflict is the working out in dramatic action of the thematic content of the play.

A play is a meaningful organization of human action, usually related to a conflict, character, or theme, or any combination of these.

THE ORGANIZATION OF ACTION IN PLOT

Because of the nature of the material of drama, a *play's structural unity depends on how its human action has been organized* and how all the other elements of the play (the characters, their thoughts and feelings, the way in which they express themselves, and all that the audience hears and sees) contribute to that organization, or *plot.*

The organization of a play's plot may be based upon several principles. Oscar Brockett has suggested three in his *The Theatre: An Introduction:*

> Traditionally, the dominant organizational principle has been the *cause-to-effect* arrangement of incidents. Using this method, the playwright sets up in the opening scenes all of the necessary conditions—the situation, the desires and motivations of the characters—out of which the later events develop. The goals of one character come into conflict with those of another, or two conflicting desires within the same character may lead to a crisis. Attempts to surmount the obstacles make up the substance of the play, each scene growing logically out of those which have preceded it.
>
> Less often, a dramatist uses a *character* as the principal source of unity. In this case, the incidents are held together primarily because they center around one person. Such a play may dramatize the life of an historical figure, or it may show a character's responses to a series of experiences. This kind of organization may be seen in such plays as Christopher Marlowe's *Doctor Faustus* and *Tamburlaine.*
>
> A playwright may organize his material around a *basic idea,* with the scenes linked largely because they illustrate aspects of a larger theme or argument. This type of organization is used frequently by modern playwrights, especially those of the Expressionist, Epic, and Absurdist movements.[32]

Of course, most plays use all three of these organizational principles to a greater or lesser degree. The last, organization around a *basic idea,* has become increasingly important in the modern theatre. This basic idea may be *social* or *political,* as in Brecht's *Good Woman of Setzuan* or Shaw's *Major Barbara,* or *philosophical,* as in Camus's *Caligula* or Sartre's *No Exit;* it may be *moral,* an examination of the values of a society or of human relationships, as in Miller's *Death of a Salesman,* Albee's *American Dream,* or Van Itallie's *America Hurrah.*

The second principle, organization around a *character,* is rare as a dominant principle, but most plays do tend to focus on one character, so that

[32]From THE THEATRE, Second Edition, by Oscar G. Brockett. Copyright © 1964, 1969 by Holt, Rinehart and Winston, Inc. Reprinted by permission of Holt, Rinehart and Winston, Inc.

this is a common secondary source of organization. Plays that focus on a character's psychology, however, like the later plays of O'Neill, have a strong sense of character as a principal source of unity. It even seems as if the action of such plays was created in order to reveal character. This aspect of psychological realism may be seen as a reversal of the classical sense of action as the main focus with characterization being only the "servant" of action.

The first type of play organization mentioned above, the *cause-to-effect* plot, is by far the most common. The shape of this type of plot can be charted as in figure 30: if we follow the rise and fall of the dynamic tension of the play as the action moves forward in time, we see a period of rising tension (what Aristotle called "the raveling,") and a period of falling tension or resolution (which Aristotle called "the unraveling.")

As in the graph, the action is often set in motion by an *inciting incident* (in *Oedipus*, the occurrence of the famine; in *Lear*, the dividing of the kingdom; in *The Zoo Story*, the encounter of Peter and Jerry). There follows a sequence of episodes or *cycles of actions*, individual scenes in which the conflict begins to heighten and complications may develop. *Each of these episodes may itself exhibit the shape of a miniature play, with its own rise and fall of tension, but each contributes in its turn to the overall shape of the whole play.*

When the conflict (and therefore the *suspense* of "what will happen?") is approaching its height, a *crisis* occurs; this is literally a turning point, an event that makes the eventual resolution of the play's conflict inevitable. This is not the same as the *climax*, which is the actual moment at which

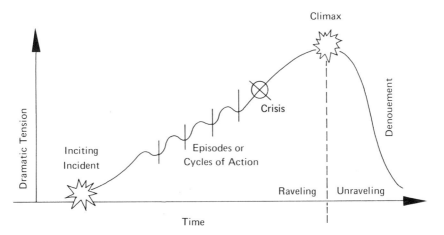

FIGURE 30   Traditional Aristotelian sectional form.

the basic conflict *is* resolved. These two moments, crisis and climax, may be quite *close* (as in *The Zoo Story,* where the appearance of the knife signals the inevitability of Jerry's death, followed shortly by the actual death) or they may be *separated* in time (as in *Lear,* in which the crisis is the banishment of Cordelia in scene 1—for after this event the rest of the action is inevitable—and the climax, which is the death of Lear at the very end of the play).

The climax is always the emotional high point of the play; the crisis, on the other hand, may be merely a structural device. In *Romeo and Juliet,* for example, the crisis occurs offstage—when Friar Lawrence's letter explaining the sleeping potion fails to reach Romeo—and is only reported later.

Following the climax, the dynamic tension of the play falls as the "loose ends" of plot and character are resolved. This section, called the denouement, may also be used to comment upon the action or even to summarize the thematic content of the play, although many plays have only a brief denouement and some have no denouement at all (for example, *Waiting for Godot* literally ends in a moment of unresolved crisis: "let's go . . . [They do not move]").

This fundamental shape of rising and falling action is of great importance to the actor, for it is also the shape of a single scene, of a section within a scene, of a single moment: it is, in fact, a fundamental shape of human energy—an orgasm, the contraction and relaxation of a muscle, and the breath itself. We see this shape in dance, in a symphony, in all the "temporal arts" in which energy flows through time.

It is the shape of life itself.

Exercise 51 Play structure polarization

I. Using the play from which your speech or scene was taken, answer the following:

A. What is the dominant principle of the play's organization: plot, character, or idea?
B. What is the *main action* of the play?
C. Does the play have an *inciting incident*?
D. What is the *basic conflict* of the play?
E. What is the *moment of crisis*?
F. What is the *climax*?
G. What is the *resolution*?

II. Prepare a movement/sound expression of the over-all shape of the play: try to "boil it down" to one gestural phrase of perhaps ten to thirty seconds duration that expresses the energy-shape of the play (as in figure 30).

III.   As you perform this polarization, ask those who watch to draw a graph of your effort-shape; how does the chart they produce compare to the shape of the play, were you to make a chart of it like that in figure 30?

Note: If you have been working alone on a speech, you should now find a partner who will join you in working on your *scene* for the remaining exercises in this book.

ACTION AND CHARACTER

Dramatic action, and the conflict or theme related to it, cannot exist without *characters* who perform the action. A character may not necessarily *cause* an action, any more than a pendulum causes itself to swing, but he will always serve as a "vehicle" or *agent* for the action in which he is involved. In this way, character is the *material* out of which action is made, and the demands of the action determine the *form* the character will take.

The way the character has been formed by the playwright is largely determined by this fact. *Characters are constructed so that they can believably serve as agents for, and sometimes even seem to cause, the action of their play.* We can call this the *dramatic purpose* of a character.

This idea of *purpose* is of primary importance. Very often actors approach their characters so personally that they begin to forget the larger purpose for which that character was created. A character as an element of a larger action has an overall dramatic function related to the plot of his play. He may serve as a "foil," frustrating the intentions of another character; he may be the spokesman for one of several conflicting points of view; he may simply serve to provide some essential information, like the classical messenger, and not be directly involved in the action himself; he may be a *raisonneur* who acts as the playwright's spokesman. There are a number of dramatic purposes characters may serve, and the true life of a character is derived *only* from fulfillment of this purpose.

No matter how "alive" a portrayal may be at any given moment, if all the moments do not "add up" to fulfill the character's dramatic purpose the actor has failed as an interpreter (however well he may have succeeded as an impersonator). In fact, the entire play is bound to fail in this case, since a play, like any mechanism, "works" only when every part has performed its job in its proper relationship with every other part. The ultimate expression of a character's dramatic purpose must live as *specific actions* contributing to the *entire experience* of the play.

Your purpose in studying the language and structure of the play and the actions of which the play is composed is to develop an understanding, a *feeling* really, of the world in which your character lives and the action and purpose that make him truly alive. As your understanding of action deepens, it enables you to become more and more *specific* about what you are doing on stage every moment, for life on the stage must be as vivid and specific as your own real life—in fact, your stage life must be *more* purposefully clear than "real" life, for why else would we need the theatre?

Lesson 13

The Hierarchy of Dramatic Action

The overall energy-shape of the main action of a play is created by the cumulative effect of a number of smaller action-patterns, each of which is in turn created by yet smaller action patterns. This hierarchy of actions begins with the "smallest" pattern, the individual *moment*. These *moments* work together to form logical units of action called *beats*, the beats working together to form *scenes*, the scenes working together to form the overall or *main* action of the play. You must analyze each of these levels as you prepare your performance.

Compare the hierarchy of dramatic activities to the structure of a piece of literature. Phrases make up sentences, just as *momentary activities* make up the smallest logical units of action possessing their own shape and meaning, called *beats;* sentences make up paragraphs, just as beats string together to make a *scene;* paragraphs work together to develop a story's main theme, just as scenes work together to express the *main action* of the play.

Each of these units of action may have the same basic shape as an entire play, each with its own crisis and mini-climax. As you examine the shaping of the play's action, you must see how each moment relates to the whole. In this way, your understanding of the way the patterns of actions interrelate will help you to develop an actable understanding of your character's action, moment by moment, permitting you to realize fully the shape and quality of each such moment of your performance while simultaneously contributing to a clear expression of the larger patterns of action formed by those moments.

You have already experienced the principles being dealt with here in the earlier section on "Shaping Movement for the Stage" in lesson 3, and you may find it useful to review this section and to repeat exercise 14 using your new understanding of how the action of a play is shaped.

Exercise 52   Shaping action; moments

Review exercise 14. Using the same principles, select a single moment from the scene you have selected, having already read the play carefully.

    A. How does this moment grow out of the previous moment?
    B. How does it lead into the following moments?
    C. What is the *shape* of this moment?

DEFINING BEATS: SAMPLE BEAT ANALYSIS

We have said that moments fit together in patterns of action called *beats*. Some think that this word was a mispronunciation of what Stanislavski called *bits* (meaning small particles) of action. We might compare moments and beats as if they were atoms and molecules: a molecule, composed of a number of atoms, is the smallest particle of matter that still has its own identifiable characteristics; just so, a beat is comprised of moments and is the smallest unit of action that has its own complete shape and specific subject.

Another way of defining a beat is to say that it is one complete link in the chain of cause and effect that moves the traditional plot; from the actor's point of view, this means that a beat is *one unit of action/reaction;* one character does something (commits an action) that evokes a reaction. The reaction, in its turn, functions as another action, evoking yet another reaction, and so the plot moves forward, with each action/reaction link in the chain being one beat.

In part 3 we will see how you can translate a beat into a unit of *playable intention or reaction* that relates to the inner life of your character, but before you can make such a translation you must be able to recognize a beat as a unit of action within the "architecture" of the play itself. Perhaps the easiest way to think of the beats within a scene is to think of making a topic outline or *scenario* of the scene; for example, in the scene from *King Lear* in which our sample speech occurs, a scenario would look like this:

King Lear, act 3, scene 4:
1. Kent tries to get Lear into the hovel: Lear refuses (lines 1–27).
2. Lear prays, realizes how little he has understood (28–36).
3. Edgar is discovered, disguised as Mad Tom, and plays out his disguise (37–62).

4. Lear relates Edgar's condition to his own, condemns the flesh for begetting evil, a sentiment and comparison that Edgar echoes (63–102).
5. Lear generalizes their condition to that of mankind, begins to tear his clothes ("expose thyself") despite the Fool's restraint (103–16).
6. Gloucester enters; Edgar, fearful of being recognized by his father, sets up a "smokescreen" of ravings (116–45).
7. Gloucester is appalled at Lear's company and condition, rebels against Goneril and Regan by offering Lear shelter and food; Lear pays no attention, converses with Mad Tom, despite Kent's urging to take Gloucester's offer (146–64).
8. Kent and Gloucester commiserate on Lear's and their own condition (165–74).
9. Gloucester again beseeches Lear to enter, but Lear wants to stay with Mad Tom; Kent suggests they all go together, which they do.

Each of these items is one beat, one link in the cause-to-effect chain that moves the scene. We will see later that each beat is also one unit of action/reaction for the characters involved, and that each of *the characters involved in each beat has a single intention or point of reaction.* It is this fact that permits the actors to translate the architecture of the scene into the thoughts and actions of their characters, and in this way all the actors may share a common understanding of how the action of the scene has been shaped. This shared understanding helps to produce clear rhythm and meaningfully shaped flow of action within the scene.

We could call this the *phraseology* of the action, and it is as important for actors to agree on the phraseology of their shared action as it is for members of an orchestra to work together so that the phraseology of each player contributes properly to the overall effect of the musical piece.

If you examine each beat from this *Lear* scene, you see that each is like a miniature play with its own crisis. Beat number 2 happens to be comprised almost entirely of the speech we have been studying; this is unusual, since a beat is usually a *transaction* between two or more characters. (We could say, of course, that there are almost two characters speaking within this speech, the "old" Lear and the "new" Lear.) In any case, we can see how this soliloquy has *its own shape* (with the crisis occurring at "O, I have taken/too little care of this") and *its own central action* (in this case, the interior action of Lear's self-realization). These are two qualities of all beats that are important to you: a beat has a central *beat action* of its own, which usually motivates a *transaction* (action/reaction) between two or more characters, and it has its own clear shape and *specific moment of crisis. If you*

*and your partners can agree on the central action of a beat and the specific shape
and moment of crisis, then you will have laid the foundation for a clear phraseology.*

Exercise 53   Shaping action; beats

Using the scene you selected in exercise 47, work with your scene
partner and

    A. Make a scenario of the scene;
    B. Select one beat and
       1. define its *beat action;*
       2. specify the *moment of crisis* it contains;
    C. Examine how this beat grows out of the preceeding beat and
       flows into the following beat;
    D. Rehearse the beat on the basis of this analysis.

SCENE ANALYSIS

We will define a "scene" as *a grouping of beats within which one major
segment of the play's total action occurs.* There are a number of other ways of
defining scenes, however: most older plays have been divided into scenes
that *usually,* but not always, fit our definition; a short play, like *Zoo Story,*
is not divided into scenes by the playwright, but it may be convenient for
the actors to do so ("the Story of Jerry and the Dog" might be thought of
as one "scene," for example). The traditional "French scene," by the way,
is merely the period of time between the entrance of one major character
and another.

According to our definition, however, we can analyze a scene in the
same way we analyzed a beat: each scene is a major item in the "scenario"
of the entire play, each has its own central motivating *scene action* (and
often a *scene conflict*), and each has its own clear shape and *moment of crisis.*
A clear sense of the scene action and placement of scene crisis will help
you to experience the scene as one flowing unit of action. One effect of
such an analysis is that the scene will seem "shorter" to you when you
perform it!

The *scene action* in the Lear scene is *to find shelter;* the individual actions
of each character in each beat can be seen in relation to this scene action.
The *crisis* of this scene is therefore at the very last moment, when Lear

agrees to go to the shelter. Only when the actors have agreed on such a shared understanding of the form of the scene can they focus their energies in the common task; they literally know then where they are going and where they are coming from.

As important as this shared sense of structure is, you must also see how each scene demonstrates some aspect of the thematic content and main action of the play, so that you are responding not only to the *form* of your scene, but to the way in which its *meaning* embraces the thematic content of the play as a whole. The scene from *Lear,* for example, moves the plot by bringing Lear to shelter (and hiding), but it also expands on two major themes: the deception of parents by their children (including the actual deception of Gloucester by Edgar's disguise) and the idea of "exposing" the truth, of knowing what is real. Compare Kent in disguise, Edgar in disguise, Gloucester betraying the commands of his queens, Lear's hallucinations, and the "genuine madness" of the Fool—in this and the following hovel scene, Shakespeare presents us with four simultaneous levels of reality, no one of which could be claimed as more "real" than another.

Exercise 54   Shaping action; scenes

Using the same scene you selected earlier,

A. How does this scene grow out of the previous scene, and how does it lead into the following scene?
B. What is the *scene action,* and how does it relate to the main action of the play? What is the *scene conflict?*
C. Examine your scenario of the beats or the scene: What is the *moment of crisis* of the scene? How is the scene *resolved?*
D. Discuss how this scene serves the *thematic* content of the play as a whole.
E. Rehearse the scene on the basis of this analysis.

PLAY ANALYSIS

In the last three exercises, you have examined a moment, a beat, and a scene from a particular play. Now apply your sense of structure to the whole hierarchy of actions in the play.

Exercise 55   Hierarchy of actions polarization

I. Play analysis

A. Construct a chart of your play, as in figure 30.
B. Select the scene within which the crisis of the play occurs and construct a chart of it.
C. Select the beat that contains the crisis, and repeat the charting exercise.
D. Construct a final chart of the specific moment of crisis.

II. Polarization. Condense your understanding of the shape of the entire play into a few massive, simple movement phrases in which you and your partner physicalize the shape of the play by enacting or dancing its main conflict, crisis, and resolution. Again, don't be literal; experience in a simplified, massive way the energy-shape of the entire play.

SECTIONAL AND LINEAR FORMS

We have been concentrating on the traditional cause-to-effect type of plot organization that has the usual Aristotelian shape of rising and falling action. This type of organization is fundamentally *sectional,* with one segment of action growing out of another, each serving its function in the overall scheme of the play's shape. In many ways, the traditional Aristotelian shape resembles the musical form of the sonata (also a common symphonic form), whose themes follow an a-b-a' pattern. Figure 31 compares the two.

	SONATA	PLAY
A	*Statement* of theme	*Exposition* of situation
		Introduction of main characters
B	*Development* and variations on theme; new keys	Cycles of action; conflict and complication mount
	Return to tonic key	Crisis
A'	*Recapitulation* of main theme	*Climax* resolves conflict; denouement

FIGURE 31   Comparison of sonata and Aristotelian play form.

Each of these sections in the sonata, as in the play, is more or less distinct, and the passage from one section to the other is usually discernible. There is another fundamental form, however, that functions on an entirely different principle than the sectional form: in music, this is called *linear* form. It was introduced in music in the nineteenth century, and we do not see its use as a dominant structural form in the drama until well into the twentieth century.

In linear form, the single main theme is replaced by a number of more or less coequal themes called *motive-lines.* The shape of the piece is achieved not by a sequence of sections but by an interweaving of these motive-lines. Compare the charts in figure 30 and figure 32 for a visual representation of the difference between sectional and linear forms.

As the charts indicate, both sectional and linear forms can provide a sense of resolution at their conclusions, but they achieve this effect in different ways. Both first arouse tensions: sectional forms through the suspense generated by conflict, and linear forms through the tensions between the various motive-lines as they interweave with one another. Both then may resolve these tensions: sectional forms by resolving the main conflict, and linear forms by allowing the various motive-lines to *converge* in one massive statement.

Perhaps the best example of linear form in the drama is Beckett's *Waiting for Godot,* in which the various motive-lines (to stay or to go, to sleep or to wake, to play a game or not, etc.) converge in the final existential question, to live or to die.

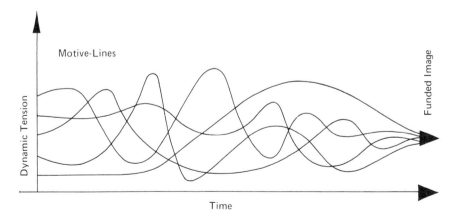

FIGURE 32   A representation of linear form.

Even in this example, however, we see that a *sectional* analysis as we described it earlier can also be of use to the actor, since the action of *Waiting for Godot* can also be viewed in terms of scenes and beats (e.g., the "tree" scenes, which recur in both acts, and the "shoe" scenes, the "carrot" scenes, the "exercise" scenes, and all other recurring scenes).

All predominantly sectional plays also share some aspects of linear form. In *Lear,* for instance, we see the recurring themes of judgment, age versus youth, naturalness, etc., flowing through the play and enriching its texture. We can say, then, that all plays share both sectional and linear structures, and that *plots* are almost always sectional in construction, while *thematic content* can usually be described in a linear way.

Exercise 56   Tracing themes

Using the play-chart you created in the previous exercises, identify the basic themes, especially those that recur several times.
Graphically lay the interweaving of themes over your sectional chart. What do you learn about the play's structure that would be useful in playing your role?

SUMMARY OF PART TWO

This concludes your examination of the text, the "actor's blueprint." From all this, do you begin to feel how the parts go together to make the whole? Aristotle described language as the material of drama; have you begun to experience the meaning, feelings, rhythms, sounds, associations, and structures of the text, and the actions that the words carry, as elements of one unified whole? In a great play, each of these elements is an organic, inseparable part of the whole; when we analyze the play, we artificially focus our attention on one aspect or another, but we must never lose sight of its place within the whole. In other words, *analysis* (the "taking apart") must always be balanced by a sense of *synthesis* (the "putting together").

Only in this way can your performance also become one unified whole, with each line, each action serving your super-objective. Remember Stanislavski's statement from the opening of lesson 12:

> In a play the whole stream of individual minor objectives, all the imaginative thoughts, feelings, and actions of an actor should converge to carry out this super-objective. . . .

In part 3 we turn to the specific techniques that will help you to achieve this by translating the results of your analysis into a purposeful and unified stage creation, the synthesis in living experience of all that your analysis of the text has inspired in you and your partners.

PART THREE

The Actor at Work

THE NEED FOR FOCUS

Imagine a bare light bulb burning in a room; the light it produces doesn't have much effect because it flows in all directions at once. But when I put a reflector behind it and a lens in front of it, I can channel most of its light in one direction, producing a greater effect. I have also made the light more controllable, for the beam of my spotlight can now be colored, shaped, and focused upon a specific objective.

The energies you possess as a human being and as an actor need the same kind of *focus,* a single direction or channel through which they may flow toward a specific objective. When your energy is focused or *concentrated* in this way, it becomes—like the spotlight beam—more easily shaped, colored, and directed; you feel more purposeful and potent because you *are* more effective.

Purposeful focus of energy has the further value of synthesizing a wide variety of skills and values, uniting them in a single action. The baseball hitter, for instance, continuously rehearses his stance, his grip, his swing, even his breathing; he studies the opposing pitchers and learns their patterns; at the plate, he takes note of the wind, the light, and the position of the fielders; but as he actually begins to swing at a pitch, he ceases to deal with all these matters separately and instead focuses his immediate and single awareness on his task. His swing becomes a total simultaneous action of mind and body into which flow all his awareness of the immediate situation and all of his rehearsed and intuitive skills. All become synthesized into a single rhythmic gesture of purposefully focused energy.

In this moment of totally focused action, he is not oblivious to the reality of his situation; rather, his focus of attention allows him to perceive the many "background" elements within his field of attention as a single flowing pattern to which he can continuously and automatically adjust as he surrenders himself totally to "being there" in his action. All his physical and psychical energies flow effortlessly through his single point of concentration into the whole field of his activity.

If he permits himself to be distracted (which means literally "turned away from the original focus of attention") his action loses its force, effectiveness, and controllability; it loses its unity and its rhythm.

You are rarely as totally focused as the athlete at the moment of making his play, but we can all recall experiences during which we were totally "tuned in" to something; think back to such a time when you were drawn beyond yourself. You felt your energies being naturally drawn forth; you felt yourself integrating with your world, which may have become, for a time at least, an effortless, simultaneous rhythmic flow of life energies out of you as well as into you.

On the stage you strive always for such an acuteness and completeness of experience. You owe such fullness to your audience as well as to yourself and your fellow actors, for whatever your *play* may be saying to them about their world, your *performance* should be reminding them of their own potential aliveness. Your art is the art of self-definition, of control over personal reality, and when you exercise your craft and art to its fullest potential you awaken in your witnesses a reminder of their own spiritual capability.

As an actor, then, you are in this respect like the athlete; *you must find a single point of focus through which your deepest energies may flow, carrying with them a wealth of rehearsed activity, intuitive skills, developed knowledge, and a continuous adjustment to the flowing pattern of your immediate reality.*

The athlete finds this focus in making his play; you find it in committing a *dramatic action.*

Once you begin to find focus through dramatic action, you will find that your energy flows easily into the scene. There it interacts (*transacts*) with the energy of others, which in turn flows back to you and becomes a source of new action. This interrelatedness of action, both verbal and nonverbal, moves the entire play; each of your character's actions causes a *reaction* in another character, or within your own character, or both. Each *reaction* serves in turn as a new *action,* causing yet another reaction, and so on. In this way, the transactions of energy between the characters in their situation moves forward the plot of the play.

It is as you begin to *experience* this flow of action that you begin to make the best discoveries, for only then are you truly being moved beyond yourself, taking inspiration from the energies of others and from the play itself, and thereby participating in a whole that is greater than the sum of its parts.

Under the influence of such an experience you can be swept beyond yourself and begin to discover not only what you already *are,* but also what you may *become* as your character, that new version of yourself, grows.

You can begin to experience such focused energy flow very early in the rehearsal process if you learn to make some tentative working definitions of action. These early definitions are, of course, liable to later adjustment or even rejection, but they are designed to help you begin exploring your scene and character through *experience* as quickly as possible. Don't think that you must do everything perfectly the first time. If you do, you will begin at once to protect yourself against the unknown of experience with the illusion of a clear intellectual plan. While your rehearsal exploration is certainly *guided* by prior analysis that gives you a sense of direction and purpose, nevertheless your rehearsal must be more than the mere enactment of your premeditated plan. If it is not, you will be doomed to achieve only so much as you can already imagine, to be only so much as you already are.

It is your ability to recognize *playable actions* that liberates you to begin a free yet efficient exploration.

Lesson 14

The Process of Action

If you recall our discussion of dramatic action in lesson 12, you will remember Francis Fergusson's statement that "we guess at a man's action by way of what he does, his outward and visible deeds."

When you begin work on a play, you encounter first the external activities of your character (the things he does, the words he speaks), since these are the things most clearly communicated by the author's text. We assume, however, that the playwright has provided activities that are natural or "organic" extensions of the character's inner action. It is your job, then, to work back from the given externals communicated by the text, through an understanding of your character's decisions and choices, all the way back to the original stimuli that motivated the action. You then must experience these motivational sources for yourself, allowing your deepest personal energies to mingle with and be extended by your experience of the character's action, then live through the whole process that leads back to the external activities required by the form of the play.

Remember that each character in a play is a source of energy having a specific function in relation to the whole; the personality of the character serves to filter that energy as it passes into the play as activity, endowing it with those qualities that make it contribute most meaningfully to the movement and purpose of the whole. The richness and vitality of this external activity will be largely determined by how well you experience the whole process of "inner" action that must precede it.

Sit for a moment and bring your attention to some need or desire; perhaps you are thirsty, or hungry, or need some fresh air; whatever it may be, allow this *felt need* to grow in you until it is sufficiently strong that you act to satisfy it.

You have acted, and by your action you have created an event. You felt a need, or what we shall call a *stimulus,* which aroused your energy and gave you purpose or *intention.* In this case, your stimulus was entirely internal, but such purely internal stimuli are very rare in the drama; in the

190

vast majority of cases, your stage stimulus will arise as a *reaction* to some external event or, even more often, to the action of another character. Having been stimulated, your aroused *needful energy* caused you to *survey alternative courses of action* by which the aroused need could be satisfied. You then made your decision to act in a certain way, your *choice*. Having made your choice, you released your pent-up energy into the outer world in the form of *purposeful activity* directed toward an *objective*. Your activity collided with circumstance and the result was an *event*.

That is the whole process of action: *a purposefully focused energy arising in response to a stimulus, which, through a process of choice, results in directed activity toward an objective, creating an event.* .

You have served as the agent of the action, since the energy of the action has flowed through you. In doing so, this energy took on specific qualities that were expressive of your character. Thus it is that on the stage, as in life, character is most vividly and truthfully expressed through action. There is an old maxim that the bad playwright *tells* you a man is a villain, while the good playwright *shows* him kicking a dog. You cannot simply go on stage and "be" a villain; you must *do* something villainous. The dynamic nature of theatre is such that you must achieve and fulfill your dramatic purpose through action.

THE INNER PHASE OF ACTION

The process of action has several phases, and each is potentially expressive of character. There is an "inner" phase in which a stimulus arouses a needful energy; this aroused energy pushes you toward a choice to act (or not to act) in order to satisfy (or to suppress) the felt need. If the character's decision is *not* to act (as it is surprisingly often), then the needful energy is suppressed and becomes a source of continued dramatic tension. If the decision is *to* act, there follows an "outer" phase of action in which the inner action of the character becomes an *observable activity.*

Let us examine the inner phase of action and the ways it is expressive of character. Think back to the simple action you just thought about, and see how your personality was expressed in each of these aspects of its inner phase:

1. *The nature of the stimulus.* What sorts of stimuli affect you most? Contrariwise, to which are you *un*responsive?
2. *The response to the stimulus.* What values were expressed in the nature of your response? What general emotional character was expressed by your response—how do you typically "take things"?

3. *The alternatives you examined.* There were presumably various ways you might have chosen to satisfy your needs and you probably, at least briefly and perhaps "unconsciously," examined each; you at least had the alternative of *not* doing anything. These alternatives were themselves expressive of your character, since they are an "inventory" of the way you see your world; perhaps there were also alternatives that you characteristically *failed* to see.

4. *The nature of the choice itself.* What values were expressed in your choice? How was it characteristic of you? What factors influenced it the most?

Since the choice of action is the crucial moment at which the inner phase of action ends and the outer phase of activity begins, it is the specific moment most deeply expressive of character. We can list a number of factors that may influence any particular decision to act, and you should carefully examine such influences as a way of coming to understand your character's world. These influential factors may be *internal* to the character, or *externally* related to the environment as created by the playwright:

A. Internal factors influencing action:
   1. Need, desire, or other internal stimuli
   2. Social background of character
   3. Ethical values of character
   4. Physiology of character
   5. Psychological peculiarities and/or "way of thinking" of character
B. External factors influencing action:
   1. Relationships with or attitudes toward other characters
   2. The social environment
   3. The physical environment
   4. Specific immediate circumstances
   5. The style or genre of the play
   6. The character's dramatic purpose in the play
   7. The demands of theatricality

The last three are clearly "actor" considerations rather than "character" factors, but it is part of your job to synthesize your concerns as a performer (to be seen, heard, stylistically appropriate, etc.) until they become an organic part of your character's world and of the character itself. All these influential factors will be examined in greater detail in the later lesson on characterization.

The process of action begins in the inner phase, and all the factors we have listed conspire to give the inner action of your character a unique and personal quality, making it different from the same impulse experienced by someone else, or different from the same impulse experienced at a different time or place.

INNER ACTION BECOMES EXTERNAL ACTIVITY THROUGH CHOICE

Once you have made the choice to act, your energy passes beyond your skin and into the outside world where it takes the form of a purposeful activity (*intention*) directed toward an *objective*. We can say, then, that the choice to act is the end of the inner, private phase of action and the beginning of the outer phase of *activity* that is public and observable to your witnesses.

The nature of the choice of action or response made at the moment of decision determines the form of the external activity that follows. It is also the moment of greatest expressiveness of character on the stage, as in life. Here is what therapist Moshe Feldenkrais has to say about the decision-making process:

> This delay between thought process and its translation into action is long enough to make it possible to inhibit it. The possibility of creating the image of an action and then delaying its execution is the basis for imagination and for intellectual judgment (choice). . . .
>
> The possibility of a pause between the creation of a thought pattern for any particular action and the execution of that action is the physical basis for self-awareness. . . .
>
> The possibility of delaying action, prolonging the period between the intention and its execution enables man to know himself.[33]

Feldenkrais mentions the possibility of "inhibiting action," of choosing *not* to do something. The decision to *not* act upon an impulse is made with surprising frequency on the stage, since it is a device that aids the heightening of dramatic tension and suspense. When a character chooses to suppress an impulse, that unresolved energy tends to build up within him and to become a source of increasing dynamic tension. In fact, if all dramatic characters chose to act upon most of their impulses, plays would be a great deal shorter and less suspenseful than they are. We will discuss this in greater detail in the lesson on emotion.

[33]Moshe Feldenkrais, *Awareness through Movement* (New York: Harper & Row, 1972), pp. 45–46.

In any case, the choice *not* to act is perfectly serviceable to the actor; it represents a sort of "temporary" crisis by which aroused energy is held in abeyance. Viewed in this way, we may say that *there are no passive characters on the stage, there are only characters who choose not to act.* Think, for instance, of the scene in which Hamlet chooses *not* to kill the praying Claudius despite a perfect opportunity to do so; does this scene lack dramatic tension or playable action merely because "nothing happens" in the gross sense? Quite the contrary, the agony of Hamlet's choice is a source of enormously compelling drama.

It is this inherently dramatic quality of a difficult decision that is the central feature of most plays (including comedies). When your character is presented with a choice, you must identify for yourself his various alternatives and come to understand his attitude toward each. In this way you can capture fully the tension of his choice, which is an important source of suspense and a profound expression of his character. In short, think not only about what your character *does*, but also about what he chooses *not* to do—for *every* choice of any significance involves negation as well as affirmation.

We mentioned that the choice to act largely determines the nature of the external activity that follows. For this reason, the moment of choice that precedes activity is the moment at which the actor makes most of his necessary *adjustments*, changes in his behavior that serve the needs of his characterization, his fellow actors, the demands of his dramatic purpose, or the requirements of the theatre itself. If the director, for instance, yells, "Louder!" you do not merely say the line more loudly. You review the choice or stimulus from which the line springs and *adjust* that choice so that the line *must* be said more loudly.

You can also make adjustments at other points within the inner phase of action. You can often change your response to your initial stimulus; perhaps *reacting* differently will produce a better *activity*. Further, since your stimulus is almost always the action of another character, you can even make adjustments by requesting a change in the initiating stimulus, by asking your fellow actor to provide you with a stimulus that will move you more readily toward the desired goal.

We make adjustments constantly in the course of rehearsal, and even in the course of performance. We make them for the sake of our audience, for the sake of our fellow actors, and for the sake of our own creativity. Every actor must be ready to assist his fellows in making adjustments, for we must give to each other whatever is needed to best fulfill our stage tasks. The action/reaction chain of cause and effect that moves the play binds the actors inseparably to each other, and each has the right to receive —and the obligation to give—what will best serve the common purpose.

It is in the inner phase of the action—in the nature of the stimulus, in the response to the stimulus, or in the nature of the choice that precedes activity—that adjustments must be made. If we alter only the form of our activity without adjusting the process from which it springs, the resultant activity will seem forced, unnatural, and incomplete.

ACTIVITY PRODUCES EVENTS

Once your inner action has, through the process of choice, become an external activity, it becomes vulnerable to many influences. Just as we were able to list possible factors influencing inner action, we can describe those factors that may influence external activity; moreover, just as the factors influencing inner action were expressive of your character's personality, so the factors influencing his activity are expressive of the world in which he lives and his relationship to that world.

Think back to the simple action you thought of at the beginning of this lesson; how did each of these items influence your activity?

1. *The physical environment.* What was the influence of your place, the time, the climate, surrounding objects, etc.?
2. *The sociological climate.* What were the influences of custom, of your status in society, of your upbringing?
3. *The social environment.* Did the actions or presence of others influence what you did?

This last is of tremendous importance to the actor. In a play, the action moves through the *transactions* of characters; your character's action may be thwarted, redirected, or supported by other characters, consciously or unconsciously. Your character's attitude toward other characters is itself profoundly expressive of his personality; in fact, you can often learn more about your character by examining his relationships with others than from looking only at him. We will examine this later, in the lesson on characterization.

Influenced by the physical, sociological, and social aspects of his environment, your character's activity collides with his immediate circumstance, including the actions of others. The result of this collision is the *dramatic event,* it is "what happens." Events are therefore the end of action, the form in which the energy springing from the initiating stimulus expends itself. The character's personality and the influential factors of his environment become part and parcel of the event itself.

Thus action and event at last become one. Prior to the culmination of

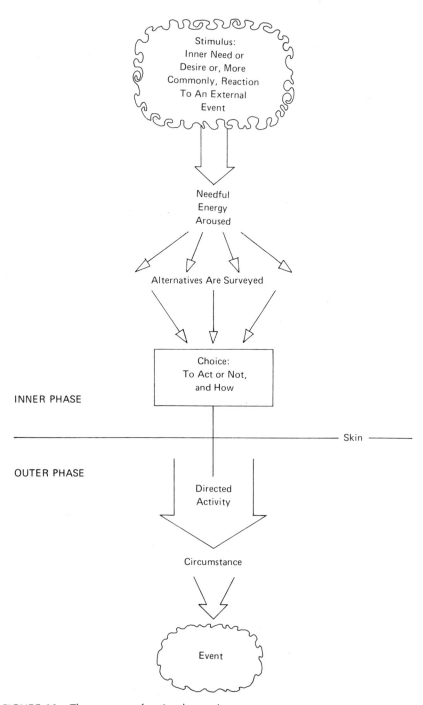

FIGURE 33   The process of action becoming event.

the process of action in an event, however, we see again (as we discussed in lesson 12) that action and events are not identical but are rather *different phases of one process.* We can summarize this process in the causal chain outlined in figure 33.

EVENTS LINK TO FORM A SCENE

As we discussed in lesson 12, the structure of most plots is based upon the causal connection of one event to another: because "A" happens, "B" happens, and so on. This interconnectedness of events produces a *flow* of action, since a skillful playwright has shaped the sequence of events so that it seems "organic" (or, as Aristotle put it, *necessary*) no matter how surprising the events may seem at first. When all the actors participating in the action experience how their individual actions support and are drawn into the flow of the events surrounding one segment of the plot that has its own central conflict and crisis, then they are experiencing a *scene.*

To fulfill its dramatic function truly, however, a scene needs more than just an organic flow: it also needs a sense of urgency, significance, or rising tension that provides *momentum.* A scene lacking in momentum feels "flabby" and fails to compel our attention: we commonly call this a lack of *pace.*

It is wise for the actors to analyze the energy-structure of a scene to discover how the playwright has guaranteed momentum. Most commonly, he will have achieved this through the use of some sort of conflict: the energy of one character may be in opposition to the energy of another (as in arguing, pursuading, or rejecting), or the energy of a character may encounter some obstacle in the situation itself (as in striving, avoiding, or even waiting). Whatever the case, the actors must experience the condition that provides momentum as part of the intrinsic reality of the scene, thus avoiding an artificial heightening of energy through merely rushing or "hyping up" the action. The real source of a scene's momentum, in other words, is within the reality of the scene itself, not in any external technique applied by the actors. A good playwright usually will have provided a source of momentum if you will only look for it.

More difficult are those scenes in which there is no obvious source of momentum, since there is no strong conflict between the characters involved. In such cases, the situation or locale of the scene may supply a sense of urgency: there may be an external "deadline" that requires that an objective be achieved as quickly as possible (someone coming, fear of discovery, etc.) or even an "internal" deadline (to say something before you break into tears, to break the news without hurting, etc.).

For example, there is a scene in Molière's *School for Wives* in which a jealous guardian, who intends to wed his own ward and has "protected" her from contact with the outside world, fears that in his absence she has had an affair with a younger man. He must find out the truth without revealing how important the matter is to him, so as not to arouse her curiosity. The scene seems difficult because she offers no resistance to him and freely answers all his questions. Yet with each answer, his fears mount, and it becomes increasingly difficult for him to control his feelings (which he releases in a number of "asides"). This scene's sense of momentum, then, comes from a purely "internal" condition—his need to get at the truth before losing control.

In some rare cases—since no playwright is always perfect in his architecture—it may even be necessary for the actors to *invent* some external or internal source of momentum for a scene. In such cases, you should examine the situation, the nature of the characters, and the locale; what *activities* might serve as outlets for your energy and provide momentum to the scene? What might this character be doing in this time and in this place, even if the playwright has not specified an activity? There are a number of characterizational or situational activities (sewing, smoking, drinking, eating, playing cards, etc.) that might help you to release energy and thereby move the scene forward.

Beware, however, of applying this principle indiscriminately. At moments of great tension or emotion, it may be that *containment* will be more effective than *release,* and at such moments *less* is truly *more.* For example, the tendency of some modern actors to thrash about during the monumental emotional crises of Classical tragedies tends only to dilute and belittle the passions of the scene. Remember that activity "spends" energy and that you must invest your stage energy with great discrimination.

In general, then, a scene will move naturally and with momentum when you and your partners have experienced its energy-structure (which is really its *rhythm*) and have felt those conflicts or conditions that drive its energies forward with a sense of urgency or significance. Any action, any activity, any emotion, or any character trait that does not contribute to the scene in this way *should be discarded* because it will only obscure, and perhaps impede, the rhythmic momentum of the scene's underlying dramatic action.

AUTOMATIC AND NONAUTOMATIC ACTIONS

So far we have been describing a process of choice that involves, however casually, conscious thought on the part of the character. There are obviously a great many things we do in life and on the stage, however, that are not necessarily the result of conscious choice. These are called "involuntary" or *automatic* responses. For example, when riding in a car and presented with sudden danger we find ourselves stepping on the brake, even if we are not driving. Characters on the stage have many responses of a similar kind: when the alarm bell sounds, Othello reaches for his sword; Sir Anthony Absolute takes his snuff when he feels the need for it; Stanley Kowalski grabs a beer when he is thirsty. These are habitual actions to which the characters give little or no thought.

It is extremely useful when approaching a role to decide early what aspects of the character's behavior and physical being are automatic to him. These are aspects of the characterization that will require a great deal of homework on your part, since it is your task to recreate the character's habits in yourself; in fact, we could describe the development of a characterization by saying that it is *the learning of a new set of habits.*

Follow this general rule: *whatever your character doesn't need to think about, you shouldn't need to think about; whatever your character does need to think about, you must think about each and every time you perform that action.*

When you consider how much of a character's behavior falls into the area of automatic response, you will see what an important area of concern this is: his voice, his walk, the way he wears his clothes, any special skills he may possess (like Othello's swordmanship or Falstaff's ability with a flagon of wine)—all these and more must become as natural and habitual to you as they are to your character. It is this kind of thinking that makes the wise Sir Anthony Absolute ask for his rehearsal cane early on, since he knows that the handling of a cane is habitual to his character; the wise Mrs. Maloprop will ask for her rehearsal skirt and wig early, and so on.

Since the formation of new habits is difficult, you see how unexamined habits of your own will be terrible obstacles if they intrude or impede the formation of habits designed for your characterization. New habits also need time to develop, so you cannot count on rehearsals alone to do the job, nor should you waste the time of the group on this sort of personal work; you must develop an early program of homework that carries the formation of these habits into your daily life—not in order to "lose yourself" in your character but to insure that you don't lose the character in yourself!

Equally important, of course, are those nonautomatic actions of your character, the things he *does* have to think consciously about. You must relive the character's process of choice each and every time you perform such an action. Too often, actors—out of laziness or ignorance—will rush pell-mell through the whole process of decision making and leap directly to the resultant activity. When this happens, the audience cannot help feeling that what they are seeing, however competent and clear its form may be, is empty and devoid of significant human content. In a very long run of a show, for instance, it is easy for an actor to go "on automatic pilot"; through long habit, he stops thinking through each decision made by his character and begins merely "going through the motions," which is sometimes humorously called "phoning in the performance."

Such a mechanical performance may seem to satisfy an audience that lacks any point of comparison, but to any sensitive theatregoer (and to any ethical actor) it will be woefully lacking in that special aliveness that separates great theatre from merely competent theatre. Your audience, your partners, and you deserve a total commitment to the actions in each performance and in each rehearsal.

An important cautionary note must be made here: the process of decision making that we have described in such detail in no way requires that your performance be ponderously slow. The making of a choice may take only a split-second; in most comedy, for instance, the tempo of the performance requires that this process occur quickly (and in truth, comic characters rarely have terribly difficult decisions to make, since the agony of moral choice belongs more to the realm of tragedy).

At the same time, almost every role will offer at least a few crucial decisions that need to be prolonged and savored in order to take full advantage of their dramatic value. Whatever pace and tempo may be required of a given scene, all deliberate choices made by your character must be relived each time they are enacted, or the performance will seem inevitably hollow.

Exercise 57   Making choices and adjustments

A. Using the scene that you and your partner analyzed in lesson 13, select a specific beat and work together to identify:

1. Your stimulus;
2. The quality of your response to the stimulus;
3. The alternatives you examined;
4. The choice you made;
5. The form of activity that resulted;
6. The event that resulted.

B. Using this same beat, examine the choice (to act or to respond) made by each of you according to the list of internal and external factors supplied above.

C. Now experiment with the making of *adjustments:*

1. Discuss what you need from each other and find the adjustments needed to supply it;
2. Consider what adjustments may be demanded by characterization;
3. Explore adjustments that might be demanded by style:
   a. do the scene as if it were a Classical tragedy;
   b. as if it were a romantic comedy;
   c. as if it were a farce;
   d. as if it were modern realism.
4. Explore adjustments that might be demanded by the theatre:
   a. do the scene for a huge auditorium;
   b. for an intimate arena stage;
   c. for a film.

In all these experiments, find your adjustments within the inner phase of action!

Lesson 15

Defining Character Action

Actions are easy to experience, but often difficult to describe. Nevertheless, forming a simple verbal description of your character's action will help you to begin work on your scene with your partner as quickly as possible; just be sure to remember that these verbal descriptions are only a working convenience, and that the true understanding of action lives in *experience,* not in *description.* At best, verbal descriptions of an action will provide a clear point of energy-focus that will, in turn, lead you more quickly to the exploration out of which the true development of a scene may grow.

We will focus our description of character action for now on a single beat; we do this because your character will, within a single beat, have a single point of intention or reaction (that is, he will be trying to do one particular thing or one particular thing will be happening to him). As explained in lesson 13, a beat forms one action/reaction link in the causal chain that moves the entire play; therefore a beat, as the smallest unit of action having its own clear shape and purpose, is the level of action that provides you with the greatest opportunity for complete focus of attention. A baseball batter will swing at many pitches, but his full attention is on the one thrown *now;* your focus of attention on your *immediate* intention or reaction within one beat is your way of "keeping your eye on the ball," even though you know that this particular action is also part of a larger pattern and must contribute to the flow of that larger pattern.

Each beat contains, in miniature, the energy-shape of an entire play: there will be a stimulus arousing your energy, just as the play has an inciting incident; this aroused needful energy will cause you to examine alternatives, just as the play has a period of rising actions and growing conflict and complexity; you will finally make a choice, just as the play will have its crisis; your choice will release your energy into activity, just as the play has its climax and denouement.

Let us examine this process by setting up a simple exercise, one beat of action that you can perform by yourself (remembering that such solo actions are very rare on the stage, where the emphasis is on transaction between characters). Assume that you feel very thirsty; your thirst grows in intensity until you must get up and get a drink. How would you describe this action in just a few words? Try it.

You probably said something like, "My action is to get a drink." But consider: was that really your inner *action,* or was it a description of your resultant *activity?* Would not a better description of your action be "to quench my thirst?"

This may seem a minor distinction, but there are several ways in which "to quench my thirst" is a more useful description of action than "to get a drink." *Thirst* relates to your stimulus in a personal way that *drink* does not; the thirst was the true initiating stimulus, while the drink was the external objective toward which your inner energy became directed once you had chosen what to do about your thirst.

From this, you learn the first principle of defining a character action: *your definition must include response to a stimulus felt by your character.*

It is possible that you might have defined your action in this experiment as "to be thirsty." This is in no way a *playable* action. The nature of drama requires that the momentum of your energy be moving into the scene through the activities that you perform; "to be thirsty" is a mere *state of being* that does not necessarily drive you forward into activity and is therefore not a very serviceable way of defining your action.

From this we deduce the second principle for defining actions: *use a simple verb phrase in a transitive form.* Avoid forms of the verb "to be," since these are *intransitive* verbs; they have no external object and their energy turns back upon itself, certainly not a good condition for an actor whose energies must continuously flow outward into the structure of his play! Strive instead for a *transitive* condition in which your energy flows toward an objective.

The third principle follows from the second: *include the object of the verb in your definition.* In our example, *thirst* is both the stimulus and also the object of the verb phrase, *to quench.* This is a very simple action, but we can provide a few more complex examples from scenes and plays mentioned earlier in this book; can you identify the characters?: *To be a success in the eyes of my sons; to convince him to enter the hovel; to persuade him to join the conspiracy; to trick him into helping me kill myself; to convince the prince that I am a gallant man.* Do you see how each of these conforms to the three principles listed above and would therefore assist you in entering into a meaningful *interaction* with your stage partners?

A subsidiary fourth principle deals with the addition of *adverbs* that specify the particular quality of the action. Usually this specific quality will be necessitated by your objective or point of reaction within the situation, or by your relationship to the other characters, or by the personality of your character. In the examples of actions we listed above, the qualifying adverbs might be: to be *completely* successful in the eyes of my sons; to convince him *out of compassion* to enter the hovel; to persuade him *deceitfully* to join the conspiracy; to trick him into helping me kill myself *as an act of love;* to convince the prince *humorously* that I am a gallant man.

As you see by these examples, the exact quality that you select for your action is often a matter more of *interpretation* than *necessity* and expresses much of your personal sense of the character. These choices will therefore be made only through trial and error as your characterization gradually develops in specific interaction with your fellow actors.

All these examples deal with active characters who have a specific intention that they attempt to achieve. But what of the so-called "passive" or reactive character? And what of those many beats during which your character is *reacting* rather than *acting?* The same principles apply, whether you are the initiator or the receiver of the energy. For example, if I am Peter listening to Jerry tell the story of "Jerry and the Dog," and we are in the beat in which Jerry comes to his decision (in the story) to *kill* the dog, I know that I must provide an external response of horror (since Jerry then says, "No, Peter, don't react, just listen"). My responsibility to motivate Jerry's line demands an activity from me; how do I define my action so as to supply the required behavior? Do I say that my action at this moment is "to be horrified" or merely "to react with horror"? Certainly not; as we discussed, these are only states of being, not playable actions. I find my initial stimulus (the thought of killing the dog), I find the qualities of my personality that make this thought repulsive to me, then I give my full attention to the immediate moment and I *allow* the natural flow of my response (now carefully prepared) to take its course. My action is "to protest with horror that Jerry intends to kill the dog." This action-description conforms to all four of our principles; do you see how?

As I said earlier, there are no passive characters on the stage; all characters are at some times acting and at other times reacting. Some, it is true, are characteristically more often reactive than active—the most famous example is Hamlet—and these are usually very difficult roles. But they become less difficult if the actor, whatever the demand for action or reaction, will translate his action into a positive (that is, *transitive*) form, as I have demonstrated.

THE FLOW OF ACTION INTO ACTIVITY

Once the choice to act has been made and the aroused energy becomes a purposeful intention or point of reaction, it changes modes from the internal to the external and becomes an *activity*. Notice however that *it retains the vitality of the original stimulus.* The activity "to get a drink" is really the outer or public form of the inner action, "to quench my thirst"; *they each describe a different phase of the same energy.* When you take the glass of water into your hand, it is no longer a mere impersonal thing; it is now the objectification of *your thirst.* Defined in this way, our external activities become total gestures arising from deep personal energies, and those objects or relationships involved in our activities become endowed with a deeply personal quality—they become extensions of us.

If you can experience the flow of energy from stimulus to event (as in figure 34) as one unbroken line, then you will understand how all your external behavior is truly the way we "deduce your action," for the whole process of action from stimulus to event is literally *your inside becoming your outside.*

Your activities on stage must always be deeply expressive in this sense, so you must learn to carry the personal energy of the inner phase of action into the outer activity that springs from it. You must experience the unbroken flow of energy from the stimulus through the decision into the activity toward the object; your full sense of your action must encompass this entire process, so that your defined action is not a static image but is rather *a name for an experienced flow of energy.*

Using our example of thirst, we can describe this process as being "how to quench my thirst?/decision/to get a drink as quickly as possible." The inner phase of action asks a question that is answered, through choice, by the external activity. Notice that our description of the external activity "to get a drink as quickly as possible" followed the same four principles that we established for describing an inner action: *a transitive verb phrase including its object and implying a personal sense of its original stimulus, perhaps specified by an adverb.*

When we experience the flow of energy from stimulus through choice into activity, we experience our action as *one total rhythmic gesture.* This flow can be summarized in four key words:

STIMULUS ⟶ CHOICE ⟶ ACTIVITY ⟶ OBJECTIVE

In your simple drinking exercise, these moments would be:

THIRST ⟶ DRINK ⟶ GET IT ⟶ SWALLOW

Each of these is a specific moment in time, but is also experienced as the unbroken flow of one deep energy. It is this entire process that you will now understand as the process of dramatic action.

We now have two ways of defining an action: one through verbs (to quench my thirst/decision/to get a drink) and the "shorthand" version using the trigger words (THIRST / DRINK / GET IT / SWALLOW). Test your understanding of all this by selecting the beat in the scene you analyzed in lesson 13: can you define your action or point of reaction? Can you define the flow of the inner action into the activity using four trigger words?

FINDING THE MAIN ACTION OF THE ROLE

You will remember the hierarchy of actions that we described in lesson 13: from play to scene to beat to moment. This same sense of large actions being comprised of smaller units of action operates within each character's action. Think of the largest unit of action first: just as a play has one underlying main action, so a role has a main action, which is its overall dramatic purpose expressed in actable terms. You already know that Stanislavski called this the super-objective of the characterization. This is sometimes also called the "through-line" or the "spine" of a character. We will use the term *main action* because it emphasizes a dynamic and outgoing quality of stage activity.

It is not always easy to describe a role's main action, since it may be very complex and may even undergo a change in the course of the play. The important thing, however, is to express it in *active* terms, and to understand how it enables the character to realize his dramatic purpose as a contributor to the plot and meaning of the play. Your description of your role's main action should not only guide you about *what* to do, but also should provide an idea about *how* it must be done in order to contribute as much as possible to the meaning of the play.

The main action often will be understood only after all the component actions of which it is made have been explored and experienced, and even then it may remain inexpressable. Nevertheless, it is the overall understanding of where the character is heading that alone can provide coherence and unity to your performance.

The action of each *scene* may be easier to grasp and to express. Usually a character will have one general action in a scene, which will be worked out through the beats that form logical units within the scene action, and the momentary actions of which the beats are made. The actor's immediate concern when performing is to fulfill each moment as it happens, but this is only after each moment has been understood as contributing to a beat, each beat to a scene, and each scene to the main action.

You can understand the interrelatedness of all your moments only when you understand the *dramatic purpose* they serve. The playwright has made your job easier, of course, by providing a multitude of actions implicit in the verbal structure of the play, and the kind of close textual analysis you have already learned will go far toward helping you to understand your character's actions on every level.

In a production of Brecht's *Mother Courage,* for example, the actress playing the role of Kattrin, the mute daughter, needed help in analyzing the action of her last scene. In it, Kattrin climbs atop a hut and beats a drum to warn the nearby town of an impending attack. The soldiers coax and threaten her in every way they can, trying to make her stop drumming. Finally, she is shot. Clearly, this scene and the action of choosing to warn the town is the climax of her entire performance, and she was having terrible difficulty with it. Yet no scene is easier to do *if* the preparation is correct. If the audience has been shown all the things that make this action understandable and indeed *inevitable,* there is almost no way the scene can be done badly.

The impact of a moment, a scene, or an entire role is the payoff resulting from careful investment in preparation. You may reap only what you have previously sown. In this case, the actress should examine each moment of her role, each of her previous actions and reactions, to see how it will contribute to this final action, since this final action embodies the ultimate development and fullest statement of Kattrin's character. It is also, of course, the final fulfillment of her dramatic purpose, since hers is the only truly *selfless* act in the entire play. By her sacrifice, by the fact that the world of the play makes it mandatory that a humane action is also suicidal, we are able to see the other characters and their world in sharper perspective.

Kattrin's dramatic purpose is to provide one glimmer of selflessness against which the avarice and callousness of the other characters and a world in which love itself has been outlawed by economic necessity may be judged. Her main action is *to observe* the various ways in which people are forced to abandon their humanity in order to "get along," and finally *to protest* what she has seen when she can no longer countenance such a world. Each of her scenes, beats, and moments must be understood as contributing to this main action.

Exercise 58 Action polarization

Use the same scene as in the previous exercises, and work again with your partner, each on his own part but in mutual discussion:

I. On the basis of the analysis you did of the play and this scene in lessons 12 and 13, describe according to the principles outlined earlier:

A. The dramatic purpose of your character;
B. The main action of your character as a translation of this dramatic purpose.

II. Define the *scene action* of your characters, then:

A. Choose an *overall pattern of movement,* a sort of rough
"blocking" expressed as principles of movement, that expresses
the *scene action* (for example, one character is trying to pry
something out of the other, so one will remain closed up or
continually in retreat, while the other pursues and attempts
various movement-strategies to penetrate the defenses of the
other. Here, the actions of *prying* and *penetrating* versus
retreating and *closing up* would be literally acted out.)
B. Choose *individual movement patterns* that express qualities or
needs of each character (for example, the aggressive character
might be *open* and *free* in his movements, while the other is
heavy and *inhibited* in his).
C. Using your individual pattern *within* the overall pattern, attempt
to recreate the shape of the scene, using *only* full organic
movement, vocal noise (not words), and uninhibited physical
contact. Each of you pursue your character actions in reaction to
the other. Be especially careful to realize the shape of each beat
and the patterning of the beats to form the scene. Use the
rhythms, sounds, and dominant sensations, which you analyzed
in part 1 of this exercise, as the *basis* for your movement and
noise, but don't try to be too specific. Concentrate instead on
the *action* of the scene.

CAUTION: *The aim of this exercise is, like the other polarizations, to
create a total organic experience of the action of the scene. Seek out every
opportunity for exaggerated movement and noise and react fully and
physically to each other. Do not be tied to "realistic" movement or even to
the type of movement that might really be used in the performance of the
scene. Your aim here is* EXPERIENCE, *not* PERFORMANCE.

III. Verbalizing the scene. When you both feel that you have
realized the shaping of the scene and have honestly communicated
real cause/effect energies to each other through your actions and
reactions, begin to allow the energies of your noise and movement
to shape themselves into the words of the scene. Don't force the
words to come, just push them a little. If your organic involvement
is complete and your analysis has been correct, the words should
begin coming as a natural extension and completion of your action.
Keep a firm sense of the *process of verbalization* as an active
decision-making one, which is an integral part of the action and
thought of the character. Be sure to respond fully to the growing
verbalization of your partner as well. Review the principles used in
exercise 36 (slow-motion verbalization).

IV.   Using the same beat you selected for the previous exercise:

A. Define your action within this beat according to the four
   principles outlined earlier;
B. Select the four trigger words that express the flow of your action
   within this beat;
C. Prepare a sound and movement polarization of this beat. This
   should be a brief, single action phrase expressed in sound and
   motion that provides you with a muscular experience of the flow
   of the action and of the *transaction* between you and partner.

V.   On the basis of this experience, begin to verbalize the beat as
in III above.

VI.   Now return to your verbalization of the entire scene and
examine your actions, beat by beat, as you continue to rehearse the
entire scene. Are you giving each other the proper stimuli? Are you
keeping the shape of the whole scene clear by focusing on the crisis
of the scene? Are you each beginning to experience your *scene action*
as *one total rhythmic gesture?*

VII.   Finally, as a way of checking the *continuity* of your
character's thought throughout the scene, return to exercise 34
(interior monologue) and use it for this scene, constructing and
verbalizing an interior monologue that carries your character through
all the transitions of thought and action required by the scene and
that *also expresses your sense of relationship to the other characters in the*
scene.

This massive exercise is the most complex and the most important in
this book. It can take weeks to perform in its entirety; indeed, an entire
acting course could well be devoted to this exercise. Do not rush, take each
step in turn; this experience can outline for you the growth of a role as it
may occur over many weeks of rehearsal. This is the stage of your work
when your expressive abilities and your analytical insights become synthesized in the experience of playable actions. It is at this juncture that the
life of your character will truly begin. All of the work which follows is
concerned with the extension and enrichment of the foundation you have
laid here, a foundation which is rooted in the bedrock of dramatic action
and dramatic purpose.

Lesson 16

Action, Emotion, and Character

What is *emotion?* The root meaning of the word is *an outward movement.* It is any activity that expresses the immediate condition of our organism and is directed toward the world outside. This doesn't mean that emotional activity is always meant to be communicative; it arises automatically out of our efforts to relate to life. There are times, of course, when we wish to make our feelings known to others, but the feelings themselves have arisen in the course of our interaction with the world, as we *move outward* and encounter either satisfaction or frustration of our intentions. It must also be this way on the stage: we do not "create" emotion; rather, it *arises out of* our outward movement or *action.*

In everyday life emotion serves many purposes. First, most forms of emotional expression are "safety-valve" activities that provide a release of tensions (pleasant or unpleasant). Since our organisms tend to seek equilibrium through the release of tensions, emotions are one of our basic adaptive mechanisms.

Second, emotional expression helps us to *realize* our condition, to objectify and clarify it *for ourselves.* By forming an emotional reaction to something, we gain some degree of understanding about our relationship to it. For example, many people are impatient with some modern theatre because they don't know whether it is "supposed to be funny or not"; they don't know how to cope with it until they decide what emotional response is appropriate. Another example is when we ask, "Are you putting me on?" If the answer is yes, we may laugh; if it is no, we may be angry. In either case, the formation of the emotion formalizes our response, and until the emotion is formed we may suspend our judgment of the situation. Third, emotion is also a *symbolic* activity that often serves to let us "act out" desires, to substitute for real success or to extend pleasure. As we shall see, most forms of emotional behavior are symbolic variations of practical activities.

Finally, some psychotherapists view emotions as a form of value judgment which we pass upon our actions. Pleasurable emotions arise from those actions which we feel are "successful" in attaining a desired goal; painful emotions arise from those actions which are "unsuccessful." Anger may arise when we feel our actions have been unjustly or needlessly prevented from succeeding; fear arises when we feel that we have incomplete control over the effectiveness of our actions.

From all these points of view, emotion is tied inextricably to action. It arises automatically from any significant confrontation with the world and will enter our consciousness unless we suppress or repress it, in which case it is not lost, but only stored until such time (if any) when it can be released.

Young actors are often tempted to admire the powerful emotional impact of the actor who loses control of himself, but you must remember that the sheer experience of emotion for its own sake is not your true purpose. An actor may feel selfishly successful if he makes his audience weep, but he has failed if his audience's weeping does not lead to a fuller, more vivid, more honest understanding of the play as a whole.

The great actor aspires to use his emotional technique to realize fully the truth of his character, in terms of the play in which that character appears. In other words, the ultimate test of a performance is not simply its emotional power, but the completeness with which it contributes to the whole play as a work of art. For the actor, emotion is a means to this end, never an end in itself.

The proper theatrical purpose of emotion is to make the action of the play and its meaning more immediate for the audience, to help them experience the character's situation and activity more vividly. Each play uses emotion in a different way; some appeal to sentiment, others try to appeal to more profound passions, and some even attempt to be "*un-emotional*" in order to focus their appeal on our reason. But in all plays, emotion on the part of the characters, whatever response is expected from the audience, helps to move and vivify the action.

THE GENESIS OF EMOTION: THE JAMES-LANGE THEORY

Near the turn of the century, two psychologists, Fritz Lange and William James, developed a theory of emotion of special interest to the actor (Stanislavski was familiar with it) because of its physical orientation.

This theory holds that an emotion is identical with its muscular symptoms. What we call "grief" is not a description of a "mental" state, but a description of convulsive sobbing, tears, shortness of breath, and erratic body tempo. Our emotion *is* its bodily manifestation; our *concept* of the emotion is our recognition of our own bodily condition.

Let's say you are stepping off a curb when, out of the corner of your eye, you see a car rushing toward you. Of course you leap back out of danger. You are afraid, but you did not jump *because* you were afraid; if you had to wait for the emotional response to motivate your action, you would have been too late. You reacted *automatically* (or viscerally) to the signal of danger. It was a direct motor response, which bypassed conceptual thinking. Then, with your heart pounding, adrenalin flowing, your breath short, you conceptualized your condition and called it "fear." In other words, your emotion did not motivate your action, your action gave rise to your emotion.

Psychologists call this "fright-flight": you do not run because you are afraid, you become afraid because you are running. While not all emotions in life are generated in this way, all emotions *do* involve a bodily symptom; without some bodily symptom, there is no emotion. When we suppress the "normal" symptoms of an emotion, it will redirect itself and reappear in some other form. Peter, in *The Zoo Story,* inhibits the direct outpouring of his feelings until they find their own release in the uncontrollable, hysterical laughter near the end of the play that he himself does not understand.

This view of emotion can help to describe the communication of emotional experience from actor to audience. It begins as simple physical imitation, the spectator's muscles empathically mirroring the actor's physical state; then, because the spectator's muscles are responding similarly to those of the actor, similar feelings are inspired in him. In this way the spectator *shares* the character's emotion, rather than simply *observing* it. If the character weeps, the spectator feels a "sympathetic" (actually *imitative*) lump in his throat; as Willy Loman shuffles across the stage, back bowed, the spectator participates physically in his exhaustion and dejection.

This same process applies to the actor playing the character: if he adopts with his *whole self* the symptoms of the character's emotion in the course of pursuing his action, the fullness of the specific emotion required will grow within him—assuming, of course, that he is completely in touch with himself and that all facets of his being are so accessible to the experience that his own activity will *resonate* in his total consciousness.

It will also help you to remember that the expressive "symptoms" of an emotion are part and parcel of the emotion itself. You needn't be concerned, at least initially, with emotional behavior; if you are able to pursue your character's action with full focus the emotion *will* arise and it *will* be communicative. As William Ball of the American Conservatory Theatre says, "Do the act, and the feeling will follow."

Another way of putting this is to say that your aim as Willy Loman is not *to be dejected,* but rather to do something *in such a way that it causes you to be dejected.* The "something" is your action or intention at the moment, *adjusted* by the way in which you perform it so as to invite the desired emotion to arise.

This is a useful attitude for you, since your script provides you with a wealth of external details to be utilized in achieving an internalization of the life of the character. A play script contains not only specified actions, but a whole range of implied adjustments or qualification of the actions embodied in its rhythms, emphases, images, and overall structure. By participating physically in these "externals" we imitate the character; through our imitation (adjusted to conform to the character's dramatic function) we can help ourselves develop a strong inner identification with him. Finally, by mastery of the techniques of stage performance we can communicate this fully realized characterization to our audience.

Here is a simple exercise to experience the James-Lange theory in operation:

Exercise 59   Action to emotion

Without thinking about it in advance, begin to move violently in some manner. Continue this movement and concentrate upon it until an emotional attitude begins to grow spontaneously from it. Allow the emotion to develop until it specifies itself. It may begin to suggest to you a situational context. Your thoughts might be something like, "I am jumping up and down. I am beginning to breathe very hard. When I make a noise, my pitch is very high and my phrases short. I sound like a little girl. I am very happy and excited. I am about to be given a present." And so on. See how far you must go to complete the process you have set in motion. In this example, you might finish with a squeal of delight and a grasping and hugging movement.

Before we move on, however, a cautionary word should be said about the essential limitations of physical expression of emotion in the theatre. We must realize the importance of context in the specification of emotion, as Robert Breen explains:

> If emotion had to be judged solely from the external expressions, it would be difficult if not impossible for us to discriminate even such widely different emotions as joy and sorrow. It is not uncommon for people to cry in joy *and* sorrow. Discriminating subtler emotions would be even more difficult were it not for the fact that the psychological situation can be depended upon to identify the emotion. ... Investigations of fear, rage, and pain showed no distinguishing features among the bodily changes which would discriminate these emotions. However, the situational responses of flight for fear, attack for rage, and aimless, uncoordinated movement for pain distinguished the emotions well enough.[34]

[34]Bacon and Breen, *Literature as Experience,* p. 34.

In other words, it is context (plot, the identification of character traits, and the audience's understanding of the situation in which the characters interact) that provides a *conceptual* understanding of the exact quality of emotion, but it is generally the nonverbal aspects of the performance (muscle tone, breathing, inflections, and so on) that provide the *power* and *believability* of the emotion. Without this nonverbal foundation, our response to a play would be superficial or only intellectual.

The potentiality of nonverbal communication is great, but don't expect it to do a job for which it is not suited; a performance that is physically and emotionally powerful but blurred in its outlines and lacking in specificity of conception is as faulty as an intellectually vivid but lifeless performance.

THE EXCITATION OF EMOTION

We have studied action and the specific way in which it operates as an energy flow from the outside world through a stimulus into our "inner world," then back out again as intentional activity. When our activity encounters circumstance we are frustrated, successful, or compromised by it, and emotion naturally arises. You have probably experienced a good deal of emotion in the previous exercises without thinking specifically about it; now we can examine this natural process in greater detail.

We earlier said, "Do the act and the feeling will follow." There are three important qualifications to be made, however. First, what *is* the action that generates emotion? Most of the overt emotional acts we might think of (for example, hitting the table when angry) are actually safety-valve actions which erupt when tension has reached a high level. They are not actions that will generate emotion so much as they are the *results* of emotional tension. One can pound the table for hours and generate little more than a sore hand; it is the underlying action, the tension, that would *cause* us to pound the table, which we must emulate if we wish to generate rage.

Second, we must perform the *proper* activity in order to generate the appropriate feeling. Playwrights generally answer this qualification for us by providing carefully designed externals, both vocal and visual.

Finally, in order to be responsive to our own actions, we must be "in touch" with ourselves. If we have not contacted ourselves, then the actions we perform will have no effect upon us. Our aim in "doing the act" and letting the "feeling follow" is to allow the internalization of our action to become *self-generating.* Our basic actions lead us in turn to fuller actions, which become the true extensions of the actions provided by the play.

We must also remember that while the actor's emotional energy is one of his basic tools, the form any emotional expression takes on stage must be consistent with the demands of the play's style. We study emotional expression in real life in order to discover the principles that underlie expressive behavior, not because emotion on stage is always expressed in the way it might be in everday life. A character of Shakespeare's and an O'Neill character might need to express similar emotions, and the actor would have to supply the same degree of emotional energy in order to vitalize the character's feelings, but probably the form in which the emotion would be expressed would be different in each case.

You can use this simple exercise as a way of testing your own ability to work from the externals of emotional expression toward a self-generating internalization. It also tests your ability to retain the energy of that emotion while transforming it into a new style of expression.

Exercise 60   Emotion adoption

From your own experience or, better, from real-life observation, reconstruct in minute detail the physical characteristics of someone's intense emotion. Consider each area of the body and its behavior. Do not neglect the breath and the general motor rhythm and tone. Do not think about the *reason* for the emotion or even the exact quality of the emotion in its completeness. Concentrate instead on the simple, mechanical manifestations of this emotion in the body. Think of the physical traits of the emotion as parts of a costume you are putting on. Beginning at the bottom of your body and moving upwards, adopt the behavior you have analyzed. Throw yourself fully into it. See if the proper emotional state begins to grow within you. Which aspects of your behavior seem to contribute most to the development of this feeling? Can you find vestiges of animal activity in each aspect of the behavior? Here is an example:

> "I am curling my toes against the floor so as to have a firm footing in case I have to spring either in attack or retreat. I am shifting my body weight forward on the balls of the feet so as to be as mobile as possible. My legs are bending so that my body can spring. This causes great tension in my calves and thighs. This bent posture is also a good defense, since several vulnerable areas of my body (my genitals, by abdomen, my neck, my eyes) are protected. I have drawn my arms in so as to protect the center of my body, but at the same time my hands are upraised for defense. My fingers are curled; this is perhaps a vestige of a time when man had claws. My shoulders have hunched forward so as to protect my neck. My jaw is very tense, and my lower jaw is thrusting out. It is as if I still had fangs and was

preparing to tear at my opponent's throat. My brow has sunk down to protect my eyes, which have narrowd to thin slits. This generally defensive posture has made me breathe in a restricted manner, because my diaphragm can no longer travel its full extent. But because of the increased need to oxygenate my muscles, I compensate by breathing more rapidly. The general tension in my body is growing; I feel a cold sweat breaking out in the palms of my hands and on my forehead. My breath is coming erratically now, and I am beginning to make guttural noises. If I attempt to speak, I find that my tone is the tone of an extremely angry person. In fact, I feel rage beginning to swell up in me. . . ."

Continue the development of this sensation by thrusting yourself more and more intensely into your physical situation. Avoid thinking about anything but your own body. As the emotional state grows, let it wash over you and extend itself to its own necessary conclusion. In this case you may perhaps finally plunge forward, slam your fist on a table, or let out a bellow of rage. A point will come when your suppressed tensions must result in overt reaction. The "emotional outburst" is an "overflow" or "safety-valve" action.

In this exercise, you may have found yourself discovering a basic sort of characterization arising from your involvement in an active emotional state. Since you took your observation of the emotion from someone else, does the realization that you now have about this emotion seem appropriate to your model? What new information does it give you? If it does not seem appropriate, what might have gone wrong? Which aspects of your behavior influenced the development of the emotion most? Try doing this exercise in front of the class, and compare their impression of your behavior with what you are feeling and with your original model. Now try the next exercise.

Exercise 61   Emotion adoption in a new form

Attempt to recreate for yourself the emotion adopted in the previous exercise, but this time try to experience it as it would be expressed by a Greek tragic hero (if it is unpleasant) or a *commedia dell'arte* character (if it is pleasant). Examine *each detail* that you observed in real life, and evaluate it in terms of its appropriateness for this new form. Should it be kept, or is it too unessential for the economy demanded by stylized forms? If it is kept, how must it be transformed? What is essential and useful in this form; what isn't? Can you experience the energy of the emotion as strongly in this new form? Is the quality of the experience different?

BREATH AND EMOTION

Most actors agree that the most effective tool we have for the communication and expression of emotion is the breath. The next time you see a performance try to become aware of the impact that an actor's breathing can have on the audience. One negative example would be the actor who breathes with great tension, who has not learned to relax. His voice is strained, and the muscular tensions are rapidly communicated to the audience, which responds with a wave of coughing and restlessness. It has "caught" his tension. On the other hand, effortless breathing can help to quell nervousness. When experiencing stage fright, taking deep breaths will help to relax you.

It is perfectly appropriate that the breath should be at the root of most of our emotional states. The word *psychology* itself means "study of the soul," and the word for soul, *psyche,* originally meant "vital breath." Common superstition is that the expiring breath of a dying man is his soul leaving his body. This is why we say "God bless you" when someone sneezes.

Besides the breath's obvious importance for life, there is another way of describing its importance in the expression of emotion. As we have said, emotion usually is the resut of our attempt to adapt to the outside world. The ways in which we most directly contact the outside world are therefore the primary means of emotional expression. Remember the space exercise in which you became aware of space moving through your body? It is through the breath that we literally bring the outside world into our bodies and then expel it again, and the way we feel about that outside world will be expressed by the way in which we breathe it in and breathe it out. Take, for example, a sudden and unexpected danger. It would seem that the physiological necessity of coping with whatever is threatening us would make us breathe rapidly in order to oxygenate our muscles, and indeed, when the initial shock has worn off, our fear is expressed by rapid and shallow panting. But our initial reaction at the time of the first shock is just the opposite: we take a sudden breath and quickly shut the mouth, and then *hold* our breath for a period of time. It is as if we are saying to the outside world, "You threaten me; you can't come in; I'm closing the door to you." This is what a psychologist might call "playing dead inside our skins."

Exercise 62   Breath and emotion

Place yourself at rest in a comfortable position. Concentrate on your breath: its frequency, its rhythm, its depth. Begin to manipulate the

breath as if you were improvising on a musical instrument.
Concentrate on the sounds and feel of the breath for its own sake;
do not think of "emotions" or "experiences." Concentrate only on
the breath. You will become aware of shifting and momentary
moods, which will play across your consciousness as a result of your
changing breath pattern.

At this level, any feelings that might be motivated by your breath manipulation would be vague and undifferentiated, and can best be called
"moods." In this undifferentiated form, emotion is simply increased energy and excitement in response to a stimulus. It is only as the emotion
develops that it begins to take on unique characteristics of its own and is
further specified and clarified by our understanding of character and situation. Just so, in this exercise, we begin to sense the germinal state of
emotion as an unspecified increase in excitement, which nonetheless contains the seed of further specification.

The particular value for the actor in tracing the development of emotion
is that it helps him to regulate the sights and sounds he produces for his
audience; he can move directly and actively into the emotional realm.
Beginning with the breath has the particular advantage of providing a
direct route to three highly expressive aspects of performance: our general
muscle tone and rhythms, facial expression, and the quality of our speech.
Continue the exercise now to explore these areas.

Exercise 63 Emotion and voice

A. Continue your concentration upon a manipulation of your
breath. Become aware of the effect that various breath rhythms have
upon the general muscle tone of the body. Explore pleasant and
unpleasant kinds of breath patterns. In breath that is short, irregular,
and rapid, you will find that an unpleasant sense of anxiety may be
produced. See how this anxiousness affects the general muscle tone
and rhythm of your body. Try moving in this state, and see how the
rhythms of your muscular functions are affected. What expressive
qualities result?

B. Now return to a comfortable position. Continue breath
manipulation. Concentrate on your facial expression. Do not attempt
to manipulate it, simply become aware of it. You will be surprised
at the rapidity of its changes and how directly the breath influences
it. Begin to make sounds. The sounds may form themselves into
articulated speech, but avoid making up speeches. Your breath
manipulation will have an immediate effect upon the loudness and

quality of your speech, and expressive inflections will arise automatically.

We see that the voice is profoundly influenced by the muscular conditions of emotion. Playwrights, knowing this, have provided rhythms, tones, and inflections useful to you in recreation of the character's emotion, and you have already learned a great deal about the emotional quality intended by the playwright by studying these aspects of the text.

Exercise 64   Breath scene

A. With your partner, work on your scene, concentrating on the shape of the emotions communicated between the characters. Use only breath and nonverbal noises. Do not pantomime or "charade" the content of the scene; your objective is to communicate intensely with each other through breath and breath noises alone. Move as actively as possible. *Do not be limited to a realistic approach to the scene.*

B. Now begin to let your breath and noise be formed into the words of the scene. The breath and noises that you produce involve an enormous number of muscles, and only when the entire body is actively participating in their production can you hope to communicate effectively. Do not think about the emotions as concepts or even memories, but focus on your breath communication.

EMOTION AND EXTERNAL OBJECTIVES

You probably found that the act of *relating* to your scene partner enhanced your emotionality. This is because in its fullest expression, emotion needs an external object toward which it is directed. If there is no external object immediately at hand, we will find a substitute. Often we will "take out" our emotion on someone who had nothing to do with the original feeling. Or, we will perform some *symbolic* action (like punching our own hand) to provide at least a symbolic external object. This is a basic problem the actor must solve when expressing emotion: what external objects or persons are available toward which he can direct the emotion? Usually you will find that a skillful playwright will have provided such an object, even though it may be only a symbolic one. In *The Zoo Story,* Peter's main function as a character is to serve as such an object, toward which Jerry directs his general *malaise.*

By seeing what the external object of emotion may be in each scene, you will discover much about the quality of the emotion and its expression. In

King Lear, for example, Lear begins by railing against individuals: Kent, Cordelia, his daughters. During his madness, he provides external objects for his emotion by imagining that he sees a convict, a justice, a grand lady, even Goneril and Regan themselves. But later on, his feelings have much more symbolic, generalized objects, such as the gods themselves. This reveals to us the way in which Lear's emotion grows beyond the limits of his immediate situation to an almost existential concern for all mankind.

The actor's problem is to localize the emotional object at each moment and make real contact with it. Here is an exercise for moving the focus of our emotion out of ourselves and into the reality around us.

Exercise 65   Emotional objects

With your partner, work on your scene several times, each time using different external objects as the vehicles through which your emotional energies flow to and from each other:

1. Use an irrelevant object: a fireplug, or chair, and so on.
2. Use a symbolic object: translate any emotional activity (like hitting the other person) into strictly symbolic activity (like tearing pieces of paper).
3. Use a verbal object: translate the emotion into words, or create an imagined object for the emotion in words (Jerry does this continually in *The Zoo Story,* using his various "stories" as vehicles for the expression of underlying emotion).
4. Use a direct object: contact each other physically. Analyze your performances. Was the most direct one necessarily the most interesting, or was more revealed when direct action was inhibited and the emotion channeled through an indirect object instead?

Now analyze the scene and see what objects have been provided by the playwright. What does this tell you about the scene and the characters?

THE DENIAL OF EMOTION

So far we have spoken of the *release* of emotions, but dramatic characters, like people in everyday life, do not act upon every emotion they feel, nor are they always consciously aware of what they may be feeling. The mechanisms of *suppression* and *repression* are often at work to deny an emotion or a desire.

Suppression differs considerably from repression; we may *consciously choose to suppress* a feeling or desire, thrusting it away from conscious awareness because it is inappropriate or untimely. Such suppression is usually intended to be only a postponement until such time as the situation becomes more hospitable to the suppressed emotion, at which time it is returned to conscious awareness and released. In another type of suppression, we may consciously choose to surrender permanently a desire or feeling. When this is a willful choice, accompanied by the necessary compensatory actions (like the deep sigh which often accompanies the decision to suppress anger), we may be successful in "letting it pass."

Repression is a very different matter from suppression, although suppression (especially when it becomes a chronic pattern of behavior) may lead us unwittingly to repression. The difference lies primarily in the degree of consciousness involved in the act. Suppression is a *conscious* choice, while repression is a *non*-conscious process. In the opening discussion of emotion, I noted that emotions automatically enter our consciousness (and, usually, are then released through action) unless they are prevented from doing so. Certain "taboo" feelings (such as elation at the failure of a competitor, or sexual feelings for a relative) may sufficiently threaten us that we establish an *un*conscious block of our awareness of such emotions. This is repression.

Repression is an automatic and therefore indiscriminate pattern of behavior, blocking not only those emotions for which it was originally intended, but many other emotions relating to the same issues, even if they are pleasurable and productive. In this way, repression permanently alters our perception of the world.[35]

Dramatic characters do repress and suppress feelings and desires but, since repression and suppression do not usually result in easily observable activity, the actor does not always have clear evidence indicating such a choice by his character. Recreating the through-line of the character's thought will help you to discover those moments when your character probably has an impulse which he chooses to suppress, which the situation does not permit him to release, or which he unconsciously represses. *Remember that stage characters, like most people, may often be feeling and wanting much more than their overt actions indicate.*

In lesson 15 you analyzed the way in which your character perceived

---

[35]For a discussion of this view of emotion, see Nathaniel Branden, *The Psychology of Self-Esteem* (New York: Bantam, 1971), chapter V.

his alternative courses of action, including those alternatives which he characteristically failed to perceive. You were actually cataloging his pattern of repression! It may be useful to deduce or to imagine hypothetically sources of these patterns of repressive behavior as a way of expanding your understanding and feeling of your character.

Exercise 66 Tracing repressions

I. During your analysis of your character's process of action in lesson 15, you probably observed blockages in your character's perception of his world. Invent a *specific* experience which could have initiated this repressive pattern. Then, with the aid of your partner, create an improvised scene which enacts this event.

II. Reread the section in lesson 5 on Body Alignment and Character. Through experimentation, translate the experience of your character's repressions into a bodily form; in what part of his body does he "store" his repressed energy? What has happened to his body as a result?

Suppressed and repressed emotions are bits of "unfinished business"; they tend to remain with us—not always in terms of specific memories, but also as *patterns of repressive behavior* which continue to affect our *present* responses to the world.

The power of stored emotions which most dramatic characters (and most of us) carry in the unconscious reveals itself in many ways. Not all behavior is a direct response to an external stimulus in the neat way suggested by the analysis of the last lesson; random or "surrogate" stimuli, and even self-generated stimuli, can evoke discharges of stored energies. Of course, cause-and-effect does usually govern stage behavior, but occasionally a character will suddenly erupt into an emotional state, or will react disproportionately to an event, because a "de-repression" is taking place. The plays of O'Neill and Tennessee Williams, for example, offer several such instances.

More common in both tragedy and comedy is a character refusing to acknowledge a situation, attempting (usually unsuccessfully) to suppress it. Molière makes frequent use of this device when he shows us someone who, like Orgon in *Tartuffe*, stubbornly refuses to believe the evidence of his own eyes. In tragic plays we find even more examples of unsuccessful suppressions; the scene in *King Lear* when Lear confronts the blinded Gloucester is one long attempt at suppression of a painful recognition. After trying to make light of what he sees ("Get thee glass eyes and like a scurvy politician seem to see the things thou dost not," and many other such black jokes), the pain begins to mount as the recognition forces itself toward Lear's consciousness ("Do thy worst, blind Cupid, I'll not love") until, as Gloucester begins to weep, Lear can keep the pain away no longer ("If thou wilt weep my fortunes, take my eyes. I know thee well enough, thy name is Gloucester"). Such admissions, especially when the playwright has shown us the agony of the attempted suppression, are enormously moving and—since they always mark a massive change in the personality of the character—are enormously revealing.

Freud and other psychologists at one time claimed that man needed his ability to suppress and repress painful recognitions in order to live happily, but from the time of the oldest Greek tragedy the drama has shown that true nobility cannot be achieved without self-knowledge, no matter how painful that knowledge may be.

THE UNCONSCIOUS OF THE CHARACTER AND OF THE ACTOR

Your personal patterns of repression and storehouse of repressed emotions are of considerable importance to you as an actor. They may cause emotional "blind spots" in your work, or may give rise to seemingly inexplicable anxieties in relation to certain roles or actions. The release of stored emotions and the removal of repressive blocks are useful to the actor not only to avoid blind spots and anxieties, however, but also to open the actor's unconscious fully to participation in his work.

Stanislavski's "psychotechnique" was created to assist the actor in tapping the resources of his unconscious and to bring emotional and sensory memories from the actor's personal history to bear upon the creation of his character. However, this is an area in which the playwright can rarely be specific, and careful deduction and a sensitivity to implication must guide you. It is all too easy to "project" inappropriate elements of your personal history and present personality into the unconscious mind of your character.

This sort of indiscriminate projection is a very common mistake, even among seasoned professionals. In any performance, the "subtext," that invisible pool of desires, feelings, and needs which color and to some extent motivate the character's behavior, is supplied by the actor. The actor bases his subtext upon his understanding of the character's behavior and upon *the uniquely personal connection which he has made between his unconscious and that of the character.* This aspect of characterization therefore requires the actor to project his deepest feelings into those of the character; this is a necessary aspect of the growth of the role, but one which must be approached with great care and patience.

The profound identification between actor and character, which Stanislavsky called *metamorphosis,* cannot be artificially forced; like any growth of the personality, it must occur organically and according to the rhythm of your personal assimilation of the experiences and feelings of the character. Even those seemingly sudden, massive revelations, which occasionally occur in rehearsal, as in life, are only the crystallizing steps in a journey of change which has its antecedence in all of your prior experience. Such massive breakthroughs occur when the marriage of conscious, unconscious, and organismic changes occurs in a blinding flash of self-recognition.

Such massive and sudden revelations are profound and exciting experiences, but they are not the only way in which growth occurs. Most meaningful personal development occurs in a much more invisible and gradual fashion. Have patience. Your character is growing as you have grown, through depression as through ecstasy, through failure as through success, through pain as through pleasure.

THE CONTINUITY OF EMOTION

So far we have been discussing emotions as if they had a beginning and ending. This is a common misconception which we should clarify. Emotion is not *periodic,* it is *continuous.* It arises from the success or failure of our attempts to adapt to the world and may be considered as our evaluation of the effectiveness of our adaptations. As such, it is continuous and immediate. It is vital to our well-being "for it not only furnishes the basis of awareness of what is important, but it also energizes appropriate action, or, if this is not at once available, it energizes and directs the search for it."[36] Emotion is an unending process, since we are continually evaluating our relationships with the outside world.

Actors often make the mistake of regarding emotions as periodic outbursts in their characters that flare up and then disappear, as the character progresses from one emotion to another. But there are two aspects of our character's emotional makeup; his *dominant* mood, which is continuous, and his *phasic* mood, which is changeable. Early in your development as an actor, you will successfully achieve striking moments of emotional expression. Such momentary emotions are only phases through which the character passes. Beneath these changing emotional phases is a continuity of expression and feeling, which is much more subtle and difficult to achieve. The momentary or "phasic" emotion is easier to achieve because it is intense and spectacular, but the test of the great performance is the

---

[36]Perls, Hefferline, and Goodman, *Gestalt Therapy,* p. 95.

communication of the dominant and continual existence of the character that underlies and gives meaning to phasic emotions.

The emotional life of our character, therefore, does not "begin" and "end," but rather is continuous, with phasic emotions swelling up to the surface at certain times. The potential for these phasic emotions, however, is a permanent aspect of the dominant mood. In *The Zoo Story,* Jerry's suicide must be an integral part of his personality. At the beginning of the play, it is a submerged element of his personality; we must not feel his potential for suicide too soon. But when, at the end of the play, it swells up, then we must realize that it has been there all along. Think of a character's emotional makeup as a complex musical chord containing many notes. As a whole, the chord has a unified sound into which each individual note is submerged. But the dynamic vitality of the character's changing life is achieved by allowing first one note, then another, to swell up until it can be picked out for its own sake. Though we may recognize it for its own sake at such moments, we also realize for the first time that it has been there all along. Examine your scene from this point of view.

Your experience with the action and the emotional responses of your character have probably begun to give you a vivid sense of his personality: it is now time to examine characterization per se, working from the foundation we have already laid. As you move on to the next lesson, do not lose sight of the work you have already done.

Lesson 17

Characterization

Our personality develops largely through our interaction with the environment. As infants our kinetic experience, the physical exploration of our world, is a major factor in our development: psychologists have found that inhibition of movement in an infant arrests the normal early phases of ego development. As we grow older, our relationships with our parents and eventually with larger social groups shape us, as do the customs, taboos, and value systems of our culture.

Our personality at any given moment in life is the *product of an accumulation of experiences and transactions* and is—assuming a healthy degree of responsiveness to life—*continually evolving* under the influence of ongoing experience. It seems logical, therefore, to assume that the personality of a dramatic character should evolve according to these same life-principles and with the same sense of ongoing evolution through the impact of experiences and transactions.

The rehearsal period should be viewed as a condensed period of growth and maturation of the dramatic character in which your creation passes from infancy to maturity. Your aim, therefore, should be to open yourself to the specific experiences, actions, reactions, and transactions of your character in his world. It is through these specific experiences that your character will develop and evolve in the same way that your own personality has grown and is continuing to grow.

We discussed in lesson 14 how the relationship between your character and other characters in his world was a primary factor in the development and expression of character. You can see how you and your fellow actors, under the guidance of your director, must strive to supply each other with the qualities of relationship and interaction of energies that will help each character to develop in the way demanded by the play's structure and meaning. We summarized this principle by saying that "we create each other on stage more than we create ourselves." We can now go on to say that since the dramatic personality evolves under the influence of experience and interaction with other characters, it is also true that *we find our own characterization primarily by relating to the events, circumstances, personalities, and actions of others provided within the world of the play.*

In short, *character grows out of action:* don't worry about "being the character" first and then doing things "because that's what my character would do"; instead, do the things your character does in the way he does them and see, under the influence of these specific actions, *whom they cause you to become!*

The playwright has guided you by constructing the outlines of your character so that you can fulfill your dramatic purpose and perform your actions believably. Your character is an energy-source within the play, and his personality serves to "filter" his energy so that it services the entire play. If you can engage your deepest energy in the commission of your character's actions and open your deepest center to the experiences and relationships of your character, you will find your energy being *transformed* under the influence of these specific experiences into the personality-structure of the character.

The criterion that guides and motivates you in this process is your understanding of your character's dramatic purpose, his super-objective. *Characterization, therefore, is a means to an end, never an end in itself.* Your creation of the character is really the *measure* of how successfully you have performed the tasks we have been studying so far, how successfully you perform certain actions in certain specific ways. In other words, the creation of character is not what you begin with, it is rather what you *end up* with when you have done all your various tasks well.

THE FOUR LEVELS OF CHARACTERIZATION

In order that their characters serve their dramatic purpose and perform their actions believably, playwrights construct their characters in a specific way. They provide their characters with certain traits relating to their actions and purposes, traits that distinguish the characters from, and help them to interact effectively with, the other characters in the play.

We can classify these characterizational traits on four levels, as suggested here by Oscar Brockett:

> Character is the material from which plots are created, for incidents are developed mainly through the speech and behavior of dramatic personages. Characterization is the playwright's means of differentiating one dramatic personage from another. Since a dramatist may endow his creatures with few or many traits, complexity of characterization varies markedly. In analyzing roles, it is helpful to look at four levels of characterization. (This approach is adapted from a scheme suggested by Hubert Heffner in *Modern Theatre Practice* and elsewhere.)

The first level of characterization is *physical* and is concerned only with such basic facts as sex, age, size, and color. Sometimes a dramatist does not supply all of this information, but it is present whenever the play is produced, since actors necessarily give concrete form to the characters. The physical is the simplest level of characterization, however, since it reveals external traits only, many of which may not affect the dramatic action at all.

The second level is *social.* It includes a character's economic status, profession or trade, religion, family relationships—all those factors that place him in his environment.

The third level is *psychological.* It reveals a character's habitual responses, attitudes, desires, motivations, likes, and dislikes—the inner workings of the mind, both emotional and intellectual, that precede action. Since habits of feeling, thought, and behavior define characters more fully than do physical and social traits, and since drama most often arises from conflicting desires, the psychological is the most essential level of characterization.

The fourth level is *moral.* Although implied in all plays, it is not always emphasized. It is most apt to be used in serious plays, especially tragedies. Although almost all human action suggests some ethical standard, in many plays the moral implications are ignored and decisions are made on grounds of expediency. This is typical of comedy, since moral deliberations tend to make any action serious. More nearly than any other kind, moral decisions differentiate characters, since the choices they make when faced with moral crises show whether they are selfish, hypocritical, or persons of integrity. A moral decision usually causes a character to examine his own motives and values, in the process of which his true nature is revealed both to himself and to the audience.[37]

PHYSICAL TRAITS

Let us examine these four levels of characterization more fully. The first level is *physical,* and while it may be the simplest level in relation to dramatic action, it is certainly of primary importance to an actor. The physical or external traits of body and voice that you present to your audience are the *only* means by which you can communicate any of the other levels of characterization. There is no "mental telepathy" in the theatre; if the audience can't *see* it or *hear* it, they can't understand it or feel it.

[37]From THE THEATRE, Second Edition, by Oscar G. Brockett. Copyright © 1964, 1969 by Holt, Rinehart and Winston, Inc. Reprinted by permission of Holt, Rinehart and Winston, Inc.

This is *not* to say that there is one right or wrong way for a character to look and sound. Except for a few essential traits demanded by the play, there is considerable latitude for an actor to use his own voice and body to best advantage in a role. For example, a skinny Falstaff is inconceivable, but are we really sure that Hamlet has to be thin? Willy Loman is described by Arthur Miller as being a slight man, yet the powerfully built Lee J. Cobb created a masterpiece in his portrayal of the salesman.

The Elizabethans believed that a person's physical characteristics expressed his personality; they would expect a man with a "bovine" face to be slow of wit. Falstaff's fatness is an important expression of the "fatness" of his spirit; generous and good-humored, but also lazy, sloppy, and irresponsible. In many ways, we still respond strongly to physical traits in this way; psychologists have actually determined that a squat or large-abdomened man (an endomorph) is indeed often easy-going, jolly, and a good "family man," while the "athletic" build (the mesomorph) and the thin, nervous man (the ectomorph) often exhibit qualities popularly associated with their types. So within very wide limits, a basic appropriateness of body to a role is advantageous, but this should never be construed as an argument for type-casting.

The physical qualities of character specified by most plays are general and malleable enough to make type-casting artistically unnecessary. Stanley Kowalski ought to have a strongly masculine physique and "animalistic" quality, and many actors who simply could not achieve these qualities would be disqualified for this role. Nevertheless, these qualities could be manifested in many ways by many actors, most of whom would have only ordinary physiques. The important point here is that while physical traits are a way of expressing the nature of the character, they do not have specific meanings of their own. The audience will usually accept *your* way of manifesting an important physical trait. Lee J. Cobb's body is solid and powerful, yet through his posture, rhythms, and muscle tone, he created a vivid impression of Willy Loman's exhaustion and frailty. Within the boundaries of common sense, what you've *got* is not as important as how you *use* it.

Your participation in the basic physical traits of the character is a powerful "trigger," which can generate a deeper sense of involvement in the thought and emotion of the character. Many actors use a walk, a posture, or a style of gesture as the starting point for their creation. No amount of intellectual or psychological analysis will replace the actual *experiencing* of the character that can occur when you begin to adopt his physical traits, assuming that these traits are accurate expressions of the other levels of characterizations, and also relate to the potential of your own body and voice.

The basis of your use of the physical elements of characterization will be provided by a careful study of the clues provided by the text. There are three main sources of such information in any text: those that (1) *are described in the stage directions,* (2) *are described by other characters,* and (3) *can be deduced from the action of the play, or from the close text analysis you have learned.* Such text analysis will supply many suggestions about the posture, rhythms, and vocal qualities of the character.

From each of these sources, you look for physical qualities which: (1) *relate to the action the character must perform,* (2) *express the personality of the character,* or (3) *relate to the style of the play.* This last point is a subtle one, but for now you can consider it on a basic level; a character in a Restoration comedy, for example, had better not slouch around like someone in *The Iceman Cometh,* and vice versa.

In relation to each of these points, you further ask yourself the crucial questions, *how will I use my body and voice to manifest the traits required of the character? What do I experience by participating in the physical traits of the character?*

You explored many of these physical principles in a general way in lesson 5: it would be wise to review them now in relation to a specific dramatic character.

Exercise 67   Physical characterization

Using the same character and scene as in the preceding exercise, work with your partner to rehearse the scene using each of the following exercises:

A. Repeat exercise 24 to select the bodily center, alignment, energy-structure, and quality of gesture appropriate to your character;
B. Repeat exercise 66 to review the repressive aspects of the character's behavior and their effect on his body;
C. Repeat exercise 27, using the list of compositional characteristics that you applied to your mask as a checklist to explore further vocal and physical possibilities in your scene character;
D. Repeat exercise 44 to be sure you understand how the words spoken by your character are an exteriorization of his thought process;
E. Consider what aids such as hard props, costume, makeup, etc. might be useful in completing the characterization.

Don't underestimate the contribution that can be made by makeup and costuming. Age and physique can be changed radically. But padding and crepe hair can only *support* a physical characterization, never *substitute* for one. Any costume or makeup depends upon the actor's skill in wearing it, while no good actor has ever *depended* upon costume and makeup. Nevertheless, such aids are respectable and important elements of your theatrical heritage, and it would be stupid to avoid using whatever can help to create a more vivid character.

SOCIAL TRAITS

This second level of characterization relates the character to his environment and the people in it. Character can be understood fully only when we understand the situation in which it operates. Even a single emotion cannot be properly interpreted without an understanding of context. This fact has been recognized by psychologists:

> The celebrated James-Lange theory of emotion as a reaction to bodily movement—for instance running away gives rise to fear or weeping gives rise to sorrow—is half right. What needs to be added is that the bodily actions or condition are also a relevant *orientation to,* and a potential *manipulation of,* the environment; for example, it is not just running, but running *away,* running away from *something,* running away from something *dangerous,* that contributes to the situation of fear.[38]

We must never, even on a basic emotional level, approach our characters in a vacuum. Only by fully realizing the situation and relationships, the objectives, the inhibitions, and the characteristic responses of our character can we fully understand the emotions to be expressed in our performance. The playwright has carefully chosen and constructed the situation in which the characters operate, and it is our job to discover the essential aspects of that situation that influence character.

Many of Tennessee Williams's plays, for example, must take place in the hot, humid climate of the south. Think what an air-conditioner would do to *A Streetcar Named Desire!* Shakespeare chose to set a play of great passion, *Othello,* in a similar climate. But beyond simple physical influences of climate, the *social* environment established by the playwright is of great importance. The society in which Stanley Kowalski moves, for example, is an active part of Stanley's character. Think over the plays you have read, and you will see how in each case the influences of the immediate locale have been carefully chosen and are indispensable ingredients in the realization of character.

Even more important than the effect of the environment is the charac-

ter's relationship to each of the other characters in the play. The relationships are a direct expression of the conflict or dramatic interaction between
the participants, and also a profound influence upon and expression of
each of their individual characters. When we examine one of these relationships, we see an extraordinary wealth of information that is in many
ways more important to the actor than statements about any of the characters alone. Your concept of a character and the determination of his dramatic function and main action must be based on an understanding of his
purposeful interaction with other characters, as expressed by his relationships.

In *Death of a Salesman,* for example, Willy has a relationship with each
person in the play: father, husband, lover, neighbor, employee, salesman.
We see Willy operating in each of these contexts, and each relationship
reveals another aspect of Willy's character. Each of these relationships also
helps us to penetrate the surface of his behavior to the underlying consistency of Willy's character.

As we define our character's various actions and points of reaction at
any moment, we must define his relationships and what they are expressing as well. Our reactions, which in turn become new actions, will grow
almost entirely within the context provided by these relationships.

As is often said to actors, "the root of what you do is in the other
people," and realizing your character's relationship to each of the other
characters provides the guidelines for your interaction with your co-workers as well as tremendous insight into the character itself.

Exercise 68   Social characterization

A. Examine your scene character and the relationships within your
scene according to the following points:

   1. *What is my character's relationship to his environment?*
   2. *What is his relationship to every other character?*
   3. *How does each of these relationships affect his dramatic
      purpose?*
   4. *How does each of these relationships affect his needs, desires,
      and intentions?*
   5. *How does each affect his actions?*

B. Repeat exercise 26 (gesture communication scene), using its
principles to "boil down" your scene into one expressive gestural
and vocal pattern that embodies your relationship and any changes
that occur in the relationship in the course of the scene's action.

PSYCHOLOGICAL AND MORAL TRAITS

We will approach the third and fourth levels of characterization as one. We must here understand the *process of thought,* which is the antecedent of action. The nature of this process is different and serves different functions in various plays. In plays where the external action of the plot itself is the dominant element of the play (as in allegories, farces, and some Classical tragedies, for example), the psychological aspect of characterization is of small importance. In fact, when the actor insists on psychologically motivating every action, even when such motivation is irrelevant to the nature of the play, the quality of the play's structure may suffer greatly. On the other hand, some plays feature *interior* action (like those of Chekhov and O'Neill), and here the psychology of the characters is the vehicle for the plot itself.

The main point is to remember that the psychology of character is meant always to serve the demands of *action,* and that the relative importance and nature of psychological characterization is dependent on the play's dramatic objectives and structure. Your analysis of your character's action and the process of decision by which his inner action flows into external activity has already provided you with the basis for understanding the character's psychology, for it is in reenacting each of his choices that you best come to understand the character's mind.

Now you can turn to the text to see the *specific* ways in which the playwright's shaping of the action leads to an understanding of the psychology and values of the character. In Arthur Miller's *Death of a Salesman,* for example, Willy, whose felt need is to be "successful," is presented by his situation with several alternatives. He could, like his brother Ben, strike off on some bold venture; or he could, like his neighbor Charley, accept his life as it is and see that in many important ways he *is* a success. But Willy is driven by the "American Dream," in which success is not internal satisfaction, but the esteem of others and the tangible worth of material possessions. Lacking the courage and independence to follow his brother's example, and lacking also the sense of self-identity necessary to accept his own lot, he finally opts for a third alternative, the suicide, which will give his insurance to his family. It is the making of this choice, and seeing how frustrations from society and from within Willy himself have driven him to this choice, that moves the entire mechanism of the play.

In the terms we have been using, Willy's *main dramatic purpose* relates to the *theme* of his play; how American society in general, and the free-enterprise system in particular, can destroy a man by filling him with false values. The *main action* that translates this dramatic purpose into active terms is Willy's constant *search for "success,"* which for him means esteem and possessions. Each scene, each beat, each moment of the role, and

Willy's thought at any moment, can be understood as contributing to this basic purpose, and reflecting this main action.

When the process of a character's decision making involves moral values, as it does in Willy's case, then we can speak of his ethical or moral characterization. When this aspect of character is important, it will always relate directly to the thematic content of the play; the moral choice confronting Willy, for example, is an embodiment of Arthur Miller's thesis regarding American society. When such moral value is attached to your character, you must shape your performance to meet its demands, though the *process* of thought involved will be the same as that we have already described. In other words, the psychological and moral levels of characterization are not different in *kind,* but only in the *values* involved.

COMPLEXITY OF CHARACTERIZATION

We have examined each of four levels of characterization. Each works in relation to each of the others, and the way in which they are put together reflects the purpose and nature of the play. Oscar Brockett indicates this:

> A playwright may emphasize one or more of these levels. Some writers pay little attention to the physical appearance of their characters, concentrating instead upon psychological and moral traits; other dramatists may describe appearance and social status in detail. In assessing the completeness of a characterization, however, it is not enough merely to make a list of traits and levels of characterization. It is also necessary to ask *how the character functions in the play.* For example, the audience needs to know little about the maid who only appears to announce dinner; any detailed characterization would be superflous and distracting. On the other hand, the principal characters need to be drawn in greater depth. The appropriateness and completeness of each characterization, therefore, may be judged only after analyzing its function in each scene and in the play as a whole.[39]

Too often we train actors as if each of them was going to play nothing but major roles, and so they attempt to turn the maid announcing dinner into Phaedra. This is not to say that the maid should not be fully characterized; she should be as fully characterized as *she needs to be.* To realize the

[39]From THE THEATRE, Second Edition, by Oscar G. Brockett. Copyright © 1964, 1969 by Holt, Rinehart and Winston, Inc. Reprinted by permission of Holt, Rinehart and Winston, Inc.

limits of a characterization and fill them completely, without allowing extraneous and irrelevant details to obscure the clear outlines of dramatic purpose and character action, is what we mean by *economy*.

Think of a great athlete whose performances you have admired. His "style," his grace and power, come from the complete *efficiency* with which every bit of his energy is focused upon the job at hand. He exhibits no movement or bit of concentration that does not directly contribute to his purpose. This is his economy.

If *your* purpose is to be a maid announcing dinner, then any energy directed toward creating qualities beyond those necessary for the fulfillment of this task is wasteful and distracting. An overly detailed performance is as disruptive as an incomplete one. This is the actor's sense of economy, and it is the hallmark of his skill and concentration.

THE DYNAMIC NATURE OF CHARACTER

Just as your personality in real life is continually changing, many dramatic characters are shown undergoing a similar process. Not all characters change, of course, despite the tremendously moving things that happen to them and the shattering discoveries they make about themselves. Oedipus, Othello, Jerry in *The Zoo Story,* and many other important characters from every type of drama undergo no essential change of character within their plays. Minor characters are rarely characterized deeply enough to undergo significant changes, and since such change usually implies some serious self-discovery, comic characters rarely change in any essential way.

When a significant change in the nature of a dramatic character *is* demanded, however, it is often a direct expression of a theme of the play, and the dramatic purpose of many characters is to undergo just such a change. In these cases, the main action should be defined in terms of the change, and all minor activities should be defined in terms of their contribution to the change.

Lear, for example, undergoes a radical change, which is expressed in three phases: his self-centeredness at the outset of the play, the suffering and madness he brings upon himself in the middle of the play, and the humility and love of humanity he has learned by the end. It is hard to imagine the Lear of the first scene praying for justice for the poor, or calling himself a "fond, foolish old man."

Yet it is this change in Lear that expresses the main theme of the play and is Lear's dramatic function. His main action changes, then, as he changes. At first, his main activity is to retire as king and still be assured of grace, comfort, and respect. All his actions in the first two acts can be related to this activity, which is frustrated by his daughters. When this desire has been completely frustrated, the second unit of action begins, as Lear himself prophesies, "O, fool, I shall go mad."

Lear's second main action is to seek vengeance upon his daughters, and the storm is at once a heavenly extension of his wrath and a punishment for his earlier pride and insensitivity. Throughout his growing madness, he seeks vengeance, this main action sustaining him until his meeting with Gloucester near the end of the fourth act, when he imagines sneaking up on his daughters, "Then, kill, kill, kill, kill, kill, kill!"

His third and last main action is expressed in his love for Cordelia, a poetic balancing, since it was his banishing of Cordelia that instigated the tragedy in scene 1. The man who was self-centered at the outset of the play has, through suffering, become completely *other*-centered in his love for his daughter at the end, and the shifting of his main actions reflects the change. Lear's change embodies the change in his world, away from the injustice of feudal society toward a more humanistic, democratic morality.

SUMMARY EXERCISE

Let us review all that has been covered so far in part 3 with the following exercise, which should take several sessions to complete.

Exercise 69   Scene work

Use the same scene you and your partner chose for the previous exercise. Considering the entire play, as well as the demands of your particular scene, consider each level of the characterization of your roles.

I. Physical. What physical characteristics are important to your role? Consider stage directions, descriptions by other characters, and information you can deduce from the purposes and actions of your character.

II. Social

A. What factors of environment are important to your characters?
B. What relationship do your characters have in the play? In this scene?
C. How do these relationships help express your characters' dramatic purposes?
D. How do they influence your actions?

III. Psychological and moral

A. Considering the entire play—
1. Does your play feature mainly external or internal action? How important is psychological characterization to it?
2. What are the needs, desires, or intentions of each of your characters? How does their relationship affect or express these needs?
3. What alternatives are available to your characters for the satisfaction of their needs?
4. On what basis do the characters choose between these alternatives? Are moral choices involved? What do their choices express?
5. How does this process of thought lead to the actions of the characters? How does it help express their dramatic purpose?
6. How detailed and complex must each of your characterizations be in order to be appropriate to the meaning, organization, and style of the play?
B. Considering your scene in particular—
1. How does the relationship between your characters affect the scene action?
2. How does the psychological process of each character affect the scene action?
a. Relate your character's immediate need, intention, or desire to the scene action.
b. What decisions does he make within the scene, if any?
c. How do his reactions to the situation or to the other character express his thought and affect the action?
3. Consider each beat of the scene and each moment of each beat. How does this organization of the scene action help express the process of thought of each character?

IV. Thought polarization. Act out the scene slowly, trying to *exteriorize* the process of thought of each character. Let the audience see your character's needs or intentions, the alternatives available to him, and the decisions he makes prior to each of his actions or reactions. In other words, physicalize *as a muscular experience* the dynamic process of thought of your character. Again, your movements will not be "realistic" or even appropriate to a performance of the scene. Instead, move so as to create *for yourself and your partner* an active expression of your character's thought. See how fully you can respond to, and participate in, your partner's thought as well; experience how the movement of the scene is produced by the interaction of the thought processes of the characters.

Like exercise 58, the Action Polarization, this long exercise summarizes what is normally a characterizational development that goes on throughout a rehearsal period. These two exercises taken together express much of the process of the creation of character and should be given thorough attention and plenty of time. It is through the process they embody that the most mysterious, magical, and spiritual quality of acting is achieved, the phenomenon of *transformation*.

Lesson 18

Transformation

The Greek play festivals were "gifts" to Dionysus, a very old god whose roots go back at least four thousand years. Also commonly called Bacchus, he is most often associated today with the Bacchic "orgies," which were actually frenzied religious rituals. It is in the nature of this ancient god that the deepest impulses motivating the theatre and the actor may be found, for this god of the theatre was himself an actor—a lover of disguise, trickery, and transformation. He is the god of potency, of the ecstatic irrational vitality that moves man as a race through time.

The development of theatre was deeply involved with the worship of Dionysus, and both center around the phenomenon of *transformation,* man's ability to transcend the limits of ordinary existence and to enter into new states of being, into extended or even separate realities. The Bacchic reveler, through wine and the frenzy of exhaustion, entered into states of expanded consciousness similar to those produced today by hallucinogenic drugs or meditation; the worship of Dionysus usually took the form of a *masked dance,* with Dionysus himself most commonly represented by the mask of a bull. Many consider the masked dancer to be the true prototype of the actor.

The mask, ancient and mysterious, is a feature of rituals and celebrations in many cultures, from the African medicine man to the Kachinas of the American Hopi Indians, to the Hallowe'en trick-or-treater. The wearing of masks seems to offer man a way of sharing in divinity and immortality for, by donning the mask of a god, the worshipper becomes "possessed" by the god.

The mask in a primitive festival is revered and experienced as a veritable apparition of the mythical being that it represents—even though everyone knows that a man made the mask and that a man is wearing it. The one wearing it, furthermore, is identified with the god during the time of the ritual of which the mask is a part. He does not merely represent the god; he *is* the god.[40]

The mask, with its mythic vitality, seizes its mortal wearer, and he feels his transitory, mortal energies inhabiting an immortal form. As Walter Otto puts it in his study of Dionysian worship:

The primal phenomenon of duality . . . the fraternal confluence of life and death. . . . This duality has its symbol in the mask. . . .

The wearer of the mask is seized by the sublimity and dignity of those who are no more. He is himself and yet someone else. Madness has touched him—something of the spirit of the dual being who lives in the mask and whose recent descendant is the actor.[41]

The wearing of masks is, in short, a celebration of that irrational vitality from which life itself springs. The ebb and flow of the life-force, the "fraternal confluence of life and death," is itself a great drama. The actor's ability to transform himself, to be "himself and yet someone else," is a testament to the continual cycle of life, the dynamism of life-energy that manifests itself in continual change and man's spiritual capacity to define his own existence.

ACTING AND MASK WEARING

From the actor's point of view, the concept of the mask must be understood in a very broad way: a mask, or the principle of maskness, is *any object or pattern of behavior that projects a sense of the self to the outside world.*

As we discussed in the opening pages of this book, your personality (from the root *persona,* or *mask*) is itself a mask, a pattern of behavior whereby you present yourself to your world: acting is based upon this everyday life principle, with important extensions and modifications.

In everyday life, you perform actions that become a mask presented to others, and your social audience responds to this mask of actions as if it were your "authentic" self; if I convince you that I am a certain kind of person, it is not necessarily because I *am* that person, but because I have

[40]Joseph Campbell, *The Masks of God: Primitive Mythology* (New York: Viking Press, 1959), p. 2.
[41]Walter Otto, *Dionysus: Myth and Cult* (Bloomington: Indiana University Press, 1965), p. 210.

performed my mask of actions successfully. Social psychologist Erving Goffman explains it this way:

> In our society the character one performs and one's self are somewhat equated. A correctly staged and performed scene leads the audience to impute a self to a performed character, but this imputation—this self—is a *product* of a scene that comes off, and is not a *cause* of it. The self, then, as a performed character is not an organic thing . . . it is a dramatic effect arising diffusely from a scene that is presented.[42]

For the ancient worshipper or actor, the mask was an object to be worn, which carried with it a vitality of its own. The contemporary actor rarely wears a literal mask, but he still creates a *pattern of actions* (behavior) that projects a persona. This pattern of actions becomes the "mask" of the created character, and when the actor puts on this mask, he is literally impersonating in the root sense of that word: *im-persona,* "going into a new mask." He is *trans-forming* himself, "going into a new form." We who watch project onto his mask of actions a sense of authentic identity.

We may define an actor as someone *who disciplines himself to enter into a new personality through his theatrical craft.*

It is never enough, however, for the actor merely to put on a convincing mask, merely to *seem* to be someone else; he must wear the mask of his character with such total commitment that he creates an independent and meaningful reality with its own deeper truth. His fundamental task is therefore a dual one—he must *seem* and also *be.* No matter how much he seems to be someone else, his creation must also have its own personal reality; it must exist not only as a representation but as a unique creation in its own right. Stanislavski called the difference between acting filled with the true experience of the actor and acting that merely emulated the surface appearances of things as "the difference between seeming and being."[43]

All periods and styles of theatre demand their own particular balance between seeming and being. Think of this balance as being represented by a mask that can be made more or less transparent, allowing us to see more or less of the actor's face beneath it. Now imagine this changeable mask as a set of postures, gestures, sounds, and actions performed by the actor, which require a greater or lesser degree of transformation of him; can you now understand how different kinds of acting, having different purposes, require different relationships between actor and character, different balances of seeming and being?

---

[42]Goffman, *The Presentation of Self in Everyday Life,* pp. 254–55.
[43]Stanislavski, *An Actor's Handbook,* p. 91.

In some kinds of theatre, the actor's own presence is a dominant element in the performance (as was the case with the virtuoso stars of the nineteenth century and is still the case with our own movie idols), and some plays, like those of Brecht, even encourage us to see the actor's own face peeking out from behind the mask of the character. On the other hand, other kinds of plays (especially realistic ones) encourage the actor to disappear completely behind the opaque mask of his character.

Whatever the balance between seeming and being required by your play, this balancing expresses itself for you as a peculiar kind of multiple consciousness. As George C. Scott put it in an interview:

> I think you have to schizoid three different ways to be an actor. You've got to be three different people: you have to be a human being, then you have to be the character you're playing, and on top of that, you've got to be the guy sitting out there in row 10, watching yourself and judging yourself.
> That's why most of us are crazy to start with or go nuts once we get into it. I mean, don't you think it's a pretty spooky way to earn a living?

This multiple consciousness of the created character, with its own identity existing simultaneously with the actor's personal identity and with his theatrical concerns, is similar to the ancient mask-wearer's experience of being "possessed" by his mask. This "being yourself and yet someone else" is a kind of controlled schizophrenia—but it is an important and potentially beautiful and fine madness.

This multiple consciousness is a feature of *all* acting: no matter how opaque the mask required by the play, we never entirely lose sight of the actor's own face; nor does the actor lose his sense of his own separate identity. If we were to lose sight of the actor's own face completely, we would also lose our sense of the duality of his existence, and the magic of his transformation would be lessened. If the actor were to lose his own sense of separate identity, he would also lose his ability to make aesthetic choice, and his "fine madness" would become pathological insanity.

Nor, on the other hand, do we ever entirely lose sight of the mask either. No matter how "transparent" a mask required by the performance, and even though the actor may momentarily drop the mask and reveal his own face, he cannot discard his mask altogether. Without his mask he is not an actor, he is only a man.

PUTTING YOURSELF INTO THE CHARACTER

A character existing only on the printed page of your script is lifeless. At first he is only an outline, an empty receptacle waiting to be filled. You must contribute your responses, give something of your own vitality, in order to bring him to life. Many external properties of the receptacle have been determined by the playwright, but you create the energy that will, for you, best fill the receptacle, best make it glow with inner life. The actor must *analyze, respond to,* and *rejuvenate* what the playwright provides. This process is a dialogue between externals and internals, each affecting the other, with the text as the initiator and eventual criterion of judgment of this process.

Though your own feelings must be engaged in the creation of the character, they must be selected and modified in order to meet the demands of the script: *you do not absorb the character into yourself but, rather, put yourself into the character.*

The way in which an actor projects himself *into* his character is not unlike the way in which we put ourselves "in the shoes" of other people in real life. Psychologists call this process *empathy.* The word *empathy* has been knocking around the theatre for a good many years. No one is quite sure what it means, and it is so misused that some critics have suggested abandoning it altogether. If we look into the development of this concept, however, we can find much that seems useful as a way of describing the actor-character relationship.

The word *empathy* was coined in 1906 to translate the German word, *Einfühlung. Einfühlung* literally means "in-feeling," and it originally described how we project muscular sensations into inanimate objects. When we look at a steeple "thrusting" up toward the sky, sense the "twisting" feeling of a spiral, or the "rolling" feeling of low hills, we are projecting these muscular feelings *into* the objects. Later on, psychologists began to use this term as a way of describing how a person can imaginatively project himself into the place of another person. When you are empathizing, you are feeling yourself "in" the place of another person, though the feelings you are experiencing are still your own, not his.

> You can share an experience with someone in the sense that you and he may experience similarly some situation which you and he have in common but what he experiences is *his* and what you experience is *yours.* When you say to a friend in trouble, "I feel for you," you do not mean that literally, since he is doing his own feeling and no one else can do it for him, but simply that you, by imagining yourself in his place, construct a vivid picture of what the situation would be like—and then react to that.[44]

The actor puts himself into the place of his character in the same way; he has, for himself, the experiences of the character. Under the impact of

[44]Perls, Hefferline, and Goodman, *Gestalt Therapy,* p. 33.

these experiences he is transformed; he behaves *as if* he were feeling what the character feels, and through this empathy a kind of "sympathetic magic" occurs, and he starts to become that version of himself that fits the reality of the character. This is what Stanislavski called the "Magic If," a process of empathy which could lead to "Metamorphosis," or—as it would be called in psychology—"identification" between actor and character.

USE OF YOUR OWN EXPERIENCE

Your own feelings and experiences are the principal materials you manipulate in fashioning a creation appropriate to the demands of a given play, but it would be irresponsible to force a character to conform to your personality. The actor's art is a very creative one, but it is not a particularly *self*-expressive one. Perhaps we should say that *the actor realizes himself by living the life of his characters.*

Since most human experience has some commonality, a good deal of your own experience will be useful in the creation of any character. But the way in which that experience is used, the configuration it assumes, must be determined by the demands of the play, not by the nature of your own being.

Remember also that most plays deal with situations that are in part extraordinary, or beyond your specific life experience. When you do old plays, for example, you are forced to relive the spirit of an age that has long since ceased to be, to behave in a way that is alien to the "natural" behavior of your own time. Even contemporary plays demand a great deal that you cannot provide from your own real experience, and it will be a rare occurrence when your own habitual manner of expression will satisfactorily coincide with the form required by a particular play.

A sense of estrangement and the thought of suicide have at some time crossed the minds of most of us, but we have not behaved precisely like Jerry, nor done what Jerry does in *The Zoo Story*. Nevertheless, your own emotional *energies,* if not the habitual form in which you express them, provide the basis of all stage creation, remembering that however much you may utilize your own experience and feelings in creating a part, you will also gain *new* experience and feelings in the process.

While it *is* necessary for you to search out all the ways in which you are similar to your character, to bring to bear all experiences that help you to understand and express the character, it would be foolish and unrealistic to ignore the many ways in which you and your character are quite different, especially in the form of your expression and that demanded by the character. These differences must be realized, accepted, and utilized.

You must isolate the aspects of your own experience and behavior that are not appropriate to the creation of the character, and extend or modify them in the act of creation until they *are* appropriate. It is all too easy to imitate a character so strongly that you project into him qualities of your own personality and experience, which turn out to be unfunctional, irrelevant, and therefore untruthful. In order to identify truly, you must get as close to the character as you can *without* losing your respect for the character's separate identity as an artistic creation with a definite purpose.

This is one of the most exciting aspects of acting: the actor is continually expanding himself, continually having experiences that are inaccessible to the average person. By feeling what it is to live in past ages, in other places, and inside of people quite different from ourselves, actors find their own lives continually challenged and expanded. The actor who looks only *within* himself for the materials of creation is robbing himself of vast riches of experience embodied within the great plays of the theatre; the actor who, on the other hand, refuses to involve himself in his creation, will remain unaffected by the experiences he merely pretends to be having.

You may enjoy testing the depths of your assimilation of your character with the following exercise. It is based upon one used by psychotherapist Nathaniel Branden in his work, and you may use it to explore spontaneously expressed feelings of your character.

Exercise 70   The character's feelings

Preferably standing before a group, place yourself in alignment. Perform your relaxation exercise; then proceed to enter your characterization as fully as you can. Imagine yourself as the character in a specific place; endow your witnesses with specific identities of persons within the character's world; then speak directly to each of these persons in turn the following phrases, allowing a new spontaneous ending to erupt each time as you repeat the phrase going around the group. Take a moment to confront and contact each person, and speak directly to him, allowing a new ending to occur for each repetition. Keep momentum and try not to allow premeditation to occur. If a spontaneous ending does not arise, simply invent one or move on.

When I wake up in the morning, . . .
Ever since I was a child . . .
When I look in the mirror . . .
Pleasure to me is . . .
I can remember . . .
The child in me . . .

I need . . .
I hate . . .
Strength to me means . . .
Weakness to me means . . .
Right now I am aware . . .
Sometimes I want to cry out to people . . .
Pain to me is . . .
I love . . .
If I could be free to do what I want to do . . .
My body . . . [45]

A tape recording of the session will be very useful to you. As you review the session, notice what you may learn not only about your character but about your feelings toward your character, and about your character's feelings toward specific persons in his world.

BELIEVABILITY AND STYLE

You must create a character who will do what he must to further the action of his play "believably," that is, *as a logical expression of his very being.* This means that believability comes from the realization of the function and form of your character within the play's structure, not necessarily from seeming "true-to-life" in an everyday sense.

In fact, a character who was "true-to-everyday-life" would seem most *un*believable in any of the great Classical plays. Even in a "realistic" play, the expression of character is heightened and selected far beyond everyday life in order to achieve an artistic purpose. So, in portraying a character, your job is *not* necessarily to be true-to-*life* but *always* to be true to your character's *dramatic purpose* and the form of the play in which he appears.

Your understanding of the play's form is an essential part of your understanding of the character, and you empathize with your character with respect for the way in which he expresses himself. To be "believable" on stage you must be more than simply alive; you must also be *correctly* alive according to the style of the play.

"Styles of Acting" is a course usually reserved for advanced students, but a realization of style should be the objective of even the earliest acting experience. One of the most pressing needs in American theatre, especially in the repertory theatres, is for actors who possess an understanding of, and the facility for achieving, appropriate style.

---

[45]Nathaniel Branden, *The Disowned Self* (New York: Bantam, 1973), pp. 111–14. This is only a small selection of the many phrases listed by Dr. Branden.

What is style? We often speak of "stylized" plays, meaning nonnaturalistic or highly "artificialized" plays. But style in its broadest sense means much more than that. It is the way in which all the elements of a play have been integrated in a form expressive of the playwright, the age in which he wrote, the social and physical theatrical environment for which he created, and the way in which his play lives for us today. It is, in short, the way in which everything is put together, the cement that bonds all the elements of the play into a unified and expressive whole.

Style, in this sense, is distinguished from *stylization. Stylization* implies exaggerated external and artificialized patterns of behavior, but *style* refers to the unique *intrinsic* properties and manner of construction of an individual play. All plays have style, not just "stylized" ones.

Plays of similar types or genres may share strong stylistic similarities. Most Greek tragedies, for example, feature a massive and highly economical form of action. Most Restoration comedies feature highly ornate, verbal humor based upon simile and puns, and extremely complex plots based upon a "sex chase." Since they come from the same milieu, it is not surprising that these plays share a characteristic set of values and emphasize certain qualities of the theatrical experience more or less than other genres. The effect of generic qualities on style is very important. Yet it is dangerous to oversimplify the effect of genre on the style of an individual play, for this kind of thinking leads to the creation of formulas by which certain types of plays "ought" to be performed.

The work of many major playwrights has been mistreated by such oversimplified attitudes about their style: Shakespeare, Shaw, Chekhov, Brecht, and Beckett, to name a few. Such generalized thinking leads to a sameness and a lack of vividness in production. We must always respect the unique and individual demands of a work as interpreted by our director. Our performance should grow organically from our attempt to meet those demands.

Your performance, and the production of which it is a part, have a style of their own. Your objective is to make the style of your performance a direct expression and extension of the style of the play. In other words, you strive to put your performance together on the same principles that provided the stylistic unity of your play.

This means that no *one* acting methodology will serve the needs of all plays. Plays of different generic types are not constructed in the same way; they are based upon different theatrical premises. You can't do Restoration comedy with the same methodology you might use for a play by O'Neill. You must recognize the demands of the work at hand and use your fundamental techniques in the way best suited to meet those specific demands. While there are many common techniques and attitudes involved in all acting, and many similarities for the actor between plays of similar types, each play presents its own problems and demands its own solutions. *You can't act a style; true style results only from doing the specific job at hand in the way demanded by the form of the play.*

SOCIAL ROLE-PLAYING AND CHARACTERIZATION

Earlier we discussed the similarities between the way in which we all "perform" in everyday life and the basic techniques of stage acting. Now that we have studied some of the many specific demands of stage interpretation and technique that make stage acting more conscious, disciplined, and structured than everyday social acting, we can return to their underlying similarities.

Erving Goffman feels that our social performance can be viewed on two levels: the image we consciously desire to project to our audience, and the impressions that, despite our best efforts, they form of us.

> Knowing that an individual is likely to present himself in a light that is favorable to him, the others (to whom he is relating) may divide what they witness into two parts: a part that is relatively easy for the individual to manipulate at will, being chiefly his verbal assertions, and a part in regard to which he seems to have little concern or control, being chiefly derived from the expressions he gives off. The others may then use what are considered to be the ungovernable aspects of his expressive behavior as a check upon the validity of what is conveyed by the governable aspects.[46]

If I appear to be listening to you with the utmost interest and concentration, leaning forward in my chair and straining to catch every word, and yet you catch me glancing over your shoulder or shuffling my foot under my chair, you intuitively compare the information I am trying to *give* you (that I am interested) with the contrary impressions I am unconsciously *giving off* (that I am bored). In this case, you judge me to be insincere; when the information we *give* and that we *give off* coincide, then we are adjudged sincere. Each of us possesses a highly developed faculty for perceiving the unconscious behavior of others, even though such perceptions are themselves often unconscious.

This description of conscious and unconscious behavior during the social performance is useful in describing the stage performance as well. If we have failed to control each aspect of our behavior on stage, including

---

[46]Goffman, *The Presentation of Self in Everyday Life,* p. 7.

those that are normally beyond conscious control, our audience will perceive behavior that may be contrary to the image we desire to create. Incomplete characterization, lack of concentration, and failure to make strong contact with our fellow actors will all result in behavior that is contrary to our desired impression, and the audience will judge our performance to be unconvincing.

Stanislavski's technique aimed at a strong subjective involvement with the life of the character and was a way of insuring that the actor's own automatic behavior was utilized in his performance, since the actor's unconscious would supposedly be fully involved with the character. Unfortunately, our automatic behavior is not very flexible or changeable; if it is never recognized and evaluated as an element of a purposeful artistic creation, it may work against us. Though in the final creation of our performance much of what we do has again become unconscious or automatic, at some time in the rehearsal period it must have been consciously evaluated and structured. If, in this way, we stage actors can bring normally unconscious forms of behavior within the realm of our discipline, we will have gained a potent means of controlling our audience's impression of our character and the convincingness of our performance.

Exercise 71   Social and stage acting

Part I: Observing Yourself. Using yourself as a subject, observe changes in your everyday behavior from situation to situation. What dramatic devices do you use to reinforce your own sanity by reminding yourself of some consistency behind these performances? You probably refuse to meet some demands made upon you by social role-playing. What are those demands; are any of them similar to demands that may be made upon you on stage? What aspects of the social situation threaten you in the same way that the stage situation does?

Examine also the relationship between your social role-playing and your role-playing on stage. What similarities and what differences are there in the two activities? What skills have you developed socially that will be useful on stage? What inhibitions have you developed socially that will be liabilities on stage?

Are there certain areas of your body, certain types of gestures, that seem further from your conscious control than others? In your own social role-playing, become aware of your "unconscious" behavior. Try to manipulate it.

Part II: Observing Others. Observe others to study the ways in which they project an image of themselves: what similarities are there between this social characterization and one on the stage? What dissimilarities?

Develop your eye and memory for particularly expressive bits of real-life behavior. Do you begin to realize how "stylized" real-life behavior often is? Can we speak of the style of a person in real life? How might this relate to experiencing the unique qualities of a character in a play, especially a highly "stylized" one?

Try adopting the behavior of people you observe. Does this help you to understand them? Does it give you new experiences and enlarge your own personality? How does this relate to adopting the behavior of a stage character as outlined by a playwright?

WHAT THE ACTOR NEEDS

We can now state a fuller definition of the actor's job: *to fulfill believably his character's dramatic function in a unified, vital, and stylistically accurate stage creation.* The three active ingredients of this definition are FUNCTION, FORM, and VITALITY.

From these three principles, we can state the actor's basic needs, which have provided the content and organization of this book.

1. In order to understand the *function* of your character and the exact quality of action demanded by him, and to know exactly what problems of style a play presents, you must know how to analyze the dramatic text in depth. Just as a musician's ability to perform a composition is dependent upon his music-reading skill and the background he brings to his music, so too, you must practice text analysis and equip yourself with a solid background in dramatic literature.

2. In order to manifest the *form* of your characterization, you need *mastery of your voice and body.* You will remain a slave to technique until you are in control of it, able to form concepts and express them without technical restriction.

3. Finally, the *vitality* of your performance is the synthesis of function and form, the focusing of *all* your energy and concentration on the playing of your role. This *role-playing* ability is at once the most basic of your actor's abilities and the most "natural" to you. If your responsiveness as an open and integrated person, your contact with your environment and fellow workers, your mastery of technique, and your understanding of the job to be done are sufficient, your natural energies will be *liberated* and *focused.* It is the liberation and focus of energy that, together, supply vitality.

Exercise 72   Role-playing

1. Using the same scene as in the previous exercises, discuss with your partner the ways in which you are each like your characters, and the ways in which you are different.

2. Discuss how the way in which your characters express themselves and the style of the play demands a different form of behavior than that which is habitual to each of you. On the other hand, what aspects of your natural behavior might be appropriate to the character's style?

3. Trace your memory to see what experiences and sensations you can remember that relate to those of your character. How might the richness of these experiences be incorporated into your performance? In what ways would they have to be modified?

4. Finally, rehearse the scene over and over again, stopping to discuss these points and attempting to project yourself further and further into the character. Check each other's behavior: are you entering into the form demanded by the character? How does each new insight into the character open up new avenues of exploration and experience?

The Working Process

Success is important to all actors, but you must ask yourself what constitutes the true measure of success. Depending on the same attitudes and techniques play after play, no matter how highly developed these techniques may become, can bring only limited artistic success; the serious actor strives to balance his desire for immediate success with the more important long-range demands of his development as an artist. In short, he approaches each new role, each rehearsal, each performance, not simply with a desire to *succeed* but with a desire to *learn.*

Every serious actor continues to develop and extend his skills with disciplined regularity throughout his lifetime. There is no real substitute for the valuable experience earned in the rehearsal situation, in meeting the day-to-day demands of preparing plays for performance and in the performances themselves. This is why the actor in a repertory company, preparing a continuous variety of roles, develops his skills much faster than the actor who works only occasionally or in long runs of individual shows.

This "learning by doing" depends, however, upon how well the actor takes advantage of his rehearsal opportunities. Many actors with the chance to work steadily choose to fall deeper and deeper into their own ruts, depending time and again upon proven gimmicks and tricks. Such actors cheat their public and themselves, wasting invaluable opportunities to expand their artistry by honestly working to solve the unique problems of each play they do. It is artistic growth that makes the rehearsal the most important of all the actor's activities. It is not simply a time to learn lines and blocking; its true purpose is to allow the creative ensemble to *explore alternatives* and to *make choices.*

EXPLORATION IN REHEARSAL

The kind of exploration that takes place in rehearsal is not only the individual actor's exploration of character, but also a group exploration of the moments that pass between characters. Therefore, besides making contact with our fellow actors, we must equally trust and make contact with the *moment* itself.

When we say "trust the moment," we mean that in any rehearsal there are a great many unpredictable variables at work, and the ensemble must be receptive to them. Rehearsal is a time of risk; the ensemble must, as a unit, step off into the unknown of the immediate moment. It is not a blind step, and much thought and preparation go into it; but at some time we must allow the flow of events driven by real contact between actors to carry us along.

Too often, actors treat rehearsals much as if they were performances, planning in great detail what they mean to do in advance. The director is thrust into the role of moderator, attempting to bring their various prefabricated performances into some kind of peaceful coexistence. The impulse to "succeed" is so strong in most actors that they refuse to risk failure at the very time when such a risk is the first order of business, as it is in rehearsal. No honest exploration is possible under such circumstances.

Of course, a great deal of "homework" must precede all rehearsal; a great deal of thought and private experimentation should accompany the memorization of lines and the other mundane tasks that the actor must accomplish outside the rehearsal hall. Never should you waste the time of your fellow actors and director by failing to prepare fully for rehearsal. But this private preparation should not result in *decision*. Your prerehearsal homework contemplates the alternatives and prepares you to explore aggressively in concert with your fellows, and mutually to respect and support the explorations of the director and other cast members.

Not all or even many of your rehearsal discoveries will result from conscious experimentation, however; you must have the courage to invite the *happy accident*. Such spontaneous discovery grows only from the receptiveness and responsiveness of each cast member to each other and to the moment.

Rehearsal is exploration, but never *indiscriminate* exploration. Any meaningful exploration has a sense of goal, which directs the outflow of energy and prevents it from degenerating into blind groping. Even though goals are rarely clear at the outset, and a good bit of the rehearsal process consists of clarifying them, there is usually in the vision of a play as communicated by the director some sense of the direction in which our exploration must go.

MAKING CHOICES

The many choices that must be made during rehearsal cannot be prejudged: we must actually *do* the thing in order to know whether it is right.

One of the most common expressions you will hear during rehearsal is "that sounds like a good idea, let's try it." Then you will hear either "that feels right," or "that doesn't feel right." "Feeling right" is a good description of how choices are made in the theatre. Your analysis and research in preparation for rehearsal will not usually lead to stage choices but will rather reveal a wealth of alternatives for exploration and establish the criteria (sometimes unconsciously) upon which the results will be judged.

Our earlier discussion of the James-Lange theory that emotions grow out of physical actions will suggest what "feeling right" really means. Any action on stage, vocal or physical, will inspire in the receptive actor certain feelings. Since his intellectual conception of his role provides some idea of what he is trying to achieve, he intuitively compares the feelings inspired by specific actions with his conceptual model, and hence makes his choice. Each decision opens up new areas of exploration, and often a rehearsal experiment will initiate a sequence of discoveries that expand conception and interpretation.

Such meaningful discoveries can be made only in the context of a rehearsal, when the participants are honestly in contact and working as a team toward a common goal. The rightness of any action will be determined by the way in which it fits into the cause-effect communication between characters, which moves the play. This places great emphasis upon the directness of the contact between you and your fellow actors, and between you and the environment created by the playwright, since it is in the light of such active give and take that all decisions will be made.

Group Exercise 10   Making connections

There is a great difference between *making* something happen on stage and *letting* it happen. We can *let* a thing happen when the energies we receive and our response to them are in perfect accord with our desired results. When this has been accomplished we *feel* the connectedness of every moment with every other moment.

Using your scene at its present stage of development, or better yet, in the intermediate stage of a real rehearsal process (with the director's consent, of course), select a scene or even an entire act and work through it. Allow any actor to stop the rehearsal at any point when he does not feel connected to the flow of the action. At this point, examine the moment or moments which immediately precede the point of difficulty; what can the other actors supply that will correct the problem?

This exercise is laborious, but it will prove conclusively that all stage moments (and all actors) are entirely interdependent and that in most cases of difficulty we must receive the aid of our fellow workers—and that in seeking this connectedness we in fact make the most profound discoveries about our work!

At best, the right moment will arise of its own accord, and no one will have any difficulty in recognizing it as the truth. The best rehearsal environment is one in which the truth can most easily arise, but there is no one way to achieve this. Some plays demand a free experimental approach, while others require methodical technical planning. The actors and their director must decide on the best approach to each particular play. Discoveries cannot be made without some aggressive investigation, and we must initiate the process in a way appropriate to the truth we seek.

Since rehearsal exploration is a dynamic process in which each decision will reflect upon all other decisions, we must decide from moment to moment how completely we ought to be committed to a certain action at a given point of time in the rehearsal process. Some actors wait a long time before making their final choices and approach their roles warily in early rehearsals, gradually filling in the full performance. Others produce at performance levels right off, though they maintain enough flexibility to avoid making final choices too soon. You will have to determine your own best approach, in terms of the disposition of the director, your fellow actors, the nature of the play, the length of the rehearsal period, and so on. As a general rule, however, an actor's output of energy should be as high as or higher than performance levels during rehearsals. The actor who lies back and plays the waiting game is usually being unfair to his co-workers, since they depend upon him for their reactions, but neither should he make final decisions too soon, committing himself to insufficiently explored and tested actions.

One way of working (though not the only one) is exemplified by Paul Scofield's preparation as King Lear in Peter Brook's production, recorded here in the assistant director's notebook:

> *First reading at Stratford.* Brook spoke of the play as a mountain whose summit had never been reached. On the way up one found the shattered bodies of other climbers strewn on every side. "Olivier here, Laughton there; it's frightening."

> Describing the enormity of the task before us, he gave one of the aptest definitions of the rehearsal process I've ever heard: "The work of rehearsals is looking for meaning and then making it meaningful." To illustrate the extent of this search, he related a short oriental fable about a man whose wife had suddenly disappeared. A neighbor came upon the man sifting sand on a lonely beach, and asked what he was doing. "I have lost my wife," he explained. "I know she is somewhere and therefore have to look for her everywhere."

The day was devoted to a straight readthrough of the play. It was a reading full of conventional verse-speaking; at times robustly acted; at other times, dully mouthed by actors torn between study of the text and performance. Paul Scofield used the reading mainly as a study-session—struggling with the verse like a man trapped in clinging ivy and trying to writhe his way through. One was immediately aware of the actor's resolve and caution. Scofield circled Lear like a wary challenger measuring out an unbeaten opponent and it was apparent from the start that this challenger was a strategist rather than a slugger.

First dress rehearsal. Scofield's Lear has slowly begun to emerge. His method is to start from the text and to work backwards. He is constantly testing the verse to see if the sound corresponds with the emotional intention. It is a peculiar method which consciously prods technique so that instinct will be called into play. The Method actor starts with feelings and then adds the externals of voice and movement. Scofield uses externals as a gauge with which to measure the truth of any given speech. He frequently stammers his lines, openly testing inflections and accents, discarding conventional readings not because they are predictable but because they do not tally with an inner sense of verisimilitude.

His concentration is a model to the rest of the company. He even asks for a prompt in character. Only when fumbling for a line does one glimpse the disparity between the man and the character, and then what one sees is a man winding painfully into a Shakespearean fiction. Underlying all the rigor of creative application, one discerns the gentleness of the man himself.[47]

Scofield's method of starting from the text and "working backward" is very close to the approach we have used in this book. It is a way to involve "instinct" and the unconscious, without losing the critical control of externals demanded of all good acting.

GETTING ALONG: THE ACTOR AND HIS FELLOWS

Your relationship with your fellow actors must be founded upon trust and mutual respect. It is so out of necessity, as each of your performances is fully dependent on what you give and receive from each other. In the very early stages of rehearsal, before close rapport has been established within the company, it is especially important that each actor make the act of faith

---

[47]Charles Marowitz, "Lear in Rehearsal," (in the program of the 400th anniversary tour of the U.S.) *Royal Shakespeare Company* in *King Lear/The Comedy of Errors* (Stratford-Upon-Avon, England: Herald Press, 1964), p. 3.

to work together toward the defining of goals with respect, trust, good humor, and a generous heart. Later on, as ideas begin to form themselves and decisions come closer, we must avoid a rigidity of attitude that prevents the organic development of a cohesive group interpretation.

Perhaps the most dangerous rigidity is exemplified by the actor who becomes an apologist for his character, arguing from the character's point of view as if every scene were "his." Group interpretation can be ruined by actors who insist upon adopting their character's point of view at the expense of the play as an artistic whole.

On the other hand, we do a great disservice to our director and fellow actors, and ourselves, if out of a false desire to get along we fail to express ourselves honestly. An actor who is *too* pliable is as destructive as one who is too rigid. Your ideas will be appreciated by your ensemble if they are presented in a reasoned, timely, and respectful fashion. One word of warning: your director must be the center of all company communication. Your feelings and ideas are best expressed directly to him, not to fellow actors in private conversations. A show must have only one director, though everyone connected with it must feel the responsibility of providing the director with ideas that may be of value.

THE ACTOR AND HIS DIRECTOR

Each director has a characteristic way of working, and it is part of the actor's job to help the director develop the most effective channel of communication with himself and with the company. Actors and directors are co-workers, not master and slave. The actor and his director, though they share many responsibilities, have essentially different functions, that are interdependent and coequal. The director's responsibility is first to the overall patterning of the play as a theatrical experience; the actor's responsibility is to bring his role to life so as to contribute best to that patterning.

There are many ways in which these responsibilities overlap and where compromise will be necessary. In his effort to shape the experience of the play, the director will inevitably need to determine certain specific actions or character traits. At the same time the actor, in his struggle to bring the character to life, must receive from his director an environment conducive to the growth of that life.

The actor, intimately involved with the life of his character, possesses insights into the life of that character which are denied the director. At the same time the director, with his overview and special position as the source of interpretation, has an objective point of view unavailable to any actor. In an effective working relationship, each will respect and value the special insights of the other and seek to join their points of view to the best possible advantage.

Even at the best, however, there are times when insoluble disagreements will occur. At such times the actor must remember that the director has assumed public responsibility for the audience's experience of the play. On his side, the actor has assumed public responsibility for the portrayal of his character within the context established by the director's interpretation, and once the interpretation has been clarified, it is the actor's responsibility to find the best possible means of implementing it. Therefore, it is ultimately the director's function to evaluate *what* the actor does, and the actor's job is to find *how* best to do it. They are equally creative artists, the director being an artist of *what,* and the actor being an artist of *how.*

THE ACTOR AND THE PLAYWRIGHT

Some playwrights (like Strindberg) have congratulated actors on creating characters that were improvements upon the originals. But even more playwrights (like Chekhov) have been shocked at finding the actor's creation bearing little relation to their conception. Some few playwrights (like Tennessee Williams) have occasionally permitted actors and directors to make changes in their basic conception of a play. Others (like O'Neill) have insisted that their plays remain uncut and unchanged. Still others (like Ionesco) have allowed portions of their plays to grow out of a "group-write" improvisational situation.

The playwright as we know him today is a recent invention, and he seems unfortunately isolated from the theatre for which he writes. In most great ages of theatre, playwrights were working members of the producing units for which they wrote. Most serious playwrights today have made an attempt to involve themselves in the day-to-day working of a production unit and to gain practical experience, rather than remaining literary artists who happen to write in a dramatic format. Unfortunately, our theatre has made this difficult, if not impossible, for most playwrights to do on a professional level, and our theatre has suffered for it. If our theatre is to prosper, we must bring the playwright back into the working ensemble.

Most of the time, we do not have the benefit of the author's presence, nor even the benefit of any clear idea about the author's intentions as expressed apart from the text itself. Under these conditions it is usually assumed that the director will take the playwright's part and, through his own exhaustive analysis of the play, will discover all necessary information that the author might otherwise supply. Some directors, unfortunately, are guilty of using texts as mere vehicles for their own creation.

In the other extreme, some directors force themselves and their actors to conform so rigidly to their notion of the author's intention that the actor finds it impossible to make a creative contribution to the production. In either case, the actor has the difficult task of maintaining his primary responsibility to the authority of the director without abdicating his sense of respect for the original text.

HONING THE PERFORMANCE

The actor often expends more energy during rehearsals than he does in performance, and he generally expends less and less energy as performances continue after opening. This is not because he begins doing his part mechanically, without thought or feeling, but because he penetrates deeper and deeper to the essence of the part. As this happens, unessential detail begins to fall away.

As the actor grows in proficiency, his energy output will also be economized. No matter how difficult the thing is, the seasoned veteran usually makes it look easy, because he knows what is essential and what is not. Our performance is usually made more effective by so economizing it as to distill it to its essential detail. This focuses the audience's attention clearly on the details that contribute most directly to the vitality of the play as a whole. This "natural attrition" of unessential detail usually occurs during a run under pressure of audience response, though there is no reason why natural attrition cannot be at work during rehearsals as well. A dual process with new actions being explored and established ones being distilled to their essence can be achieved simultaneously.

While the performance is being honed, the actor reserves a level of his consciousness for evaluation of his choices; this is what George C. Scott meant by "the guy sitting out there in row 10." No matter how deeply involved the actor is with his action and character on one level, the wise actor reserves a barely sufficient portion of his consciousness to evaluate the appropriateness and effectiveness of the character's behavior in relation to his overall dramatic purpose. He depends on his director to supply a truly objective viewpoint during rehearsals, and in performance his reading of the subtle reactions (or "feedback") of the audience supplements his own critical faculty.

A NOTE ON AUDITIONS

Finally, we must discuss the point at which the actor's job usually begins. Auditions are a painful but necessary part of the actor's life, and if it is any consolation, directors dislike auditions even more than do actors. The initial casting of a play is one of the most influential steps in the determination of interpretation, and yet the director must make these crucial decisions when he has only minimal acquaintance with his actors' work. Most directors have their own audition techniques, some of which can be rather disarming.

Some directors ask the actor to perform a few speeches of different types, and the actor should have at least three or four carefully chosen and prepared audition scenes, including comedy and tragedy, poetic and modern styles. About two minutes is a good length for each. The speeches should be chosen to demonstrate your abilities to the best advantage, and it is wise to avoid the standard audition speeches. It is difficult to evaluate an actor's work, or even to listen to him, when he is doing the sixteenth speech from *Richard III* that day.

Other directors prefer to have actors read scenes from the play at hand. Time, in this circumstance, allows only minimal preparation. Some actors can give polished cold readings with only a few moments work, but directors are usually suspicious of this; many times these slick cold-readers fail to develop much beyond their initial reading. On the other hand, some competent actors are so slow of study and such late bloomers that they are at a hopeless disadvantage in most audition situations. Directors therefore are as much interested in your past experience and reliable references about your work as they are in the immediate audition, and you should be, prepared to provide this information in an organized and attractive resumé and composite picture.

Auditions will be much more enjoyable if you approach them without a sense of competitiveness, but rather as an opportunity to communicate your potential to the director. Remember that the auditioners are under even greater pressure than you, since there is a great deal riding on the wisdom of their choice. Your objective should be to assist them in making their choice honestly. Whether or not you are cast or get the particular role you wanted, auditions challenge you to face great pressure with integrity and a willing spirit. Auditions do not test your artistry so much as they test your usefulness to the director for the specific task at hand. Moreover, the opinion formed of you at an audition may be important at some future time; it is therefore important that you honestly present your best abilities and avoid falsifying yourself for the sake of the particular instance. The question young actors most often ask about an audition is, "What do they want?" A much better question would be, "How can I best show them what I am?"

THE LIFE OF THE ACTOR

The deepest, most ancient root of the actor is his exemplification of man's need and ability to define his own existence. The actor's ability to wear his mask with consummate skill is itself a kind of potency, a kind of power over the future. While the play may teach us something about who we are, it is the actor's ability to be transformed that teaches us something about *whom we may become.*

The actor's ability to redefine himself before our very eyes reminds us of our own spiritual capacity for self-definition, and thus the theatre becomes a celebration of the vitality of man and of the ongoing flow of life.

Sensing the capacity of the theatre to help enrich our spiritual lives at a time when we have great need of such spiritual revivification, we have begun to explore more than ever before the full richness of the experience that may pass between actor and spectator, and the way in which the theatrical moment can resonate in the totality of our being, affecting our lives long after the curtain has fallen.

The Western actor's horizons are thus being continually broadened, and the art of acting has begun to encompass not only an expanding range of performance techniques and possibilities, but a renewed sense of ethical and spiritual purpose as well.

It is a wonderful time to be an actor.

> The actor cares,
>   but not for himself;
> The actor shares,
>   but does not exhibit;
> The actor loves,
>   but does not court;
> The actor receives,
>   but does not take;
> The actor's joy
>   is in the truth;
> See not who he is,
>   but whom he has become.

Sample Speeches

From King Lear, *Act III, Scene 4, by William Shakespeare*

1. Poor naked wretches, wheresoe'er you are,
2. That bide the pelting of this pitiless storm,
3. How shall your houseless heads and unfed sides,
4. Your loop'd and window'd raggedness, defend you
5. From seasons such as these? O! I have ta'en
6. Too little care of this. Take physic, pomp;
7. Expose thyself to feel what wretches feel,
8. That thou mayst shake the superflux to them,
9. And show the heavens more just.

Also see page 264.

From The Zoo Story *by Edward Albee*

1. It's just . . . it's just that . . . (*JERRY is abnormally tense,*
2. *now*) . . . it's just that if you can't deal with people, you have
3. to make a start somewhere. WITH ANIMALS! (*Much faster now, and like*
4. *a conspirator*) Don't you see? A person has to have some way of
5. dealing with SOMETHING. If not with people . . . if not with
6. people . . . SOMETHING. With a bed, with a cockroach, with a mirror
7. . . . no, that's too hard, that's one of the last steps. With a
8. cockroach, with a . . . with a . . . with a carpet, a roll of toilet
9. paper . . . no, not that, either . . . that's a mirror, too; always
10. check bleeding. You see how hard it is to find things? With a street
11. corner, and too many lights, all colors reflecting on the oily-wet
12. streets . . . with a wisp of smoke, a wisp . . . of smoke . . .
13. with . . . with pornographic playing cards, with a strongbox . . .
14. WITHOUT A LOCK . . . with love, with vomiting, with crying, with
15. fury because the pretty little ladies aren't pretty little ladies,
16. with making money with your body which is an act of love and I
17. could prove it, with howling because you're alive; with God. How
18. about that? WITH GOD WHO IS A COLORED QUEEN WHO WEARS A KIMONO AND
19. PLUCKS HIS EYEBROWS, WHO IS A WOMAN WHO CRIES WITH DETERMINATION
20. BEHIND HER CLOSED DOOR . . . with God who, I'm told, turned his
21. back on the whole thing some time ago . . . with . . . some day,
22. with people. (*JERRY sighs the next word heavily*) People.*

Index

The index has been prepared to avoid duplication with items and ideas already identified in the table of contents or table of exercises.